Screening the Holocaust

Jewish Literature and Culture
Series Editor, Alvin Rosenfeld

ILAN AVISAR

Screening the Holocaust

Cinema's Images of the Unimaginable

Indiana University Press

BLOOMINGTON AND INDIANAPOLIS

MANUFACTURED IN THE UNITED STATES OF AMERICA

Library of Congress Cataloging-in-Publication Data

Avisar, Ilan, 1951–
    Screening the holocaust.

    (Jewish literature and culture)
    Bibliography: p.
    Filmography: p.
    Includes index.
    1. Holocaust, Jewish (1939–1945), in motion pictures.
I. Title.   II. Series.
PN1995.9.H53A95   1988   791.43'09'09358   87–45400
ISBN 0-253-30376-1
ISBN 0-253-20475-5 (pbk.)
1 2 3 4 5 92 91 90 89 88

CONTENTS

Acknowledgments

This book involved a decade of continuous research and writing. Any work that lasts a life span of ten years owes much to the assistance and support of many individuals and institutions. The research was enhanced by courses on Holocaust films that I taught at Indiana University with the aid of the Department of Comparative Literature, Film Studies, and the Jewish Studies Program, and at the Ohio State University, the Department of Judaic and Near Eastern Languages and Literatures and the Melton Center for Jewish Studies. Acknowledgments are also due to the Museum of Modern Art in New York, the Library of Congress in Washington, D.C., the Abraham Rad Contemporary Jewish Film Archives at the Hebrew University in Jerusalem, and the College of Humanities at the Ohio State University.

Special thanks go to Terry Geesken and Mary Corliss of the Museum of Modern Art/Film Stills Archive for helping with the photographic illustrations. The illustrations are reproduced with permission of The Museum of Modern Art/Film Stills Archive.

I wish to express my special appreciation to Alvin Rosenfeld, whose stimulation and encouragement helped to bring this book to completion. I am also grateful to Harry Geduld, whose guidance was invaluable in the early stages of this work, to Arieh Ben Menachem, Karen Bodner, Edward Dmytryk, Henry Fischel, Annette Insdorf, Arnost Lustig, James Naremore, Nan Miller, Deb Munson, Charles Silver, and, especially, to my wife, Batia, and my children, Idan and Mor, for enduring and sustaining.

Introduction

Of all the events of modern history, none is more compelling and disturbing than the Holocaust. The enormity of the Nazis' attempted genocide of the Jews haunts the contemporary mind with crucial historical, ethical, psychological, and theological questions. Works of art constitute a major sphere of cultural reflection and metaphysical scrutiny, but in dealing with the Nazis' unimaginable atrocities and the systematic extermination of millions, artists encounter critical aesthetic problems involving the adequacy of art and literature to record, interpret, and evaluate the historical event.

The present study rests on two assumptions: first, that the Holocaust was a unique or an unprecedented historical experience; and second, that as such it poses new kinds of problems and challenges to those who seek to reflect upon and transmit its singular character. These special challenges lead to a new and distinct Holocaust discourse, which is nevertheless closely interrelated with the entire cultural discourse of the post-Auschwitz era.

The Nazi assault on the Jews was an unprecedented crime for several reasons. The victimization was of nearly inconceivable magnitude—six million innocent people and two-thirds of European Jewry, including the whole of Jewish culture in eastern Europe, were wiped out by the Nazis and their collaborators. Hitler's intent to exterminate an entire people is incomparable to any other episode of malice in the annals of human history—the word "genocide" was coined in 1943 to denote the ongoing crimes against the Jews. Unimaginable atrocities were carried out in the heart of western civilization by one of the most civilized nations in Europe, aided by technological achievements ostensibly designed to foster human progress and a higher quality of life. Thus, contrary to any notions regarding the premises and promises of enlightenment and modern development, the Germans created a diabolical kingdom of death using the very accomplishments of the human spirit in science, the arts, philosophy, and social studies to destroy as many innocent people as possible. Further, the genocide program was carried on for an unusual length of time, whether we reckon this span to have been the twelve years of the Third Reich, or the six years of World War II, or the four years of the massive killings of Jews and others. Each of these periods lasted to an extent that indicates a disturbing inability on the part of humanity to overcome the eruption of extreme evil, while historical evidence demonstrates damning universal indifference and complicity. The Holocaust also revealed to us the limits of human experience under the harshest conceivable conditions. The creation of a functioning system or micro-society in the Nazi hell, which forced the inmates to survive through bizarre adjustments and unbelievable trials, is one of the most staggering phenomena of the concentration camp universe. Finally it is important to remember that the planned genocide was directed against the Jews, the people who brought the world monotheism, the Ten Commandments, Jesus, and in modern times Freud, Kafka, and

Einstein. The attempt to wipe out the people who played such a crucial role in the evolution of western culture suggests not only a fierce and inhuman attack against innocent victims, but also an abysmal self-destruction that threatened the very foundations of our civilization.

To begin to contemplate the cultural implications and critical significance of the Holocaust, one must first be thoroughly aware of the unprecedented character of the actual events. The facticity of the Holocaust, understood in terms of the unsettling facts and details of historical accounts, is a special challenge for any artistic discourse on the subject. For many sensitive minds, the essential gap between art and the extraordinary atrocities of World War II is unbridgeable. Works of art are, in the first place, in a different ontological status than the authentic experience, which means that the transition from history to art is not an act of direct transmittance but actually a translation into a different order of human experience. Hence George Steiner advocates silence as the adequate response to the unspeakable.[1] Moreover, artistic work is based on some kind of formal organization of raw experience, leading Wiesel to declare: "Auschwitz negates any form of literature, as it defies all systems, all doctrines. . . . A novel about Auschwitz is not a novel, or else it is not about Auschwitz."[2] Finally, the aesthetic response to the embedded artistic formalization usually involves feelings of pleasure and satisfaction. But Adorno sees the possibility of deriving aesthetic pleasure from the actual atrocities as "barbaric,"[3] and Michael Wyschogrod believed that "art is not appropriate to the Holocaust," because "Art takes the sting out of suffering."[4]

These attitudes cannot be underestimated, and they require theoretical explication. The reservations regarding the discourse of art are very serious, but their final conclusions are unacceptable. For if indeed art is inadequate to deal with the Holocaust in any meaningful manner—intellectually stimulating or ethically constructive—then we face a colossal cultural scandal. Those concerned with the aesthetic distortions of the extreme historical experience cannot call for the elimination of one of the major spheres of human expression, which could and should play a critical role in imprinting the Holocaust's significance on the post-Auschwitz mind. At the same time, from an artistic point of view the claim that Auschwitz is beyond art means a terrible admission that our culture has been incurably maimed by the Nazi horrors. For even if we don't share today the romantic exaltation of art as the most important human activity and of the artist as the legislative spirit of cultural development, we must still recognize art to be the most important act of personal and social self-examination, as a crucial means of communication of thoughts and sharing of human experiences, and as the special mirror of the moods and limits of the human spirit and its major concerns in any given period. My work is rooted in the recognition of the crushing impact of the Holocaust on our cultural self-esteem, but at the same time it is rooted in a refusal to accept a nihilistic attitude in regard to the potentials and values of human faculties vis-à-vis this crisis.

The purpose of this study is to examine how cinematic art meets the crucial challenge of dealing with the extraordinary nature of the Holocaust, focusing on the adequacy of the medium to record, transmit, convey, interpret, and evaluate the historical event. Through a detailed analysis of selected works representing serious attempts to deal with the subject on the screen, we shall highlight cinema's specific potentialities, strengths, and limitations, and the variety of stylistic strategies and thematic concerns displayed by the most significant Holocaust films. I have chosen to deal with the treatment of the Holocaust in cinema, for film can be a mode of artistic expression, a rather complex idiom used by serious minds with contemporary metaphysical concerns and sensitivities, or a form of mass entertainment designed to please large audiences by catering to escapist melodramas, resorting to rather crude signs of communication (e.g., the stereotype, clichéic symbols, familiar narrative formulas), and yielding to popular demands and conventional taste to assure commercial success. But for our purposes, these differences contribute to the clarification of the Holocaust discourse in more inclusive terms, covering the modes of high art, popular expression, and sociopolitical manifestations.

The present study is highly eclectic, drawing upon a broad array of sources and methodologies. It includes research in film history, aesthetic discussions, literary and film theory, thematic analysis of abstract ideas, and sociological studies. The discussions will involve a great deal of textual criticism as defined by Tzvetan Todorov with respect to poetry: "It must be done in such a way that the principal traits of the object are not omitted and indeed emerge more evidently. . . . All the constitutive and pertinent elements of [the work] . . . will be identified: then their relative disposition, and finally a new presentation of the same [work], a presentation that allows us to penetrate more deeply into its meaning."[5] In the case of films, especially most of those discussed in this book, there is a special need for a detailed explication and analysis of the individual works. That is simply because the filmic texts are not as readily available as are their literary counterparts, and furthermore many of the Holocaust films are out of circulation for the large public. (It is hoped that the present study will bring about a change by inducing interest in some of these unjustly neglected works.) Thus the primary concern of this research is twofold: first, to highlight theoretical issues of representation and presentation; and second, to provide critical analysis of significant films, many of which have been neglected. In light of Annette Insdorf's book *Indelible Shadows: Film and the Holocaust*, an intelligent but general survey of almost every film related to the subject, I propose to submit an in-depth analysis of selected films, chosen on the basis of their artistic merits as well as their relevance to the theoretical topics being discussed. Finally, there will be a number of detours to consider more fully the important points raised by any of the films studied here. Since the Holocaust is not merely a topical subject but a searing historical experience, individual responses call for a variety of critical approaches rather than a conventional or even rigid type of genre study. The various subjects deserve special attention; they indicate fundamental metaphysical attitudes that cannot fall into a coherent thematic study. Some of the issues discussed in this research include, for example, the comparison of the Holocaust to hell, the imposition of tragic vision on the actual atrocities, and the mythologization of the historical experience.

The different chapters are geared toward the goal of trying to define the distinct discourse of the Holocaust. The characteristics of this discourse basically stem from the unprecedented nature of the event, and from the compelling factual sources. The imperative to be truthful determines one chief trait of this discourse, namely that its assessment involves references to and the integration of historical material with critical exposition. In this vein I will focus on three main categories: representation, presentation, and comprehension. The first involves the aesthetic problematics of achieving an adequate representation of the original reality. The second category is more political in nature, referring to the need to present correctly the role and identity of the participants in the historical drama. The third involves the challenge of trying to understand why it happened, how it was allowed to happen, and the profound implications of the unsettling experience to our human culture.

In general, cinema is a formidable tool for recording historical events, communicating information, spreading familiar ideological views, or conveying propaganda that is either conservative or subversive, and it is also a rich medium and a complex formal system used by artists to express inspiring visions. My study analyzes how film functions in each of these categories; hence, the underlying unity is guided by theoretical considerations, examining in a systematic way the basic elements of the medium and their usage in cinematic treatments of the Holocaust. The discussion is cumulative in the sense that the different chapters add up to a progressive clarification of the discourse. Thus in chapter 1 we analyze documentary approaches and the basic mode of visual-photographic representation; in chapter 2, film narrative when it subordinates naturalistic representation to a dramatic form; in chapter 3, the stylization of the historical narrative within the sphere of a total fictional diegesis; in chapter 4, the accommodation of the historical material to extrinsic sociopolitical concerns and realities; and finally, in chapter 5, the attempts of distinguished artists to present intriguing dianoia, focusing on the study of character within the concentrationary universe.

There are other distinguishing elements in the Holocaust experience which also underlie the structure of this study. In the first part (chapters 1–3) I discuss the special reality of the concentration camp universe, with its unique system of terror and its extraordinary atrocities, and in the second (chapters 4 and 5) I focus on the hideous and unprecedented program of genocide against the Jewish people. In addition, the discussion of films in the context of national cinemas has a special bearing for our subject. Movies made in eastern Europe, western Europe, and the United States are the products of different societies with their own cultural traditions and distinct modes of cinematic production. Moreover, the experiences of World War II have left different impressions on the three major forms of film production in the western world. The stylistic and ideological constrictions of Hollywood have been only slightly affected by the actual atrocities, no doubt because most Americans had no direct contact with the events of the war. Individual auteurs of western Europe experienced the triumph of barbarism in their civilized societies and witnessed the cruel uprooting of the Jews from their local environment. The socialist countries of eastern Europe had the greatest proximity to the horror, since the death camps, the ghettos, and the massive extermination process took place in their midst. Thus, the three largest chapters in this study discuss cinematic works made in the context of distinct national mentalities, specific historical experience during World War II, and different modes of film production.

The immediate post-Holocaust literary generation shied away from the subject of the Holocaust as a source for fiction narratives. The literature on the Holocaust has been dominated by writers committed to its accurate transmission. (Ventures into non-realistic modes of expression were carried out mostly by survivors, e.g., Kosinski's *The Painted Bird* or Tadeusz Borowski's *This Way for the Gas, Ladies and Gentlemen;* the autobiographical backgrounds and the author's direct personal experiences were indispensable complementary factors affecting the appreciation of these works as authentic and in their own way truthful to the historical experience.) Inevitably, though, Holocaust literature in the future will be created by authors who had no direct contact with its reality and will therefore demand a new critical approach. The examination of the films discussed in this study will highlight the first attempts made by artists who, as it happened, worked in film and used the Holocaust as a subject for their fictional art. Their triumphs and failures, the possibilities and limitations of the communicative and expressive medium, can tell us about how our culture comes to grips with the terrible events and will give direction to any future commemoration and comprehension of their crucial meanings.

Screening the Holocaust

CHAPTER I

The Photographic Image
and Cinematic Documentation

Genuine works on the Holocaust are rooted in the necessity to furnish truthful pictures of the unprecedented horrors, and they attempt to convey to the beholder the unsettling degrees of human suffering and human evil in the Nazi universe of atrocities. To be sure, different creators have adopted different strategies and styles to achieve these goals. But since they all share the same impulse of achieving adequate representation of the experience, we need to define the critical principles which can contribute to the avoidance of inadequate representations in the form of compromising distortions or reprehensible falsifications. In this opening section I will discuss the problematics of the Holocaust representation in art and literature, and apply the conclusions to the key faculties of the filmic expression.

Lawrence Langer, in his seminal work *The Holocaust and the Literary Imagination*, argues that the unique character of the Holocaust experience demands artistic disfiguration of the represented material. Choosing Picasso's *Guernica* as his artistic model, Langer bases his thesis on the following arguments. First, the Holocaust represents a reality so fantastic and so extraordinary that it defies our basic notions of empirical reality, the raw material of every mimetic art. It was an "experience under circumstances in which death is more 'real,' a more accurate measure of existence—gruesome as that may sound—than life."[1] Langer concludes that "the moment one speaks of the 'reality of the Holocaust,' one is compelled to include its 'unreality,' since the two co-exist as a fundamental principle of creation."[2] Hence, contends Langer, "To establish an order of reality in which the unimaginable becomes imaginatively acceptable exceeds the capacities of an art devoted entirely to verisimilitude; some quality of the fantastic, whether stylistic or descriptive, becomes an essential ingredient of *l'univers concentrationaire*."[3]

Secondly, for Langer, realistic accounts are limited by conventional patterns of thought and therefore cannot penetrate the darkest recess of human experience. Thus, he dismisses "most of the autobiographies concerned with *l'univers concentrationaire* [because they] numb the consciousness without enlarging it and providing it with a fresh or unique perception of the nature of reality."[4]

Finally, Langer prefers the literary disfiguration because of its effect on the reader. He reaches this conclusion in response to Adorno's famous dictum that "to write poetry after Auschwitz is barbaric"—a position stemming from the recognition of the awful disparity between the horrors and moral chaos of the Holocaust and the aesthetic pleasure one derives from artworks inspired by it. Langer believes that "disfiguration, the conscious and deliberate alienation of the reader's sensibilities from the world of the usual and familiar, with an accompanying infiltration into the work of the grotesque, the senseless, and the unimaginable,"[5] can eliminate the possibility of aesthetic pleasure.

Langer's view is highly problematic. The possibility of totally eliminating aesthetic pleasure is questionable. Langer supports it by stating simply: "Such a sense of disfiguration has always governed my response to Picasso's *Guernica*."[6] However, with the exception of the above quotation on the effect of disfiguration on himself, Langer never develops the concept which he postulates as the cornerstone of his critical attitude. Langer, I feel, is fundamentally biased against realism, which he considers to be simply devoted to the surface of things, lacking the vision of more profound, fantastic, or more disorienting existence. Thus, in discussing Hermann Kasack's *The City Beyond the River* (1947), he finds that its "chief limitation is probably a *total* reliance on the descriptive techniques of realism to evoke an unrealistic atmosphere."[7] The celebrated *Anne Frank: The Diary of a Young Girl*, according to Langer, "is in actuality a conservative and even old-fashioned book which appeals to nostalgia and does not pretend to concern itself with the uniqueness of the reality transforming life outside the attic walls that insulated her."[8] And by the same token, survivors' accounts or other diaries which set out simply to record historical moments are condemned as uninspiring.

But the Holocaust challenges the artist with unsettling facts vis-à-vis artistic, "inspirational" impulses. For, after all, what inspiration, pretension, or "consciousness enlargement" could there be in the face of such total terror? As Alvin Rosenfeld asserts, "one of the major functions of Holocaust literature [is] to register and record the enormity of human loss."[9] Telling the truth, unembellished and unmodified, is both a *mitzva*, a moral commandment to know, and then to remember and not to forget, and, as Wiesel once stated, also "a *matzeva*, an invisible tombstone, erected to the memory of the dead unburied."[10]

In addition, the Holocaust's extraordinary nature poses an enormous aesthetic problem and a special challenge to artists and writers committed to giving a truthful account of the events in naturalistic terms. Langer completely ignores a whole trend in modernist literature which revised nineteenth-century realism by stripping away old conventions and returning to the raw material of reality to seize and grasp its ontological dimension. Sidra Ezrahi, in her book on Holocaust literature *By Words Alone*, mentions Erich Kahler's discussion in *The Tower and the Abyss* of the

"New Factuality," which "differed radically from the old realism in that for the meticulous, almost loving detail which conveyed a 'devout' attitude towards nature, the post-expressionist realism substituted a 'cruel, indeed even vicious over-stress of facts. . . . ' In literature as in painting, this crass, bold precision suggests that a bitterness or profound sadness had replaced the reverent attitude of the old realists toward the external."[11]

Ezrahi points out that "much of the fiction of the Holocaust is a version of inherited conventions of realism [which] serves, like the documentary literature, to render the experience so familiar that it becomes a shared historical resource."[12] Yet, the chief problem that many authors face is convincing their readers that the recounted stories are indeed truthful accounts of real events. Some go beyond the mimetic work to make a statement pleading with the readers to acknowledge the verity of the described material. Pierre Julitte introduces his novel *Block 26: Sabotage at Buchenwald* with the assertion that "it is, from the first word to the last, a true story."[13] Likewise, Anatoli Kuznetsov begins his *Babi Yar* with the statement: "This book contains nothing but the truth."[14] Rosenfeld discusses the strategy adopted by John Hersey in *The Wall* and Leon Uris in *Mila 18*, two works on the Warsaw ghetto uprising whose narrative springboard is the "recovery" of historical records. "Both Hersey and Uris," observes Rosenfeld, "in projecting fictionalized 'historians' of the ghetto as their frame narrators, have obviously aimed to capture something of the authority that belongs to the eyewitness account of events that we find in the best of the diaries and journals."[15]

In summary, the issue of representing the actual historical experience is crucial in light of the serious gap between fact and fiction, and in that respect it is connected to the broader issues of the limits of artistic mimesis. However, in the case of Holocaust representation, the problem assumes a special dimension because of the unique character of the targeted reality whose details are fictionally bizarre and its facts often beyond belief. Or, as Rosenfeld puts it, "when fact itself surpasses fiction, what is there left for the novel or short story to do?"[16] One literary approach strives to strip away the appearance of fiction in order to gain the authority of factual and truthful accounts. Another approach strives to undermine the aesthetic effects of poetic devices. For example, Michael Hamburger described a movement that he labels "new austerity" of poets/survivors who profess a poetry which is both anti-metaphorical and antimythical.[17] An impressive illustration for such poetry is provided in Rosenfeld's analysis of Jacob Glatstein's poem "Smoke," describing the fate of a Jew in the Holocaust and his transformation in the crematorium chimney. Notwithstanding the poem's suggestive power and connotative implications, Rosenfeld's conclusion is that "we must disown the figurative use of language . . . and interpret literally: the Jew has become smoke and a similar fate will overtake his wife and children."[18]

But still, a poem is a poem. What about those works whose authors/survivors attempt to re-create their searing experiences in the words of prose language written on the bare page? Primo Levi's memoir *Survival in Auschwitz*, one of the best accounts of the concentration camp universe, demonstrates the author's painstaking concern that his story, written from the distance of time and place, is indeed an adequate representation of the past horrors. Levi's anxiety is expressed in a distrust of the very basic elements of his communication, the words themselves:

> Just as our hunger is not that feeling of missing a meal, so our way of being cold has need of a new word. We say "hunger," we say "tiredness," "fear," "pain," we say "winter" and they are different things. They are free words, created and used by free men who lived in comfort and suffering in their homes. If the Lagers had lasted longer a new, harsh language would have been born, and only this language could express what it means to toil the whole day in the wind, with the temperature freezing, wearing only a shirt, underpants, cloth jacket and trousers, and in one's body nothing but weakness, hunger and knowledge of the end drawing near.[19]

So far we have outlined the general problematics of Holocaust literature in reference to the issues of the relationships between art and reality. Primo Levi touches on the most fundamental issue when he questions the qualifications of the basic means of literary expression, namely words and language, to adequately portray the authentic horrors. Theoretically cinema has an advantage over literature in the quest for realism. Compared with words, the photographic image is a better means of objective representation and has a stronger immediate and sensuous impact on the viewer. The extraordinary power of revealing and arresting photos rests on a complex mental process whereby the visual perception is associated with the knowledge that what is seen is the result of objective recording, and hence the content of the picture is immediately recognized as a piece of authentic actuality. This recognition is at the heart of the fascination with the image, especially when the picture exhibits extreme human situations. Roland Barthes has reflected on the nature of that fascination:

> "The effect it [the photograph] produces upon us is not to restore what has been abolished (by time, by distance) but to attest that what I see has indeed existed. Now, this is a strictly scandalous effect. Always the photograph astonishes me, with an astonishment which endures and renews itself, inexhaustibly. Perhaps this astonishment, this persistence reaches down into the religious substance out of which I am molded; nothing for it: photography has something to do with resurrection . . . what I see is not a memory, an imagination, reconstitution, a piece of Maya, such as art lavishes upon us, but reality in a past state: at once the past and the real."[20]

Historical photos have been key instruments in transmitting, spreading, and impressing the events of World War II. Since many of the Nazi atrocities were literally unbelievable, the photographic image has become an indispensable evidence of this awful past. Throughout the war, many moments of extreme horror were captured by the camera's eye. Moreover, the history of the Nazi era and the events of World War II unfolded before the scrutinizing lenses of legions of photographers. In those years each major power appointed a special governmental agency to handle cinematic productions on the war, such as illustrative newsreels, informative documentaries, propaganda pieces, and morale-boosting pictures. David Roskies, in the beginning of his recent book *Against the Apocalypse*, com mented that "with vigorous planning and methodical execution, they [the Nazis] left the world with only a freak show of atrocity—motion pictures, even—by which to remember a civilization [i.e., of east European Jewry] more than a millennium old."[21] The Canadian poet Eli Mandel, a veteran of World War II and the author of a number of remarkable poems on the Holocaust, reflected on his work in a recent article "Auschwitz—Poetry of Alienation." Mandel refers to "those awful *photographs* towards the end of the war as the liberation occurred during the Spring of 1945 and the evidence of the camps began to manifest itself before the eyes of the astonished and horrified world."[22] These photos helped the poet to define his feelings and even shape his literary attitudes toward the Holocaust. He confessed: "I felt a furious bafflement, the need to write, the impossibility of writing. . . . For me the camps were part of history. Pictures. Those awful photographs. The obscene evidence emerging from mass graves as World War II ended."[23] Finally it is significant that Yad Vashem, the Holocaust museum in Jerusalem which has become a shrine of commemoration of and identification with the victims, is composed mostly of series of enlarged photos recording and exhibiting the persecutions and mass killings.

There is a rich body of photographic heritage of World War II that is immediately evoked in any reference to the period. Some commonplace images such as pictures of Hitler, the swastika, and the symbol of the SS are essential icons of the Nazi era. Indeed Hitler's picture has become a favorite illustration for the idea of ultimate human evil, while SS items incarnate the most extreme forms of totalitarian intimidation and repression. Photographs of barbed wires, watchtowers, barracks, chimneys, and smoke evoke the most hideous products of Nazism, the concentration camps and the death camps in eastern Europe. There are also a few remarkable pictures, whose content is more dramatic than iconic, residing in contemporary consciousness as the quintessential moments of Nazi atrocities. The most recurrent images include the liberated prisoners at Buchenwald, multitudes of shadows of human beings lying on the three-story bunks inside long, dark barracks, wearing dazed eyes and striking skeletal bodies; the gate at Auschwitz, with its satanically deceiving title *Arbeit Macht Frei*; and, perhaps the most famous picture of the Holocaust, ironically taken by a Nazi photographer following the final liquidation of the Warsaw ghetto, featuring a small boy raising his hands with horror before the arrogant, overpowering German soldiers. In *Against the Apocalypse*, David Roskies provided an impassioned analysis of this image.

On the face of it, the photo . . . taken by a German army photographer in the last days of the Warsaw ghetto, admits no analogies. Everything about it is disturbing. Armed soldiers are rounding up ordinary citizens. The victims, with their hands raised awkwardly in surrender, face every which way: the soldiers, the camera, the side, but not each other. Everyone is carrying something, as if, at this late date, there were still somewhere to go. And then the eye fixes on the child, so neatly dressed, so bewildered. Whose child is he? It doesn't matter, because they will all eventually perish. Yet the child alone is surely all of us, the adult made a child by the Holocaust that no one can explain to us. And the child is alone, too, because no one seems to be coming

after him—or is even concerned that he keeps his hands up; he couldn't do anything
with his hands down, anyway. He seems, then, to be at once imitating the adults and
volunteering himself as one. So the Isaac motif is here, but now Isaac goes alone to
Moriah.[24]

Susan Sontag emphasized the effect of that image on the obsessed modernist mind
of the post-Auschwitz generation. In her review of Ingmar Bergman's classic film
Persona, Sontag claims that Bergman's reference to the Six Million is not topical,
nor is it part of what she calls an "ordinary left-liberal propaganda—but rather the
famous photograph of the little boy from the Warsaw Ghetto [plus a TV newsreel
of a Buddhist immolating himself], are for Bergman, above all, images of total
violence, of unredeemed cruelty. It's as *images of what cannot be imaginatively encompassed or digested* that they occur in *Persona*"[25] (emphasis mine).

In cinema it is primarily the documentary film whose content and effect rest
on the revealing and arresting power of the photographic image. The Holocaust
reality encompasses extreme situations of massive suffering, endurance, survival,
resistance against hopeless odds, countless atrocities, and the unique Nazi style as
a totalitarian regime with its own version of social order and cultural orientation,
all of which offer a wealth of challenging material for film documentation. Indeed,
there are thousands of documentaries on all aspects of World War II. However,
whereas each one of these works is usually a moving exposition of a particular
aspect of the period, the unique problematics of the Holocaust representation
cannot benefit from a discussion of most of these works, for their underlying approach is journalistic, featuring places, reporting on events, and allowing survivors
to tell their personal stories. They often touch on the great moral issues inherent
in the historical experience, but they do not attempt to explore them or to tackle
the formal problems involved in an effective presentation of the full meaning of
the concentration camp universe. We will deal now with four notable documentaries to further explore the possibilities of the cinematic medium to transmit or
transmute the unsettling facts of the Nazi period. The films are *Night and Fog* (*Nuit
et Brouillard*, directed by Alain Resnais, France, 1955), *The Sorrow and the Pity* (*Le
Chagrin et la Pitié*, directed by Marcel Ophuls, France, 1969), *Triumph of the Will*
(*Triumph des Willens*, directed by Leni Riefenstahl, Germany, 1934), and *Shoah*
(directed by Claude Lanzmann, France, 1985).

Alain Resnais's *Night and Fog* constitutes a special cornerstone in the cinematic
treatment of the Holocaust. The following study of *Night and Fog* is both descriptive
and analytic, designed to provide an exposition to the main problematics involved
in expressing the Holocaust in sight and sound: the basic historical facts, the
available photographic material, strategies of mise-en-scène and editing, and the
crucial thematic concerns implied in any serious reflection on the subject.

Alain Resnais was commissioned in 1955 to prepare a compilation film on
the Nazi atrocities. He had already distinguished himself as a sensitive and skillful
director in his earlier court-métrage films on Van Gogh, Gauguin, and Picasso's
Guernica. With such background Resnais was concerned that his work might involve excessive stylization and artistry at the expense of faithfulness to the reality

of the death camps. Not having firsthand experience with the past reality he had set out to record, Resnais declared: "I did not dare to make this film by myself: I was never deported myself."[26] He therefore requested Jean Cayrol, "a novelist and poet whose whole conception of life and art was conditioned by his concentration camp experience, "[27] to collaborate with him and prepare the script. The collaboration between Resnais and Cayrol is palpable throughout the film and achieves a special effect: the viewer becomes aware of the simultaneous presence and the double perspective of the former inmate and the visitor, the actual witness and the curious spectator, the encumbered survivor and the meditative artist.

Jean Cayrol and Alain Resnais begin *Night and Fog* by addressing the most fundamental problem of any Holocaust representation, the difficulty of reaching the horrific past from a distance of time and of reconciling the unbelievable atrocities with current perceptions and patterns of thought. The opening images of a beautiful and peaceful landscape in the Polish meadows are strikingly incongruous with the knowledge that this innocent-looking land was the setting of past horrors. In the Auschwitz camp today the camera moves at a walking pace, passing rows of barbed wire while the narrator comments: "The blood has dried, the tongues are silent. The blocks are visited only by a camera."[28] This emphasis on the distorting present sights, rather than being a general statement of an artist struggling to cope with a difficult and elusive subject, is the expression of the profound frustration and anguish of any sincere attempt to face the Nazi horrors and to apprehend the unspeakable and unimaginable.

The transition to the past is sudden, marked by a change in music from the slow pastoral flute to violins pizzicati and soft drums, and from color to black and white. "1933—the machine gets underway," a clue to the beginning of the Nazi era. The shots from *Triumph of the Will* show military parades and processions with swastika banners emblazoned DEUTSCHLAND ERWACHE. Himmler reviews the marching columns, Hitler in an open car salutes the troops, and Streicher punctuates his speech with a fist. The appearance of those figures and their order is significant. Heinrich Himmler, head of the SS, is shown first as the chief engineer of the concentration camp system; Hitler, the Fuehrer, is in the middle as the most central figure in the Nazi network of evil; and Julius Streicher, editor of the notorius *Der Stuermer*, a semipornographic Nazi magazine which specialized in racist propaganda, represents the poisonous source of fanatic racism, responsible perhaps more than anything else for the attempted "Final Solution." Pictures of faithful Nazis from Leni Riefenstahl's *Triumph of the Will* —throngs of bare-chested men lowering their spades in unison to their sides, and endless masses of highly disciplined uniformed people—complement the brief exposition of the Nazi state.

The notion of blind obedience and its evil consequence is underscored in a cut from Riefenstahl's figures with the spades to pictures of workers building a concentration camp. In painful irony, the narrator proceeds to describe the details required for establishing the setting for the horrors; the building of death camps involved contractors, estimates and competitive bids, and even concern with architectural style. In the only potentially humorous moment in the film, a series of watchtowers shows with darkly ironic voice-over commentary: "Swiss style; garage style; Japanese style; no style at all." We finally see the finished camp extending for miles with endless rows of barracks. Our guide notes: "Nothing is missing but the occupants."

Providing those occupants was the next step in the genocide process. "Rounded up in Warsaw, deported from Lodz, from Prague, Brussels, Athens, from Zagreb, Odessa, or Rome," informs the narrator as newsreel footage shows people being herded by soldiers. Most of them are Jews, identified by the Star of David sewn on their clothes. The scenes at train platforms juxtapose the arrogant behavior of the Nazis with the helpless situation of the victims. Children, bewildered and frightened, hurry along the platform. A woman in a chair is wheeled to the train. Multitudes of people are put into cattle cars. A terrified girl peers through a crack in the door. At the same time, the guards are seen performing their duties effectively but quite casually. Some examine papers, others chat, even enjoying the spectacle. The soldiers lock the doors with their rifles and the officers impassively watch the departing trains.

The nightmarish "relocation" process is narrated against the background of one such rushing train. "Sealed trains, bolted. One hundred deportees to every car. No night, no day; just hunger, thirst, suffocation, and madness."

The arrival scene provides a visual image of the film's title: a train steams into a depot, glowing in the night, soldiers await with guns poised in the fog. The watchtower's presence is ominous; next to it is the entrance with its welcoming slogan: *Arbeit Macht Frei*. We see a startled face, "It is another planet." The humane world is left outside the barbed wire, and inside humanity is quite literally stripped away. The first order is to undress; numerous prisoners in the camp yard attempt to cover with bare hands their humiliating nakedness.

The initiation process is conveyed by a series of images of prisoners shaved, numbered, tattooed. The inmates' classification leads to an exposition of the camp hierarchy. The Jews are at the very bottom. Then come victims of the Night and Fog Decree, political prisoners, common criminals, and, above them, the Kapo; still higher is the SS, and highest of all, the Commandant.

After another interlude, dealing with the memory and incomprehensibility of the concentration camp universe—"what remains of the reality of these camps— despised by those who made them, incomprehensible to those who suffered here . . . we can only show you the shell, the shadow"—the film presents the daily routine. In the Kindgdom of the Night daily life was worse than a nightmare. Appropriately, then, this section begins with the nocturnal state of the camp, dark photographs of the watchtower and the barbed wire. These silent icons say nothing of the real horrors. However, "This is all that is left to us to evoke a night shattered by screams, by inspections, by lice, a night of chattering teeth." In "the other planet" daily life begins with death—at dawn there is first a roll call to check on those who died during the night. The inmates are then taken to slave labor under extreme conditions that would kill many more; but early in the morning the satanic minds provide music for the victims—a conductor is leading a small orchestra as Nazi guards supervise prisoners marched outside the camp.

Nature inflicts additional hardships on the wretched prisoners. They struggle through the muddy snow or suffer under the burning sun. They work in underground factories filled with smoke and steam. The death toll from these unendurable conditions is seen in a number of score sheets. The enormity of the Nazi slave labor system is seen through pictures of an endless flight of steps, accompanied by the information that "three thousand Spaniards died building this staircase that leads to the Mauthausen quarry."

The theme of food is introduced as "the obsession which rules his [the inmate's] life and dreams." The starved prisoners line up for food distribution. The narrator refers to those "who are too weak to defend their ration against thieves" but the image reveals a moving glimpse of two prisoners sharing the same bowl of soup, testimony to the continued presence of solidarity among inmates even under the harshest conditions (this shot was clearly taken after the liberation).

The part of the film dealing with the inmate's experience culminates in a reference to the Musselmen, a term for those living skeletons who yielded to the unbearable conditions and lost the desire to live. "They wait for the wind or snow to take them. At last to stretch out somewhere, anywhere, and at least have one's death to oneself."

In the Kingdom of Death, food, though precious, was barely life-sustaining. The soup provided by the Nazis forced convulsive excretion. Color pictures of the latrines and their approaches mark the transition to the depiction of the world of the Nazi perpetrators; it is *anus mundi*, whose resemblance to any ordinary society is absurd yet terrifyingly real. The camp had a symphony orchestra, a zoo, a greenhouse, an orphanage, and even a legal system, using gallows and an empty courtyard with a bullet-riddled wall for executions. Even cultural symbols are meticulously preserved. The most revealing image of the satanic combination of civilized society and base evil is Goethe's oak tree at Buchenwald. The tree was not destroyed during construction of this camp designed to destroy people, "because they respected the oak tree." The inmates provide art and artifacts, creating "toys," "sculptures," and "manuscripts." There was a hospital providing the illusion of real beds and care, but in reality "you ran the risk of death by infection. The medicines are a mockery, the dressings were paper. The same ointment is used on every sore. Sometimes the starving eat their dressings." But worst of all was the surgical block where SS doctors and nurses performed experimental mutilations on human guinea pigs. Some of the victims shown here were castrated men, a patient whose hand had been burnt to the bone, and a woman revealing her shriveled limbs.

Is it hell? Not for everyone, since there are those within that infernal reality who conduct a quite ordinary life. The Kapo's room is spacious and neatly organized, containing a comfortable bed, desk, chairs, and night lamp. The Commandant lives in a villa, relaxing in his home with his wife and dog. They host guests, who chat, drink, and laugh while another couple plays chess. Part of their pleasures center around the camp's brothel, which houses better-fed female inmates. These women too, the narrator reminds us, are "prisoners still, like the others doomed to death." The camps, containing tens of thousands of inhabitants, became functional societies, with class divisions, a justice system, medical services, and forms of entertainment. But this apparatus is really an infernal mirror image of ordinary society. The presence of the camp brothel reminds us that the Holocaust "presented a blatantly new model of government—the concentration camp—in which the freedoms of both political and sexual life were denied almost absolutely to the subject class and indulged in to the point of perversion by those who ruled."[29]

And this society had been designed and created for one purpose—the annihilation of millions of human beings.

The liquidation process is introduced with a series of twelve photos of Himmler's visit to Auschwitz. The striking aspect of this sequence is not the individual responsibility of a Himmler, but the painstakingly careful design of the camp, geared to efficient destruction; as the SS chief himself stated, "We must destroy, but productively."

The killing process actually began in the deportation trains. The deportees were lined up for miles, and inside the boxcars the extreme overcrowding and subhuman conditions claimed their death toll. Nearly twenty percent of all deportees perished in those infernal trips. The first systematic mass murders were carried out by the *Einsatzgruppen*, the special mobile killing units of the SS. We see the infamous photos of naked women and children, helplessly facing their killers in the vast fields of eastern Europe, and the narrator emphasizes with pain: "These pictures were taken a few moments before extermination." After two million Jews were cold-bloodedly machine-gunned by the *Einsatzgruppen*, a new mode of extermination was introduced. "Killing by hand takes time. Cylinders of Zyklon are ordered." These brief statements summarize it all. Any elaboration on the details and considerations involved in the Nazi decision to employ gas to exterminate millions of innocent victims would stretch logic to its demonic limits.

The gas chambers constitute a terribly palpable purgatory between life and death, the most concrete reality to ever approach the transcendence of death. The actuality of the gas chamber was not only beyond human reason but also outside the realm of transmittable human experience. Millions of people went through it, and although it represents a significant moment in human history, there is not a single person left alive to tell what truly happened there. But in spite of its unique epistemological status, the chamber of death has, strikingly, a quite ordinary appearance: "Nothing distinguished the gas chamber from an ordinary block. Inside, what looked like a shower room welcomed the newcomers. Their hosts closed the doors. They watched." The language in this passage is remarkable: "hosts," "welcomed," "newcomers," "what looked like a shower room," are all expressions of extraordinary euphemism and understatement. But can there really be adequate words for the unspeakable? "The only sign—but you have to know it—is this ceiling, dug into by fingernails. Even the concrete was torn." Notice that Cayrol never spells out what the sign signifies, because it is, in the words of George Steiner, "the kind of thing under which language breaks."[30] Resnais's camera focuses on the present look of what at first seems like a shower room. It steadily advances inside and then moves up to show the gouged ceiling. The scratches on the ceiling mark the defeat of human struggle against matter. The camera movement itself becomes more expressive, slowly going upward, slightly changing its course as if looking for something beyond the concrete, perhaps following these silent traces of immensurable pain to register an anguished appeal to distant heaven.

The final stage in the extermination process was the incineration of the dead bodies. The available photos of the open pits show mounds of bodies burning and faces that are smoking ash. This is hell on earth. This hell was assisted by human technology; the drive for efficiency led to the development of the ovens and crematoria, which are introduced in color shots of their present form. The camera moves slowly as the open doors feature the infernal dark mouths which had swallowed millions of people. Mountains of spectacles, clothing, shoes, and women's hair convey the monumental magnitude of the death factories. But the ultimate dehumanization of the Nazi evil is evidenced from the exploitation of the human "material." The narrator's voice breaks. "From bodies . . . But there's nothing left to say . . . From bodies, they wanted to make . . . soap . . . As for skin. . . . " And the camera reveals figurative sketches inked on dried skin.

When the Nazis are defeated, the liberating forces discover in the camps piles of corpses scattered over the ground. They are in various degrees of mutilation and decay. The Nazi legacy is a pyramid of dead heads with eyes opened or holed. The visual shocks in this sequence culminate with pictures of Allied bulldozers shoving the corpses into mass graves (taken in Bergen-Belsen). Is that the meaning of "Ashes to Ashes, Dust to Dust; For dust thou art, and unto dust shall thou return"? The pictures of the tangled masses of dead moved by the bulldozers into the pits provoke dread and horror and not a glimpse of religious affirmation.

The images of death and destruction are so shocking that the attempts to restore justice after the war seem pathetically incongruous. To add insult to unspeakable crime, in the postwar trials, the individual perpetrators deny any responsibility. The Kapo, the officer, the Commandant, they all rise and declare: "I am not responsible." There is more puzzlement and agony than bitter irony in Cayrol and Resnais's question, "Then, who is responsible?" The issue cannot be resolved by putting the blame on a few individuals. The final image, constructed of pictures of naked, mutilated corpses, strikingly resembles Rodin's *The Gate of Hell*, or the infernal portion of Michelangelo's *The Last Judgment*. Indeed, the enormity of the Final Solution not only shattered the concept of justice in the human realm but also challenges the very notion of Providence and divine justice.

The epilogue of *Night and Fog* warns, admonishes, pleads with us to remember and to not forget. The backdrop is the camp's relics, broken watchtowers, crematorium ruins, and the expressionistic and almost abstract figures of twisted wires, cracked concrete, and a crumbled chamber.

The crematorium is no longer in use. The devices of the Nazis are out of date. Nine million dead haunt this landscape. Who is on the lookout from this strange tower to warn us of the coming of new executioners? Are their faces really different from our own? Somewhere among us, there are lucky Kapos, reinstated officers, and unknown informers. There are those who refused to believe this, or believed it only from time to time. And there are those of us who sincerely look upon the ruins today, as if the old concentration camp monster were dead and buried beneath them. Those who pretend to take hope again as the image fades, as though there were a cure for the plague of these camps. Those of us who pretend to believe that all this happened only once, at a certain time and in a certain place, and those who refuse to see, who do not hear the cry to the end of time.

Night and Fog is the most inclusive film about the concentration camp universe. In only thirty minutes Alain Resnais and Jean Cayrol provide a devastating picture of this world, achieving both a forceful documentary exposition and a serious scrutiny of its main problems. Admittedly, Night and Fog does not concentrate on the genocide against the Jews. It chooses instead to highlight the era's inhumanity. We should make it clear at this point that the Holocaust is characterized by two cardinal axes. The first is the attempted genocide of the Jews, the harvest of millennia of western antisemitism, carried to its diabolical extreme by Hitler and his henchmen; the second consists of the incredible horrors and atrocities committed by the German Nazis and their collaborators, mostly in the concentration camps and the death camps. Obviously, the two facets of the Nazi era are interrelated, for the assault against the Jews was the primary force behind the Nazi bestiality and their inhumanity. However, Resnais and Cayrol cover the basic historical framework of the process of human destruction, the crucial moments of deportation, arrival at the camps, initiation, and first selection, culminating in the major forms of extermination—Einsatzgruppen machine-gun killing, suffocation and starvation to death in the trains, extermination in the gas chambers, and finally incineration. The inmate's daily routine and the organization of a pseudosociety in the camps receive special attention because the main themes of Night and Fog are human endurance, the mechanism of evil, and the ultimate demonstration of inhumanity and dehumanization. The underlying moral impulse throughout is that postwar generations are obligated to remember the Holocaust, even though the enormity of the crime is unimaginable and inexpressible.

The most significant feature of Night and Fog is the interweaving of past and present. For the survivor (Jean Cayrol) who revisits Auschwitz ten years later, the benign colorful environment presents an unendurable contrast with the former atrocities. For the filmmaker (Alain Resnais), the innocent-looking countryside conceals the past and poses a frustrating obstacle to reaching the truth. This obstacle is overcome by employing and exploiting the contrast itself. Resnais's film is dominated by a dialectical approach leading to a series of binary structures and counterpoints that govern the use of editing, the treatment of the texture and the content of the image, techniques of camera movement, textual narration, and accompanying music. This dialectic is rooted in the basic conflict between humanity and inhumanity, whose unprecedented consequences the film sets out to depict, and conforms to the sharp moral dichotomy between the tortured victims and the arrogant victimizers who inhabited together "the other planet." Finally, the dialectical approach indicates a special dynamic attitude toward the past from the standpoint of the present, signifying the attempts to penetrate the Kingdom of the

Night through the fog of the present, and the moral obligation not to let this fog make us forget the Nazi horrors.

In *Night and Fog* the past is shown in authentic footage of black-and-white photography, while the present is filmed in color. The war period is rendered mostly through montage of still photos or short shots, whereas in the present the camera moves slowly in long takes of tracking shots and pans. The postcard beauty of the present is accompanied by pastoral flute music, whereas the marching Nazis are shown to the sounds of pizzicati and drums. These stylistic differences correspond to the sharp contrast between the two periods. The black-and-white still photos record a reality of frozen time where death's rigidity reigns, while the rapid succession of black-and-white images conveys its pervasive violence. The elaborate camera movements show that, unlike the frozen fragmentation of the past, the contemporary situation is fluid and unformed.

The connection with the incongruous present is established when the viewer is made to realize that today's rich green grass rises from the soil fertilized by the gray ashes of millions. So the current reality, for all its beauty and serenity, must be subjected to serious scrutiny. The extreme long shots of the contemporary setting always include elements of the concentration camp universe like railroads, barbed wire, and barracks as dissonant reminders of the awful past. Other shots focus on ruins, twisted wires, the black tongs in the crematoria, often projecting semiabstract forms and highly expressionistic effects, such as the dark ovens' "mouths," black latrine holes, and the darkness underneath crumpled buildings. The camera movement itself is also a highly expressive device. In the first part of *Night and Fog*, the camera moves along the corridors and through the latrines, giving a sense of the magnitude of suffering, the endless number of victims. Near the end of the film the tracking shots are no longer straight and smooth. The camera moves in all directions, literally trying to see more and to explore. Inside the gas chamber, the camera surveys the gas tanks, the steel door, the valves and nozzles on the pipes, and as the narrator mentions that the sign of previous horrors is the scratched ceiling, the camera moves closer to show the torn concrete, producing an almost abstract expressionistic image. Likewise, in the ovens the doors hang open, but the emptiness of the ovens is black and frightful; the camera moves along the ovens, pausing for a moment on a dark wall, comes out of the darkness and tries to peep into the ovens, into the darkest core of the destruction process, while the metal tongs used to carry the corpses into the ovens are in the center foreground of the frame, with a pair of handles very close to the camera as if threatening to pierce the viewer's eyes.

In spite of the consistent separation of the past from the present, Resnais's ultimate purpose is to have the viewers learn about the past, remember the horrors, so that from the safe and almost idyllic position of the present we can attain an approximate sense and feeling for what truly happened. A totally dichotomous system of contrasts and juxtapositions would fail to bridge the two worlds and might alienate the spectator from the material presented in the film. The major unifying factor here is the calm and restrained rhythm of *Night and Fog*, achieved mainly through the soundtrack, with the soft suggestive voice of the thoughtful narrator and the background music. The crucial moments of history and the extreme expressions of agony are counterpointed with soft music. The marching Nazis and the massive hysteria of Hitler's followers are not accompanied with the expected martial sounds of drums and trumpets but with the rather ironic pizzicati and background tremolos. Hanns Eisler, a German composer who had collaborated with Brecht and fled Germany after the Nazis' rise to power, wrote the original music for *Night and Fog*, following Resnais's advice that "the more violent the images are the gentler is the music."[31] Henri Colpri, who edited *Night and Fog* with his wife Jasmine Chasney, has written in *Cahiers du Cinema* on the use of music in *Night and Fog*.

The film opened with, over the credits, a long melodic phrase, ample and moving, the resolution of which was left in suspense. This theme reappeared linking the 'before' and the 'after' of the concentration camp universe only at the very end where this time, marvelously, it is resolved. The other important motifs were the deportation theme dominated by the brass and the heart-rending concentration camp theme. To contrast with the imposing staging of the Hitlerian marches, Eisler used high-pitched pizzicati. Later the pizzicati accompanied one of the results of Nazis: the huge camps, the typhus, the corpses buried by bulldozers, the SS become prisoners in their turn.[32]

The soundtrack reveals also another distinct moral strain in *Night and Fog*, which is Resnais's concern with resisting the infiltration of the Nazi legacy into his own work. The problem exists for the simple reason that most of the documentary pictures available were made by the Nazis themselves. Thus, to avoid the rigid categorization and itemization characteristic of the Nazi compulsion for order, Resnais maintains a fluid pace of exposition and an almost undetectable cinematic organization of the historical facts. The narrator's language conveys this perhaps more eloquently than anything else in the film. Unlike the deceptively straightforward Nazi slogans—"Cleanliness Is Health," "To Each His Due"—the narrator's tone is cryptic, questioning, almost distrusting the power of words to describe or explain. The Nazis used words to distort reality, to inflame their masses, and to rain death and destruction. The narrator's uncertainty is honest, agonized, and touching, and he succeeds in creating a specially intimate connection with the viewer.

The choice of the film's title also reflects the distortion of word meanings in Nazi slogans. The Nazis adapted the common German idiom "bei Nacht und Nebel davon gehen," meaning to get away or to escape under cover of darkness or the night, to designate one of their rules of terror, the "Night and Fog Decree." William Shirer described that Nazi practice:

Of all the war crimes which he claimed he had to commit on the orders of Hitler "the worst of all," General Keitel said on the stand at Nuremberg, stemmed from the *Nacht und Nebel Erlass*—"Night and Fog Decree." This grotesque order, reserved for the unfortunate inhabitants of the conquered territories in the West, was issued by Hitler himself on December 7, 1941. Its purpose, as the weird title indicates, was to seize persons "endangering German security" who were not to be immediately executed and make them vanish without a trace into the night and fog of the unknown in Germany. No information was to be given their families as to their fate even when, as invariably occurred, it was merely a question of the place of burial in the Reich.[33]

Nazi usage has poisoned this neutral linguistic expression. And in direct opposition to the Nazi message of disappearance, in their usage of "night and fog" Resnais and Cayrol intend a perpetual warning to remember and beware lest the German crimes vanish into fog and darkness.

Setting out to document the horrors of World War II, Night and Fog mentions the years 1933 and 1945 to mark the beginning and end of the Nazi era. But this film is not a documentary on a specific period. The treatment of the subject develops without adhering to chronological sequence. The moral impulse behind Resnais's ahistorical approach is that in assuming the definite historical frame of time one might easily dismiss the Holocaust as a past event, extraordinary and singular but also irreversible and unrepeatable, a nightmare to be exorcised and forgotten. Furthermore, the ahistorical approach is a key to understanding the concept of the concentration camp universe. The horrific aspect of the Holocaust is that it took place over a period of years; it cannot be dismissed as a sudden human disaster. Over the years of its happening, the Final Solution ceased to be a dramatic unfolding of unexpected events, a tragically fatal chapter in the story of human history, but became rather a continuous state of affairs, requiring endurance, adjustment, and acceptance of the fact that every day thousands of innocent people were being slaughtered. Hence the term "concentration camp universe," which emphasizes the synchronic dimension over the chronological one, and gives away the infernal nature of a rather monstrous mirror reflection of the ordinary world.

There is still one potentially major deficiency in Night and Fog. In their pondering of the issues of inhumanity, responsibility, justice, and the memory of the Nazi atrocities, Resnais and Cayrol ignored the causal core of the concentration camp universe, namely, the attempted genocide of the Jews. One critic raged that Night and Fog "suffers from a terrible flaw. It is a film about universal genocide and the particular Holocaust that omits the Holocaust. It forgets the Jews."[34] Resnais and Cayrol, it should be noted, never mention Germans or Germany either. Still, in my opinion, the distortion is minimal, nor is there any vicious attempt to falsify history. It is not true that "the script never mentions the Jews—not once."[35] Referring to the potential victims who live in blissful ignorance during the rise of Nazism in the thirties, the narrator talks about a "Stern, a Jewish student from Amsterdam," although the English subtitles somehow fail to give the full identity of Stern. Moments later, when we see those "rounded up in Warsaw, deported from Lodz, from Prague, Brussels, Athens, from Zagreb, Odessa, or Rome" it is clear from the pictures and the Jewish stars on their clothing that these victims are Jews. In particular, the first image in this sequence, the frightened Jewish child raising his hands before a German trooper during the liquidation of the Warsaw ghetto, is one of the most well-known photographs of the Holocaust.[36] Also, when the hierarchy inside the camp is discussed, the viewer understands that those wearing the Jewish star are at its bottom and are the most miserable victims.

The flaw of *Night and Fog* is not one of distortion or even of totally ignoring the Jewish suffering, but rather a failure to present the assault against the Jews as an essential pillar of the Nazi phenomenon. Unfortunately, this failure is not uncommon in world cinema. The antisemitic policies of the Soviet Union, for instance, have led to the suppression of references to the Jewish victims, not only in the postwar Soviet film but also in literature and even in special memorials erected to commemorate the victims of World War II. The first line in Yevtu-shenko's celebrated poem "Babi Yar" refers to this injustice, and Yevtushenko's poem is anything but the exception that tells about the norm. It is possible that Resnais and Cayrol also sensed comparable political pressures, unrelated to official antisemitism but similar in their effects. The 1956 Cannes Film Festival refused to show a Polish documentary on the Warsaw ghetto, *Under the Same Sky*, following vehement German protests. *Night and Fog* was banned too, in the same film festival, for including a five-second shot of a French gendarme in a French concentration camp. In his book on Alain Resnais, James Monaco points out that "this visual evidence of collaboration was intolerable to the authorities. After two months of negotiations, the producers of the film agreed to alter the image (and the evidence of history) by covering the gendarme's uniform."[37] Evidently, then, the mid-fifties were not the right time to deal forthrightly with the victimization of the Jews, the crimes of the Germans, and the complicity of the local populations throughout Europe. However, notwithstanding specific political climates and social attitudes, *Night and Fog* fails to consider the direct connection between the perennial cultural malaise of antisemitism and Auschwitz, nor does it mention clearly the genocidal assault against the Jewish people.

The failures of *Night and Fog* are especially disturbing in light of its remarkable achievement of giving both an unmatched descriptive introduction of the con-centration camp universe and a reflective warning on the dangers of inhumanity. *Night and Fog* is an outstanding documentary because it is embedded with unabashed moral rigor, yet it is first and foremost a striking exposition of the Nazi universe. The successful duality stems mainly from the filmmaker's relentless commitment to the documentation process and the inherent power of the filmed material. The overall effect is a moving work which does not betray the unique character of the Nazi atrocities with formal or thematic indulgences imposed on the subject. How-ever, an inevitable degree of stylization is involved in any cinematic discourse which might affect the perception of historical truth or distort the authentic nature of the concentration camps. Resnais's concern with the ethical implication of having a distinct style imposed on the Holocaust material is treated in the scene exploring Nazi concern with the architecture of the camps' watchtowers. Marsha Kinder and Beverle Houston explain the significance of this sequence:

> Both the cutting pace and the commentary emphasize the variations in architectural style. As a result, the barbed-wire barriers, also present in each shot, may be ignored. This ironic attention to variations in external style emphasizes Resnais' awareness of how easy it is to ignore the pervasive horror that went on inside these buildings. He underscores the point that the style of the film gives us a selected and distorted vision

of reality. . . . The main theme of this film is that we must never forget what happened in Germany. Yet there is full awareness that this is an extremely difficult demand because, as the film itself suggests, it is almost impossible to retain or recapture the reality of the past.[38]

Consequently, Resnais's film usually relies on the arresting power of its documentary photos without any additional stylization which might only cheapen or trivialize the authentic enormity. Resnais's artistic austerity applies to his complete reverence to the documentary content of the image, whereas his self-reflexivity and stylistic strategies of expressive montage and counterpoints are motivated by the pervasiveness of the ultimate moral purpose of *Night and Fog*, to commemorate the suffering of the Nazis' victims lest they be forgotten. Likewise, the metaphysical aspects are never exploited to present impressive truisms or words of wisdom. *Night and Fog* is permeated by the issues of life and death, humanity and inhumanity, justice, evil, and even theodicy, but the narration avoids any blatant didacticism. The narrator's voice is remarkably different from the traditional postures of the documentary films that spew out facts and truisms with "Voice-of-God" authority. Instead, Cayrol's language is marked by understatement, and the narrator's voice is cryptic and uncertain, confiding to the spectator the reality of the horrors.

Andrew Sarris maintains that *Night and Fog* is "the only film on the Nazi era to have truly transcended its subject without betraying it."[39] Sarris's concept of "transcending the subject" refers to stylistic strategies and patterns of vision that are usually imposed on the actual material in any filmic discourse. *Night and Fog* is both factually informative and intellectually—perhaps more accurately, ethically—stimulating, highly revealing and powerfully suggestive. In short, the triumph of Resnais's film is that it transcended the fact in its complex impact on the viewer while remaining factual. *Night and Fog* employs coherent formal devices to intensify the potential effects of the filmed material and to press home its crucial moral and metaphysical aspects. James Monaco claims that the unconventional documentary techniques employed in *Night and Fog* are designed to achieve "the leverage provided by the irony of distancing."[40] Monaco fails to explain what he means by the expression "irony of distancing," and to clarify its application to *Night and Fog*. What we see in this documentary is undoubtedly horrible and shocking. But Resnais exercises a supreme artistic restraint—not an ironic distance—when he features the visual horrors. Viewers always reach a point of saturation when they see images of atrocities. Exceed this point and their reaction is bound to be negative—too emotional, mindless, and even convulsive (e.g., nervous laughter, or even perverse pleasure.) At the same time, as François Truffaut once pointed out, "we're not going to 'feel better' after seeing *Nuit et Brouillard*; quite the opposite."[41] Indeed, the power of this film is that despite the employment of rich and complex cinematic language, the message is enhanced while avoiding the effect of pleasing aesthetics or the special gratification of indulgence with profundities, two standard reactions to works of art that in the case of the Holocaust threaten to desensitize or deflect the beholder's consciousness. Resnais is careful never to exploit the sensational effects of the extraordinary pictures and, in my opinion, he achieved a nearly perfect equilibrium between the perception of visual horrors, the absorption of their context, and reflection on their significance.

Compared with *Night and Fog*, Marcel Ophuls's celebrated *The Sorrow and the Pity* is the epitome of a "lean documentary honesty." And yet Ophuls's film exerted a tremendous impact on many people in the seventies in regard to their perceptions and awareness of the events of World War II. In four hours and twenty minutes Ophuls chronicles the history of France under the Nazi occupation. Focusing on the plight of the inhabitants of Clermont-Ferrand, a small industrial city near Vichy and the home of Pierre Laval, the French prime minister of the collaborating Vichy regime, the film highlights main events and features characteristic social phenomena during the war such as collaboration, complicity, resistance, and the incidence of antisemitism.

In *The Sorrow and the Pity*, Ophuls shows history through the recounted experiences of a selected but highly representative group of characters. "The cast," as Pauline Kael put it, "is made up of the known, such as Pierre Mendes France, Georges Bidault, Anthony Eden, and Albert Speer, and the unknown who are principally from the . . . city of Clermont-Ferrand."[42] Those figures include a French Fascist— former member of the Waffen SS; a middle-class pharmacist— the embodiment of the average French citizen who remained passive during the war; a couple of peasants—former members of the resistance; and a handful of more minor characters featuring the range of French reactions to the German occupation as well as a crosscut representation of the gamut of French society. At the same time, the focus on individual characters leads to relentless examination of moral decisions in extreme political situations and how these decisions stem from the world views, value systems, and personal traits of different human beings. Thus Ophuls's work actually transcends the specific concerns of French conduct during the war and touches on serious existentialist dilemmas. The ultimate concern is with the issues of responsibility and justice—the climax of the film involves the cruel punishments imposed on the collaborators, and the senselessness of this reaction in light of the general apathy of the public during the war years, which was no less complacent with the Nazi policies. While dealing basically with the same problems that tormented Resnais and Cayrol in *Night and Fog*, Ophuls was able to throw more light on the intricacies of the moral dilemmas by examining particular cases of individual behaviors with which the viewer can better identify. Furthermore, in dealing with the French situation Ophuls achieved an intellectually valuable distance from the shocking atrocities of the death camps. For the moral issues involving those who gave orders, those who took orders, those who suffered, and those who went on as before were the same kind of problems faced by the people who inhabited the darkest core of the concentration camp universe.

Ophuls's method is to pose general questions and let the interviewees relate their feelings, opinions, and personal experiences with little interference, avoiding any verbal interrogation or even ostensibly embarrassing questions. The characters selected to appear in the film are mostly open and a few of them strikingly honest, providing fascinating details on their motives and experiences. The prosperous pharmacist, against the background of apparent domestic happiness, self-assuredly explains his reasons for remaining apolitical during the war. The former German officer who was stationed in Clermont-Ferrand shows pride in his war decorations. The resistance fighters include a pair of silent and formidable farmer brothers, a bohemian aristocrat who tells of his opium smoking habits, and a homosexual who became a British secret agent because he wished to prove that he was brave like other men. The personal stories are complemented by wartime documentary footage providing a vivid picture of the period. But the old film clips are not merely illustrative. They constitute an additional source of vital information, and they illuminate the historical context and the coherence of vision. In particular, the director accomplishes an ironic interplay between pictures of the past and present reflections. The authoritative documentary sections expose characters who refuse to come to terms with the disgraceful past of the French nation or with their own shameful conduct during the war. The camera in the present steadily focuses on the interviewees, scrutinizing their facial expressions, and it thus achieves a special impact on the viewers—conveying an ironic, mocking attitude toward those few who lie or express no remorse, and, on the other hand, a confiding, intimate relationship with the honest ones. All this leads to the remarkable achievement of *The Sorrow and the Pity*—the projection of highly individualized characters whose fascinating personal dramas, through the special rapport created with the camera and the viewers, enliven a past which the French nation had been trying to ignore and forget.

Still, *The Sorrow and the Pity* tells a story well known to any beginning student of World War II. The film is essentially, in the words of James Roy MacBean, "a low-keyed, even bland, 'liberal' examination of the Nazi occupation and the French collaborationist regime of Marechal Petain."[43] For example, the movie ignores the French Communists' support for the Germans during the period of the Nazi-Soviet pact (until Hitler invaded Russia), nor does it highlight the close ties between the Catholic Church and the Vichy government. Nevertheless, Ophuls's documentary had enormous influence. It shattered "one of the most highly cherished political myths of Gaullist France—the myth of *la resistance*,"[44] and prompted a national self-exploration which continues into the present. (One special cinematic genre, called by the French *cinema retro* to designate the boom of contemporary French movies on wartime France, was directly augmented by *The Sorrow and the Pity*.) In the early seventies, French society was fiercely debating the content of the film. The Gaullist establishment was especially furious with the "unpatriotic" work, whereas young people throughout the world were fascinated by the range of human reactions to extreme historical situations. All the uproar notwithstanding, MacBean correctly observes that "what is ultimately most remarkable, then, about *Le Chagrin et La Pitié* is simply that such a politically vacuous film should be capable of stirring up such big political waves."[45]

What, then, truly made *The Sorrow and the Pity* such a remarkable work was neither political defiance nor any compelling artistic vision but simply the basic potential power of the cinematic medium—the direct or candid registration of truthful incidents and characters by the camera. The chinese proverb "a picture is worth more than ten thousand words" comes to mind here. In addition, the dialectical editing enhances the effect by juxtaposing the interviewees' accounts with wartime documentary material. Moreover, unlike the historical studies in print, film can display the process of the historian's research by showing us witnesses and participants of the historical drama. The cinematic encounter with them registers a special artistic impact of emotional involvement, and also puts the viewer in the position of investigator by gradually exposing the viewer to the interviewees' experiences. Ultimately the viewer judges those experiences through the gain of knowledge and emotional identification. The distinguished scholar Stanley Hoffmann expressed his reaction to the film in the following statement:

> Like all works of art that probe the truth about a society, *The Sorrow and the Pity* is a mirror presented by the authors to their audiences. How sharp a mirror a movie such as this one turns out to be, compared with novels or even with plays, not to mention memoirs or histories! The printed page, or words on a stage, are no substitutes for the faces, voices, gestures of "real" people. No written flashback has the power that explodes on the screen when a scene from 1940 and a scene from the present are juxtaposed, showing the same man at thirty years' distance. No narrative, no fictional reconstruction matches the newsreel or the live interview. Especially when the subject is nothing less than a nation's behavior in the darkest hour of its history, it isn't surprising that the reactions should be so passionate. In skillful hands of clever people, movies or television films can be formidable weapons.[46]

The Nazi documentary *Triumph of the Will* complicates the problematics of movies as mirrors and throws light on the possibilities of use or misuse of films as weapons. Indeed, by manipulating pictures and impressions while exploiting the sensuous effect of the camera's recording and the spectators' instinctive acceptance of its content as factual and actual, the cinematic medium has been employed as an effective instrument of communication and a formidable tool of propaganda. Vladimir Lenin, in the wake of the Russian Revolution and the consolidation of Communist power, had set the tone with his oft-quoted reference to film as "the most important art." Hitler and Goebbels, two cinema addicts and awesome masters of propaganda, were anxious to exploit the medium's power. In 1934 Hitler commissioned one of his favorite film figures, the German actress and director Leni Riefenstahl, to prepare a movie on the Reich's party convention. Using thirty cameras and a staff of about 120 members and enjoying the unlimited support of the Fuehrer, Riefenstahl was set to record the week-long Nazi convention in Nuremberg in September 1934. The product of her endeavors, *Triumph of the Will*, has become one of the most famous, or infamous, documentaries of all time.

Triumph of the Will begins with a series of bombastic statements: "On September 5, 1934, 20 years after the outbreak of the World War," "16 years after the beginning of our suffering," "19 months after the beginning of the German renaissance," "Adolf Hitler flew to Nuremberg again to review the columns of his faithful followers." The presentation of Hitler's flight leaves no doubt about his function as the divine savior of his people. His plane emerges out of the cloudy sky, its shadow hovering on the roofs and streets of the medieval city of Nuremberg, and he descends from above like a God visiting earth. After this impressive beginning, with its eschatological overtones, most of the film consists of endless rallies, speeches, and military parades. The political leaders, Hitler's henchmen, preach blind obedience to the Fuehrer, whose masterly postures continually evoke images of a godly presence. Ritual festivities and ceremonies featuring spades, torches, and huge banners contribute to the sense of religious ecstasy. The film's power derives from the monumental demonstrations of hundreds of thousands of followers whose uniformed appearance and gestures are almost uncanny; the organization of multitudes of faceless people and emblems in groups of huge geometric forms is visually stunning. The soundtrack consists of Hitler's speeches, brief slogans stated by Nazi leaders, lots of drum beats, and the orchestrated massive roars of *Sieg Heil*, as well as music combining Wagnerian motifs with many neo-Wagnerian heroic themes, German folk melodies, martial music, and, of course, party anthems.

Leif Furhammar and Folke Isaksson, in their book *Politics and Film*, declared: "Leni Riefenstahl's *Triumph des Willens* is one of the greatest achievements, perhaps the most brilliant of all in the history of film propaganda. It is a magnificently controlled work of art, and, at the same time, a document on an event captured in all its terrifying immediacy."[47] The film is magnificent and extraordinary, but in this statement Furhammar and Isaksson still made two significant mistakes. *Triumph of the Will* is a failed propaganda film. Although Hitler liked the film, in Nazi Germany "it was not successful with the general public and was not used very widely as propaganda."[48] Secondly, Riefenstahl's film is not a document of an authentic, immediate event. Riefenstahl's remark that "the preparations for the Party Convention were made in concert with the preparations for the camera work"[49] is one evidence that, in Susan Sontag's words, "the historic event served as the set of a film which was then to assume the character of an authentic documentary."[50] Siegfried Kracauer noted that cinematic techniques such as editing, camera movement, and mirror shots "built up a faked reality that was passed off as the genuine one."[51] And Sontag referred to some of the most blatant fakes in this film: "Indeed, when some of the footage of Party leaders at the speakers' rostrum was spoiled, Hitler gave orders for the shots to be refilmed; and Streicher, Rosenberg, Hess, and Frank histrionically repledged their fealty to the Fuehrer weeks later, without Hitler and without an audience, on a studio set built by Speer. (It is altogether correct that Speer, who built the gigantic site of the rally on the outskirts of Nuremberg, is listed in the credits of *Triumph of the Will* as architect of the film.)"[52]

Ironically, these fakes and others do not diminish the expository power of Riefenstahl's film, which is to this day the most revealing documentary on Nazism. Richard Barsam in his apologetic *Filmguide to Triumph of the Will* points out that the work "is surprisingly free of reference to the specific evils which we associate with the Nazi doctrine; the speeches, for example, have been edited to the most general statements about growth and progress. There is no reference anywhere in the film to extermination of the Jews or to conquest of the world."[53] Well, Hitler, who, as noted before, did love the film, was more perceptive about the unique quality of Riefenstahl's approach. For the fact is that the relatively general speeches are overshadowed by the film's visual power and its distinct aesthetics, so much so that the viewer is literally assaulted by Nazi ideology. The crowd scenes, for example, convey through their visual awesomeness the negation of the individual and exalt Fascist human regimentation; the low-angle pictures of Hitler and the alternation and contrast between his personal presence and the expressed admiration of the participants and spectators are nothing but a relentless glorification of a godlike leader demanding complete submission to his will and his doctrines; the camera work is characterized by the caressing and sensual pans of Hitler's face in the only film in which Hitler agreed to be featured; in terms of mise-en-scène, the medieval steeples, sculptures, and venerable façades which "are glimpsed between fluttering banners and presented in such a way that they too seem to be caught in the excitement"[54] are designed to evoke the Nazi cultivation of the Wagnerian-Teutonic myth of the German past. Indeed, Triumph of the Will contains a number of pictures that have captured the true essence of Nazism for posterity. Some of the most memorable moments include the ecstatic uniformed multitudes cheering Hitler; the delirious youth swearing loyalty to the Nazi state; and the Fuehrer, accompanied by Himmler and Lutze, marching toward a distant platform between hundreds of thousands of uniformed soldiers choreographed like black squares on a huge white setting.

It should also be noted that Riefenstahl displayed an ample concern about the specific political goals of the 1934 Nazi rally. Following the "Night of the Long Knives," the Hitler-ordered murder of Ernst Rohm, leader of the SA, and scores of his followers, Hitler was anxious to demonstrate party unity. The famous picture of the distant figures of Hitler, Himmler, and Lutze, the latter being respectively leaders of the SS and SA, signifies the theme of unity. Brian Winston pointed out that the director organized the material in accordance with Hitler's attempt to appease the SA, to cover up his role in the massacre and to vaguely suggest that whatever happened was historically justified. Winston mentions the account of an eyewitness, a contemporary American diarist who was present at Nuremberg, who reported that the SA seemed unimpressed. Adds Winston, "Riefenstahl helps along this rather poor performance of the big lie in action by emphasizing the dazzling spectacle of the setting."[55]

Finally, beyond the general vices implied in Riefenstahl's Fascist aesthetics— i.e., the pervasive feelings of dehumanization, regimentation, fanatic obedience, and the cult of the Fuehrer—one can sense in this film the pregnant, specific horrors of Nazism, the sinister ambitions that have been edited out by Riefenstahl but which were to materialize in World War II in colossal calamities. In other words, many pictures in Triumph of the Will foreshadow the specific atrocities of World War II. Furhammar and Isaksson observed: "Beyond the Führer and the masses under his spell lie the victims. The smoke from the torches recalls the smoke from the gas ovens [sic]. Behind the well-drilled columns of fair-haired youths we sense the ghostly parade of prisoners from Stalingrad. Behind the triumph stands defeat."[56]

There is another important fact about Triumph of the Will that makes it an

ominous foreshadower of horrors to come, or, looked at differently, with our hindsight today, that compels the contemporary viewer to associate Riefenstahl's film
with Auschwitz. Triumph of the Will was made in Nuremberg, and as Furhammar
and Isaksson maintain, "It is significant enough that it was in Nuremberg that
Hitler called the Reichstag to a special session and in 1935 presented the so-called
Nuremberg Laws, which were unanimously approved, to deprive German Jews of
their citizenship and forbid marriages between Jews and Germans."[57] Let us not
underestimate the pointed significance, for according to many, "the die was cast
with the passing of the Nuremberg Laws. The rest was a matter of fantasy."[58] And
as historian Lucy Dawidowicz observed, the channeling of violent antisemitism
into official law took place "on the occasion of the annual NSDAP [Nazi party]
congress in Nuremberg,"[59] that is, on the first anniversary of the making of
Riefenstahl's film. In summary, Triumph of the Will, like the antisemitic films
produced in Germany in 1941 (Jew Suss, Der Ewige Jude) to encourage the Nazis
to perpetrate the Final Solution with zeal and efficacy, is an indispensable part of
the Third Reich.[60] (When Alain Resnais shows in Night and Fog the picture of
the multitudes cheering with spades, immediately followed by photos of the camps'
construction, the editing suggests also a direct connection between the 1934 documentary and Auschwitz.)

Triumph of the Will proves that there is no necessary correlation between the
physical image and the recorded reality, and that aesthetic vision plays a crucial
role in defining the film's status as a truthful document. For what we have in
Riefenstahl's work is originally a false documentary—posing staged sets as authentic
immediate events—ending up as a potentially subversive propaganda work; instead
of being a eulogy to Nazism, the film exposes, on its audiovisual aesthetic level,
the basic evils of Nazism and it "provides insights into events which were to
culminate a few years later in Warsaw and in Auschwitz, and end on the gallows,
at Nuremberg."[61] Indeed, there is no other film whose footage has been used so
extensively in other cinematic works or has directly inspired other cinematic versions on subjects related to Hitler's era. From Chaplin's The Great Dictator and
numerous propaganda films of World War II—already during the war years Luis
Buñuel attempted to create an anti-Nazi film based exclusively on footage from
Triumph of the Will—until recent treatments of Nazism, filmmakers have incorporated footage taken directly from Riefenstahl's work or designed scenes and shots
which have direct visual bearing on the early Nazi film. At the same time, Triumph
of the Will is an extraordinary example of how cinema can reflect the nature of
political realities and social inclinations, how formal aesthetics mirror profound
moral, or, for that matter, immoral tendencies.

Both Triumph of the Will and The Sorrow and the Pity demonstrate the formidable
power of the film discourse to transmit reality and affect perceptions and attitudes.
Ophuls's candid camera approach relies on the veracity of objectively recorded
scenes and moments. He uses historically documented facts to enhance the present
critical vision while his main goal is to expose the full and unembellished truths
of the historical situation. Riefenstahl's work is a part of a big show resorting to
blatant fakes to fit propagated ideological vision. But the excessive concern with

appearance ultimately betrays the truth of its essence. The movie's undeniable content derives from our acceptance of the cinematic medium also as the producer of a sensual discourse that signifies and connotes meanings beyond the mere external appearance of things. This notion, coupled with our knowledge of the direct connection between the Nazi actuality and its embraced aesthetics—its essentially Fascist vision that relies on specifically patterned sensible attractions to imprint its ideological indoctrination—renders Triumph of the Will as an outstanding mirror to the monstrosity of Nazi Germany. In its arresting visual power, Triumph of the Will is a cinematic document for one of the most compelling subjects of our time, and yet, by its very essence, it is a demonstration of extreme falsehood in the service of extreme evil.

The title of Claude Lanzmann's monumental film, Shoah, suggests a comprehensive approach to the subject of the Nazi-attempted genocide of the Jews during the years of World War II. ("Shoah" usually means great catastrophe; in Hebrew culture today it has come to designate the Final Solution and is the linguistic equivalent of "Holocaust.") In this respect Lanzmann's program recalls Alain Resnais's Night and Fog (1955), or even Gerald Green's teledrama Holocaust (1978). However, Shoah and Holocaust present two antithetical approaches to the subject. While the contrived fiction of Holocaust resorted to the standard conventions of popular teledramas in order to reach a wide audience, Lanzmann's epic work is distinguished by its exploration of cinema language, resulting in an uncompromising film with special qualities necessary for an adequate apprehension of the authentic experience. Shoah also stands in sharp contrast to Night and Fog, Resnais's semi-impressionistic thirty-minute documentary, which is both a cinematic masterpiece and the most powerful exposition of the past Nazi horrors. Shoah neither adds nor eclipses Night and Fog, for it has different concerns, offering a novel and challenging approach to the subject.

Despite its remarkable length, Shoah is highly selective in its choice of subject matter. The lapses may have justifiedly irritated some critics. The context of World War II, and in particular the Russian front, receives little or no attention;[62] surprisingly, there is no reference to the mass murders by the Einsatzgruppen following the Vehrmacht invasion of Russia. I regretted especially the lack of any treatment of the persecution and humiliation of the integrated western Jews, most conspicuously the fate of the German Jews. One of the essential dimensions of the Holocaust is the wartime conduct of the "enlightened" societies in the west with its critical implications in regard to the value of the premises and promises of western civilization. There is only an allusion to the Allies' inaction and indifference in long shots of Washington and New York in the sequence when Jan Karski, former courier of the Polish government-in-exile, describes the infernal reality of the Warsaw ghetto. The treatment of the Warsaw ghetto lacks proper historical perspective, which is a little bit confusing, and perhaps even anticlimactic, because it is presented at great length after the detailed accounts of the killing operations in the death camps. Also in dealing with the Warsaw ghetto, Lanzmann's consistent avoidance of wartime pictures becomes a real deficiency. We are left with rather impressionistic and expressionistic descriptions of eyewitnesses, whereas the ar-chival footage that exists on the ghetto provides a piercingly realistic representation of the infernal horrors.[63]

The Nazi crimes and horrors have been documented before, in film, in lit-erature, in historical accounts, and even in dramatic presentations. One has to recognize, however, that the vast magnitude of the Final Solution rules out the possibility of a totally inclusive treatment of the historical experience in any one individual work on it, regardless of discipline, genre, or the work's size. We can only define the specific premises, concerns, and expectations of the individual work, and only then can we criticize its lapses. *Shoah* is not a document of past events; it is definitely not a peep-show of horrors, nor is it a monument commemo-rating the Holocaust. The long interviews with survivors, with former Nazi guards, and with eyewitnesses from the local population of wartime Europe summon memo-ries of the past in order to explore the unique character of the genocide.

In *Shoah*, Lanzmann created a film of extraordinary length without using archival footage. Clearly the nine and one-half hour movie is not so long because of the scope of the subject matter. Lanzmann began the editing process with 350 hours of film. Thus the length of the film ought to be considered as a meaningful artistic choice, just as the lack of wartime pictures cannot be regarded as a decision based on mere expediency. The avoidance of archival material reflects the film-maker's determination to view the past in terms of the present, to concentrate on and to explore the legacy of the Final Solution. Lanzmann attempts to draw the contemporary viewers into the special orbits of the original experience—in what-ever degree possible—by demonstrating its presence in our culture and by high-lighting its relevance to our existence in the present. In light of these concerns, the length of the film becomes an ingenious device. It defies the normal tempo of viewing movies, characterized by the expectation of a beginning, a middle, and an end and the experience of suspense, climax, and closure, which ensure some kind of a cathartic effect. Instead, it imposes a state of mind which confronts agonizing, occasionally unbearable recognitions on the spectrum of possible human behavior and moral decisions under extreme situations, painful reflections on the cultural implications of the genocide, and a special deep frustration at the failure of the mind, in its perception, understanding, or imagination, to apprehend the scope of the crime and the unsettling details of its atrocities.

Shoah gravitates relentlessly to the core of the Nazi crimes and horrors. Lanz-mann focuses on the death camps of Chelmno, Belzec, Maidanek, Sobibor, Tre-blinka, and Auschwitz. The Nazis planned, built, and organized these camps specifically as killing centers, in contradistinction to the elaborate system of con-centration camps for those considered undesirable or dangerous by the Nazi regime. (The concentration camps most notorious for their brutality and subhuman con-ditions were usually located in Germany and Austria—Bergen-Belsen, Dachau, Buchenwald, and Mauthausen—and their reputation has caused many to confuse these camps with the death camps.) The apparent thrust of *Shoah* is to reveal and document the shocking atrocities of the genocide program, including the meticulous methods employed by the Germans when performing their heinous crimes. More important, though, the film features this inhuman system in order to examine the baffling humane behavior of the main participants in the historical trauma, be they victims, victimizers, or bystanders.

Knowing the strengths and weaknesses of his medium, Lanzmann skillfully avoided a meditative discourse and concentrated on those aspects of the human experience which the movie camera records and explores most effectively. The recounted details of the horror and their incarnation in physical items are essential to grasping the unsettling singularity of the Jewish genocide and the atrocities of the concentration camp universe. Lanzmann adopts Raul Hilberg's position that the factuality of the Holocaust, understood in terms of its concrete, haunting details, makes up the core of any ethical or intellectual reference to the event and takes precedence over any abstract moralization or intellectual speculation about meaning and cultural implications.

One major aspect of the Holocaust's legacy is the concrete evidence which was left over, such items as original documents, the railroads and the actual trains used to transport millions of victims, the kind of trucks which served for the initial gas killing, and the camp sites—the real settings of the crimes. In *Shoah*, these are shown again and again, as dumb witnesses hiding unbearable secrets. Lanzmann's manifested fascination with an authentic Nazi form regulating the deportations of the Jews is not because of the document's specific historical value—as was mentioned before, *Shoah* is not a historical documentary and this aspect is irrelevant to Lanzmann's work. Rather, Lanzmann conveys the full amazement and wonder of holding a concrete item that came from "the other planet." On the screen we see the photographed document; but as Barthes once pointed out, the photographic image has the magic impact of ressurection.[64] Indeed, the cinematic medium's photographic image is the most effective means to transmit the reality of the unreality of the death camps—unreality in the sense of unbelievability, of the logic of annihilation. The recurrent pictures of the deportation trains and the camp sites have the effect of an obsessive concentration on the real that threatens to become unreal (and, for the revisionists and other neo-Nazis, also untrue). Gradually they become also the subject of dramatic recognition and assume new dimensions, and they are invested with the increasingly gained knowledge of what truly happened there.

If the inanimate objects form the past provoke amazement and wonder, the presence of those persons from "the other planet" inspires awe and trembling. In *Shoah* the people who remember function not as mere instruments to inform us on what they had witnessed. Lanzmann uses his camera to record the acts of recollection and narration of the personal stories. He presents individuals and groups whose entire lives were shaped by the Final Solution, so that acquaintance with them today tells us about the legacy of the events in the concrete human dimension of emotions, desires, anxieties, fears, traumatic memories, and attitudes. Alternating between victims, bystanders, and a few Nazi perpetrators, the viewers can see how the attitudes of the last two groups played the crucial role in the implementation of the genocide. Indeed, these former Nazis and complacent bystanders display tremendous insensitivity and loathsome poses of evasion, creating unbearable tension, disbelief, and outrage when their present positions are expressed against the background of past horrors. Lanzmann, however, cleverly avoids any explicit and simplified moralization. He ostensibly devotes his work to the examination of the minute details which had made up a tremendous crime. But the moral outrage is provoked when we realize that thinking minds and human attitudes, and not only physical force and impersonal bureaucratic efficiency, had made that crime possible.

Regarding the survivors, Lanzmann chose to interview mostly those who were members of the "sondercommando," the special detail units who had to work for the Nazis and who were often assigned the task of disposing of the countless corpses. It would be absurd and heartless to view them as collaborators. It is indeed impossible to judge them, and at times even to understand them. Their ghastly experiences stun our imagination, and their humane presence—the scrutinizing camera brilliantly captures their minute gestures and rich facial expressions—is sharply contrasted with inhuman events that are ghostly and infernal. Usually the most terrible things that happened to the victims are recounted at the end. But the buildup is not of a narrative structure; it is not the curiosity and suspense of "what will have happened." There is, however, a dramatic development: like all strong characters in drama, the survivors appear different at the end of their stories, evidently as a result of emotional and mental crises which they undergo in the filming process. The magic of Lanzmann's documentary is that it captures these changes in their full authentic force. The laughing eyes of Rudolf Vrba are incongruous and disorienting as he describes the "logical system" of Auschwitz, but his expression changes radically when the former inmate assesses the scope of the liquidation and the possibilities of resistance. Philip Miller appears heartless when he describes in a methodical, relentless discourse how corpses were undressed and shoved into the Auschwitz crematoria. But when he recounts the fate of a transport of compatriot Czech Jews, the seemingly emotionless man suddenly breaks, weepingly telling of his decision to join them in the gas chamber. (The film accomplishes a remarkable real closure—Philip Miller was persuaded by the other victims to remain alive to tell their story.) Abraham Bomba seems at first a relaxed and confident vacationer on the beaches of Tel Aviv. He talks about Treblinka with an almost defiantly sharp and measured diction. But then the former barber who shaved Jewish women inside the gas chamber chokes and breaks when he recalls how a fellow barber was made to perform the grisly task on his own wife and sister. The long moments of silence which record his desperate efforts to regain composure constitute one of the most memorable sequences in the history of cinematic documentation.

The section with Abraham Bomba, the barber from Treblinka, is the most powerful scene in Shoah. But it is the scene in front of the Church in Chelmno, featuring Simon Srebnik, the sole survivor of the the first phase of extermination in Chelmno, which provides the most intriguing moments and which best illustrates Lanzmann's original treatment of the subject.

Srebnik was a young boy of thirteen when he was deported from the Lodz ghetto to the extermination center in the village of Chelmno, by the Narew River in the heart of Poland. He was not executed at once, because the Nazis decided to exploit his melodious talent. For over two years the Jewish boy's voice was a source of sentimental folk music, both German and Polish, and was heard all over the Polish village. Toward the end of the war the retreating Germans shot a bullet into the head of every remaining Jew in the camp. Srebnik was the sole survivor of this execution—the bullet missed his vital brain centers.

Forty years later, Srebnik and Lanzmann's crew visit Chelmno. It's a small provincial place with only two large-size buildings, an old castle and the local church. The castle was the site of the German headquarters, and the church was used to concentrate the Jews before their liquidation in the gas vans. The scene which unfolds takes place in front of the church. It is a special occasion for the villagers celebrating the birth of the Virgin Mary. The background includes the imposing façade of the church, and a frontal view of the open arched doors reveals the worshipers inside. A group of elderly people demonstrates gladness to see Sreb-nik, uttering words of compassion when they recall his sufferings in the past. They are curious, but more ostensibly very friendly. Srebnik is treated like a celebrity returning to visit in his old hometown. The impassioned but insignificant pronouncements from the crowd go on for a while. Srebnik is in the middle of the group, looking ahead with a seemingly embarrassed smile and continuously nodding in an apparent affirmation of the nostalgic recollections of this strange group. His expression never changes as the gruesome details of the killing are recalled by the enthusiastic villagers. He continues to smile and nod as they explain that the Jews' suitcases were full of gold, and that all this happened to the Jews "because they were the richest!" They even describe how the Jews moaned and cried, and how "they [the Jews!] called on Jesus, Mary, and God, sometimes in German." Evidently all of these bizarre comments and stories are part of the collective memory of the Polish villagers. At one point they encourage Mr. Kantarowski to tell what a friend told him about what happened in Myndjewyce, near Warsaw. The crowd's urges create a suspenseful expectation, and Mr. Kantarowski steps forward to tell the following story:

> The Jews there were gathered in a square. The Rabbi asked an SS man: "Can I talk to them?" The SS man said yes. So the Rabbi said that around two thousand years ago the Jews condemned the innocent Christ to death. And when they did that, they cried out: "Let his blood fall on our heads and on our sons' heads." Then the rabbi told them: "Perhaps the time has come for that, so let us do nothing, let us go, let us do as we're asked."[65]

Mr. Kantarowski doesn't think that the Jews were killed to expiate the death of Jesus, or that Christ sought revenge. According to him: "The Rabbi said it. It was God's will, that's all." But at this point the crowd has been aroused. Srebnik is still standing in the middle, smiling and nodding, very much like a dummy clown. The old woman, who appeared earlier as the most enthusiastic receiver of Srebnik's unexpected visit, states: "So Pilate washed his hands and said: 'Christ is innocent,' and he sent Barrabas. But the Jews cried out; 'Let his blood fall on our heads!' "

Lanzmann said of Srebnik that "he was terrorized as a child and he is terrorized still." Like most other camp inmates, Srebnik had to master the technique of self-effacement in order to survive: hiding emotions, suppressing desires, and just trying to endure the threats of his environment. Under the Nazis the survival struggle became paramount and total. The tragedy of Srebnik is that he cannot be liberated from its traumatic effects. The tragedy of our civilization is that it contains the elements which arouse his traumatic symptoms today. For Srebnik's awkward behavior cannot be explained exclusively in terms of his past. We gradually recognize that he responds to stimuli which impel him to reincarnate his past behavior of extreme self-effacement. Thus we can understand Srebnik's passivity and strange facial expression, but at the same time we ought to realize that we have indeed been witnessing a scene of victimization whose contemporaneity is all the more frightening as it makes perceptible how the Holocaust had been possible.

In Lanzmann's special documentary, that scene, like many others, is distinguished by its dramatic rather than its expository unfolding. It focuses on relationships between characters and their development according to a pattern of conflicts and crises. It also develops themes in line with the progress of the action, finally reaching a climax and some sort of a resolution. At the end we are affected by the action of the present, which elicits the moment of dramatic recognition, while the knowledge of the past only invests it with additional insight and emotion.

In the beginning of the scene, the church foreground is charged with dramatic tension. Initially the incongruity between the religious services and our knowledge of the church's function during the war is the source of dramatic irony, further underscored by the transition from the recounting of Srebnik's wartime singing to Mr. Kantarowski playing the church organ, which opens this scene. We anticipate or even hope for an explanation which will help us reconcile this uneasy contrast. Perhaps the worshipers will inform us about a deep, genuine, and continuing compassion toward the Jewish victims, whose liquidation began in their house of prayer. We may even see a special mark commemorating the terrible tragedy. Thus the occurrence of the conflict is unexpected, and it develops as an actual drama unfolding in front of the recording camera. After all, Srebnik was apparently asked by the filmmaker to come to the site of the death camp in order to help us understand what went on there. He was a prisoner of the Germans, and the Poles, who lived under the yoke of German occupation, did not participate in the killing process. Moreover, the local villagers remember Srebnik and his beautiful singing, and his reappearance initially evokes some nostalgic memories for these folks.

It turns out that Srebnik is more like an Ibsenite ghost who threatens the tranquillity of what we eventually realize was a community totally complacent with the Nazi crimes against the Jews. The villagers are highly selective in their memories. At first they seem to ignore the grim context of Srebnik's experiences. However, when the fate of the Jews is no longer avoidable, the dramatic shock is that the villagers turn vicious. The new attitude is not the result of any defense mechanism to shelter them from the horrors of the past; it is the expression of an active support for the Nazi genocide of the Jews! Indeed, the encounter between the survivor and the villagers triggers the kind of conflict which was at the root of the genocide program. The next disturbing realization is that the church no longer provides an ironic contrast, juxtaposing the message of love and grace with the support of, or at least acquiescence to, such atrocities; it has become instead a source of inspiration for the villagers' insidious attitudes.

There is a common impression that Lanzmann is interested only in technical details and measurements, an allegation supported by the constant explanations of Raul Hilberg. His opening remarks actually serve as the keystone to the film: "In all my work" states Hilberg, "I have never begun by asking the big questions, because I was always afraid that I would come up with small answers; and I have preferred to address these things which are minutiae or details in order that I might then be able to put together . . . a picture which, if not an explanation, is at least a description." After arguing at length that in historical perspective the Nazis' specific invention was the notion and practice of the Final Solution, Hilberg suggests "a logical progression, one that came to fruition in what might be called closure, because from the earliest days, from the fourth century, the sixth century, the missionaries of Christianity said in effect to the Jews: 'You may not live among us as Jews.' The secular rulers who followed them from the late Middle Ages then decided: 'You may not live among us,' and the Nazis finally decreed: 'You may not live.' "66

Shoah informs us about the existence of seemingly milder forms of prejudice, the social and traditionally religious anti-Jewish sentiments. But the church scene in Chelmno demonstrates why antisemitism is fundamentally different from all other manifestations of the universal phenomenon of prejudice. It is something else because of its deep cultural roots and its deadly consequences. The fact that the Polish villagers' slurs on the Jews' wealth and power are expressed by those who had witnessed their extermination and then took over their property illustrates the monstrous dimension of antisemitism; the resort to Christian dogmas justifying the killing of Jews conveys its demonic nature. It should be noted that after Auschwitz, a significant number of distinguished Christian thinkers acknowledged the complicity of the history of Christian antisemitism in the incidence of the Holocaust. Referring to the centuries of Christian "teaching of contempt" toward Judaism—the Jews rejected Jesus, God rejected the Jews, the Jews killed Christ, the Jews are doomed until the end of time—the Catholic Eugene Fisher writes that "without the negative stereotyping of Jews and Judaism, it is unlikely that Hitler's manic anti-Semitism would have fallen on such fertile soil in Europe."67 Protestant theologian Franklin Littell maintains that the idea of supersessionism is the "cornerstone of Christian anti-semitism which already rings with a genocidal note."68 The death camps were the culmination of manic antisemitism—and the mystery of Auschwitz should not mystify this basic truth. This assertion with its implication of Christian responsibility is the core of *Shoah*'s interpretive impulse.

If Lanzmann then managed to present in his factual film a powerful drama with its meaningful setting, characters, action, climax, and thematic concerns, he also used the cinematic medium to explore a critical aspect of the Holocaust—its time dimension. The length of *Shoah*, the repeated pictures of the camp sites, the recurrent shots of the trains (suggesting a metaphorical journey into the past), and the numerous long takes which identify screen time with real time give away the special status of the fourth dimension in Lanzmann's work. The importance of the theme of time in the discourse on the Nazi crimes was manifested also by Alain Resnais in *Night and Fog*. The underlying structure of Resnais's classic documentary is the alternation between the black-and-white, frozen images of the past and the fluid and deceptively colorful pictures of the present. But the strength and impact of *Night and Fog* derive from the visual presentation of the concentration camp universe. Resnais added to that the expression of his profound anxiety about the eroding effects of time, and warned against the forgetfulness of the event in the name of justice and the need for a better world.

The work on *Shoah*—the process of filming the material was a significant act, as we are reminded in moments that foreground the camera work—made Lanzmann disenchanted with this kind of sentimental idealism.[69] The filmmaker has a curious harsh presence, and he occasionally adds sordid comments which neutralize the outburst of sentimentality. Working on his film one generation after the genocide happened, Lanzmann realized that the significance of the event lies not in its straightforward, didactic, moral lessons, but rather as a traumatic cultural shock, which has been enhanced, and not diffused, by the passage of time. Lanzmann's treatment of the historical events is sombre and often even anguished (and he skillfully avoids the pitfalls of pornographic fascination with the vistas of horror and atrocities). He seeks to penetrate the veil that threatens to mythologize the Holocaust and to place the event outside real, historical time. He features intriguing characters who display paradigmatic patterns of behavior in the universe of atrocities. Yet these characters have a very real presence as they are recorded by the truthful camera, and moreover their palpable presence is in the present in the sense that we watch modes of memory and strategies of attitudes toward the event. The disturbing revelation is that the prejudice and hatred that brought about the Holocaust did not vanish with the fall of the Third Reich, that the wounds of the victims are as painful as ever, and that our cultural fabric can thrive with large pockets of terrific human insensitivity to the enormous crimes. These reasons alone mandate that the Holocaust should be an obsessive event, an event in relation to which time moves backward in the sense that the progress of time grants it more attention, interest, and greater significance. (The medical field can provide the analogy of a gradual mental response to a traumatic shock or a severe accident like an amputation.)[70]

Finally, time was a specific attribute of the Final Solution which made it radically different from any other historical moments of great disasters. The Nazi-attempted genocide of the Jews took place over a substantial length of time. Many Germans like to refer to the Nazi era as "an avalanche." But the twelve years of the Third Reich, the six years of World War II, the four years of systematic extermination of millions of Jews were periods of such length as to indicate that there was a crucial process of adjustment and accommodation on the parts of those who were either victimizers, bystanders, or victims. It is indeed a terrifying realization that there were those who killed thousands as their daily activity and way of life, that many others carried on with their normal routine right next to the killing centers, and that there are those few who survived—for years!—in a world designed to bring about their destruction and extermination. To my mind the main accomplishment of Lanzmann's work is that he was able to elicit from the interviewees the manifestations of attitudes and character traits that help us understand how they functioned in the genocide program. This was not an easy task, to be sure, not with those who now dread to open their deep scars, and not with those who attempt to rationalize their complicity in the crimes. Yet in many moments in the film we see a transformation of a character who relives the past. The exceptional length of Shoah, especially the very long takes, is necessary to re-create and display this process of change for some key participants. The most remarkable example is perhaps the church scene in Chelmno, which shows the transformation of a group of Poles from a congregation of provincial, religious villagers into a bunch of vultures thirsty for Jewish blood.

Shoah is not a documentary film, but rather it is an outstanding document, for it calls attention to its own presentation rather than serving as a window representing another reality. Although the focal point of reference is the victimization of the Jews during the years of World War II, those individuals who inform us on the past are usually more fascinating because of their behavior in the present. Shoah's most remarkable qualities—the palpable presence of the death camps (a demonstration of the sites, not their evocation), the personal dramas which unfold with powerful authenticity, the engagement with the moral implications of contemporary attitudes toward the attempted genocide of the Jews—offer a unique cinematic experience, challenging the viewers to appreciate the traumatic effects of the past by confronting its symptoms in the present. Lanzmann's film is a monumental contribution to the discourse of this most crucial and most crushing human experience that we call the Holocaust or Shoah.

Night and Fog. The Survivors.

Night and Fog. The Victims.

The Sorrow and the Pity. Guilt and shame of collaborators and bystanders.

Triumph of the Will. The picture of the Messianic Fuehrer reveals an ugly, fanatic tyrant.

Triumph of the Will. The monstrous incongruity of Riefenstahl's art: the innocent-looking face of the admiring girl is framed by the towering presence of Hitler's henchmen, while the swastika occupies the center of the frame.

Triumph of the Will. The climax of the Nuremberg rally and of Riefenstahl's film: Hitler, with leaders of the SA and the SS at his side and the multitudes of faceless Nazis arranged in a frightening perfect order—soon they would be led to try to destroy the world in an orderly fashion.

The Last Stop. The arrival at Auschwitz.

The Last Stop. The roll call. The actual survivors reliving their experience in film, with an incongruous cinematically made-up attractive woman in the center.

Kapo. The harsh conditions in the Nazi labor camp.

Kapo. The improbable love affair in a concentration camp (Susan Strasberg and Laurent Terzieff).

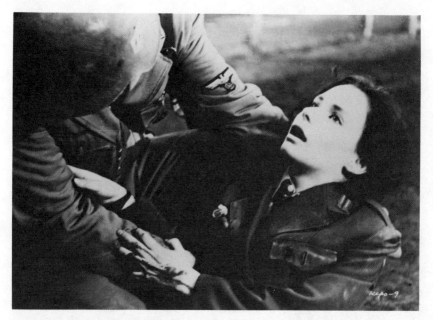

Kapo. The martyr's death of Edith redeems her sinful survival to fit the neat, conventional moral order of the story.

Taken by a Nazi photographer after the liquidation of the Warsaw ghetto—the power of pictures as historical evidence and iconic message.

CHAPTER II

The Discontents
of Film Narrative

The documentary films discussed in the previous chapter demonstrate the formidable power of cinema to register historical events. We also noted that photos are not merely mirrors or records of reality—they actually possess a crucial iconic dimension, evoking through their content and form deep meanings beyond the appearance of things. Indeed, many outstanding Holocaust pictures project powerfully suggestive visions by illustrating the full pathos of the victims' predicament, or they symbolize the unsettling degree of the era's inhumanity, or, as in the case of Triumph of the Will, they convey the essence of the Nazi menace and its corruption of human nature. We now turn to examine the most prevalent form of filmic discourse, the narrative film, in which the photographic image functions as a basic component whose independent qualities—iconic or recordlike—are subordinated to the flow of the story line.

Storytelling is rooted in basic human urges of curiosity and fictionalization. However, despite Aristotle's famous dictum that plot is the soul of drama, traditional literary criticism held narrative to be "merely the 'hook' on which the artist hung his more meaningful thoughts and patterns."[1] Recent literary theories seek to shift analytical emphasis to the structure and essence of narrative. Nevertheless, as Christopher Williams points out, the study of narrative "is an area which has been scandalously neglected in film criticism."[2] Even so, in popular cinema, regular feature-length movies rely primarily on story for their appeal and effect. In this section we shall briefly discuss the essential features of narrative and explore how the very act of recounting the Holocaust in a narrative form might limit or distort vision and representation.

Narrative art is often applied creatively to tell the stories of historical episodes and real events. Narrative is the construction of an action, composed of a series of events, forming a coherent structure with clearly discernible beginning, middle, and end. The artistic organization of the narrative units is the plot; the plot involves the acts of selection, ordering, and determining the duration and frequency of significant events and is designed to establish sequential and/or causal relationships between these events or narrative units. The implications of narrative structure are critical for our discussion because authors of Holocaust stories usually take the material for their work from the reality of the historical experience, and they organize or plot the varied story elements. But in doing so they abide by the inherent rules of the narrative form, or, as structuralist narrative theory maintains, they arrange events and incidents in accordance with the operations of the narrative discourse, the basic modus of presentation. Stephen Heath summarized: "Narrativization, the process of the production of the film as narrative, is the operation of the balance, tying up the multiple elements—the whole festival of potential affects, rhythms, intensities, times, differences—into a line of coherence (advance and recall), a finality for the repetition."[3]

Ultimately, the discourse produces an aesthetic object which, for one thing, is characterized by the achievement of an artistic unity whose mastery and perfection inevitably generate aesthetic pleasure. Referring to the aesthetic gratification of narrative plotting, Henry James observed: "The prime effect of so sustained a system, so prepared a surface is to lead on and on: while the fascination of following resides, by the same token, in the presumability *somewhere* of a convenient, of a visibly-appointed stopping-place."[4]

Characters are an essential component of narrative, for they emerge from the structural system of the story and their qualities affect the movement and nature of the system. Vladimir Propp, "whose pioneering work . . . has served as the point of departure for the structualist study of plot,"[5] has called narrative function an act of character, defined from the point of view of its significance for the course of the action. Henry James had previously made his famous statement: "What is character but the determination of incident? What is incident but the illustration of character? What is either a picture or a novel that is NOT of character?"[6] Indeed, usually the dramatic action revolves around the story of a remarkable character. This crucial element provides the explicit human dimension of narrative art and generally entails an anthropocentric vision.

The connection between characters' ethical qualities and their fate and function in the story forms the basis for the expression of a moral vision. Authors always invest the characters with a certain moral charge, but they can also manipulate readers and viewers by bestowing a sympathetic protagonist with the characteristics of their political views while defining the antagonists as the negative force representing the positions opposed to their own. In the case of the cinematic medium, most films gear toward the narrative action featuring the struggle between "good guys" and "bad guys" and culminating with the triumph—physical or spiritual—of the good. This formula, however, is usually the springboard to the fostering and manipulation of ideological attitudes ranging from blatant propaganda to more subtle means of influence.

The main substance of popular films is made of the plot and the movement of dramatic action. The elements of character traits, thoughts, setting, and references to actual realities are generally secondary to the flow of the action, whose primary function is to create suspense, lead to a climax, and prepare for the film's ending. Moreover, filmmakers usually cater to popular taste. In particular, Hollywood has perfected a stock of cliché-ridden narrative actions which have proven to have enduring popular appeal; many of the acts are taken from melodramatic literature emphasizing love stories, protagonist heroics, and happy endings.[7] Such formula films led to the attacks of "liberal high culture and Marxist influenced modernism . . . [against] the swamp-like fascinations of the narrative, whose manipulations are seen as deceiving by entertainment."[8] Christopher Williams contends that "the pleasures that narrative methods provide need to be recognized, and indeed shifted towards the center of discussion, rather than deplored or condescended to."[9] Nevertheless, one can clearly see how, in the case of the genocide of the Jews, the combination of narrative pleasures with tragic history is deplorable, and there are, to be sure, numerous films which subject the Holocaust to popular trivialization. But to illuminate the fundamental or theoretical aspects of the problem, we will study three notable works which, despite good intentions, were compelled to fall into the "swamp-like fascinations" of narrative art. In the following discussion I will focus on three essential aspects of narrative form: the stimulation of expectations and their gratification in a coherent structure; the inducement of emotional involvement with the fate of the characters; and the insertion of ideological positions by means of manipulating the reader's or viewer's emphatic reaction to the actions of the dramatic agents.

At the end of World War II liberators and survivors realized that they had witnessed the most awesome atrocities ever enacted on earth. The unbelievable degree of bureaucratic destruction and inhuman bestiality led to the recognition that the horrors of Auschwitz must be faithfully documented, be transmitted to the ignorant, and issue a warning that such things must never happen again. Along with numerous documentaries and newsreel footage that circulated throughout the world, there were a few narrative movies that sought to combine conventional cinematic codes with genuine realistic resources to commemorate the Nazi atrocities and pay tribute to their victims. Not surprisingly, two of the most outstanding works on the subject were made in Poland, the one country in Europe that was hit the hardest by the German evil and had firsthand experience of the core of the Nazi hell, for the Nazis built all of their six extermination camps on Polish territory.

In 1947, Wanda Jakubowska, a former Auschwitz inmate, returned to the death camp to create a film about its horrors which she entitled *Ostatni Etap (The Last Stop* or *The Last Stage)*. The script of *The Last Stop* was written by Gerda Schneider, who was also a former inmate. The dialogue is spoken in German, Polish, Russian, and French, as was truly the case in the babel of Auschwitz. For the most part, the narrative aims at dramatizing key aspects of life behind the barbed wire, showing scenes of roll calls, arrivals of new transports, selections, and truckloads of victims being taken to the gas chambers. Significantly, the depiction of the extermination process is limited to the appearance of flames and the smoke in the distance, and this is consistent with an honest re-creation of the survivors' perspective.

The approach to characters emphasizes the sharp moral and immoral qualities of victims and victimizers in the camps. The portrayal of both Nazis and inmates as individual human beings highlights the cynicism of the former (when they meet to discuss more efficient ways of exterminating "inferior" races), the brutalities of the Kapos (who seek to please their masters and also satisfy their own sadistic tendencies), and the ruthlessness of some inmates (who exploit their power and connections at the expense of fellow inmates). The victims display both solidarity and antagonism when they struggle for survival. However, while the script follows typical aspects of the camp experience, forceful dramatic moments prevent the action from becoming too general or schematic, and their shocking content reveals their authenticity by reminding us how "the other planet" defied normal human expectations. For example, the film begins with a prisoner giving birth to a baby. The newborn is summarily executed, but the grieving mother is comforted by her fellow inmates that in Auschwitz it is "better" this way because it increases the survival chances of the mother. The crushing irony of this incident has additional significance, for childbirth, the act which signifies more than anything else the promise of life, becomes a prelude to death. Later we see a new group of Polish women arriving at the camp. Believing they are in a labor camp, they sing folk songs to accompany the hard work. An SS guard does not like it. He calls one of them over, throws his hat a few yards away, and orders the woman to retrieve it as if she were a dog. As the woman obeys, he raises his gun and shoots her. When he reports this as shooting a prisoner trying to escape, he is rewarded with a special vacation—this is Auschwitz justice.

The soundtrack also illustrates the disconcerting reality. When the Russian doctor—a brave leading figure who distinguished herself in defying the Nazis by telling a Red Cross visiting commission the truth about the extermination camp—is being brutally tortured, her interrogators play Russian folk music. And when the prisoners are being marched to their death, the women's orchestra plays classical music of Beethoven and Brahms. The climax of the exposition of camp reality depicts the selection of Jewish women who are loaded onto trucks to be taken to the gas chambers. The scene unfolds with almost unbearable realism. There is little brutality, because of the powerlessness and resignation of the victims. The Nazis are quick and efficient, and the women are herded, like cattle, to their liquidation. Still, the monumental criminality of this moment is not overlooked. One woman yells to a French nurse, "You must live to tell everyone what happened to us." But the young nurse boards the truck too, and as the trucks move off she begins singing the "Marseillaise," and is joined by the others in an act of defiance. Then, there is an unusually long fade-in, and the next scene begins with the inmates singing Russian folk songs celebrating the victory at Stalingrad.

The film's second part starts with that triumphant note. It features one pro-tagonist, Marta Weiss, a Jewish interpreter modeled after a true legendary figure named Mala who had taken advantage of her job as interpreter to assist the local resistance and was eventually caught and killed by the Nazis. Marta enters into the concentration camp universe as a newcomer, and through her eyes we witness the initial selection to the gas chambers and we see the crematoria flames.

The film's narrative deteriorates when Marta assumes the role of a heroine in a conventional action drama. She and another resistance fighter accept the task of publicizing the Nazi atrocities, and their radio broadcast is the climax of this story line. However, the heroics involved in achieving this triumph look too trite and fictional. When Marta is fooling a Nazi guard in order to make contact with the resistance member, she seems to enjoy her act like an Errol Flynn in an early-forties Hollywood war movie. The romance that develops between Marta and the resistance fighter fulfills narrative expectation but is extrinsic to the camp's harsh realities. The heroics of Marta seem about to end in her public execution. But the film's finale turns into a complete fantasy. At the gallows, a knife is slipped into her hands, and Marta releases herself. She delivers a moving speech against tyranny and human cruelty, stirring an uproar among the prisoners and sparking a massive defiance of the Nazis, as Allied planes fly over the camp signaling ultimate triumph over the forces of evil. Then Marta kills herself like a martyr, uttering her dying words: "You must not let Auschwitz be repeated."

The Last Stop is most remarkable thanks to its mise-en-scène. Jakubowska found Auschwitz to be a field of beautiful billowing green grass and wild flowers covering the wartime mire, much the same as Resnais saw it eight years later. She restored the original filth of the grounds and the buildings and shot many dark scenes to express the shrouded quality of the Kingdom of the Night. The visual presentation of the setting seems palpably authentic. Using twenty-seven featured players and about thirty-five hundred extras, most of whom were former prisoners of the Third Reich, Jakubowska shot her film in Auschwitz itself. Many of the participants in this production relived their past traumas, adding an outstanding dimension of authenticity. It is reported that "everything about Auschwitz was restored with such frightening accuracy that during lunch hours the prisoners would go to eat five by five. In groups of five was the way they were commanded to fall out by the Nazis. The mass scenes were so realistic that the extras hesitated to break their lines until told to do so."[10]

But the film also illustrates one of the impossible goals of realistic re-creation, to feature characters that look like the human shadows of Auschwitz hell. The healthy appearance of most of the prisoners in this film is in sharp contradiction to the pictures of the living skeletons in the Nazi camps. In addition, Jakubowska actually made up her actresses to beautify them, presumably as a result of uncritical adoption of cinematic conventions. Feminine makeup, combined with the Hollywood style of three-point lighting in close-ups, transforms certain Auschwitz scenes into a human drama of attractive characters set against the incongruous backdrop of a concentration camp. Still, Jakubowska's cinematic craft often yields wonderful results, including many unforgettable scenes and pictures. For example, the scene of a new shipment of Jews approaching the camp: the train advances through a foggy night as soldiers await it on one side of the track with their guns ready. As the train drives forward, its smoke fills the screen, foreshadowing the doom of the new victims. Alain Resnais used Jakubowska's image of the train entering the camp on a foggy night, staged as it is, to show the moment of arrival at "the other planet," in addition to exploiting the impressive visual content as an illustration for his film's title. Indeed, The Last Stop is a special landmark in the history of the Holocaust film, directly inspiring many other works on the subject and constituting a source of cinematic quotations for films like Night and Fog, The Diary of Anne Frank, Kapo, The Passenger, and others.

Unfortunately, in The Last Stop the forceful re-creation of life in a death camp is replaced by trivializing melodramatic action. The initial loose mosaic structure that featured revealing and startling factual events gives way to traditional clichés of conventional heroics in the spurious context of good guys/bad guys conflict. In conclusion, though, despite these deficiencies, the film's apparent authenticity, deriving from the actual location and the firsthand experience of those involved in its making, and the manifested passionate plea to remember the incredible inhumanity of Auschwitz grant The Last Stop the semblance of quality as well as moral authority.

The other postwar Polish Holocaust movie, Alexander Ford's Border Street (1948), focused on the plight of Polish Jewry in the Nazi period. The Jews of Poland undoubtedly suffered the most during World War II. Over ninety percent of Polish Jewry, nearly three million people, perished under the Nazis. Indeed, the Germans initially created the death camps to facilitate the liquidation of the Polish Jews. Yet, of all the ordeals of that once most vital and prosperous community in Europe, the erection of the Warsaw ghetto was perhaps the most tragic experience. The Nazis crammed about half a million people into a few blocks of the Polish capital, inflicting a gradual extermination through slave labor, starvation, and plagues that hit the population very hard because of the extreme overcrowding and the lack of decent medical facilities. At the peak of the oppression the mortality rate reached five thousand per month. Following the decision to pursue the Final Solution policy, the Nazis organized massive deportations that sent most of the ghetto inhabitants to their immediate death in extermination camps, mostly to Treblinka.

The Warsaw ghetto encompassed the harshest conditions outside the Nazi death camps and the greatest trial of Jewish endurance. Despite instances of collaboration, the Jews of the ghetto managed to cling to their cultural tradition, maintain human dignity, and form mutual assistance funds and organizations. Then, against all odds, in the final phases of the ghetto liquidation a handful of desperate men and women staged a heroically hopeless revolt against the Germans. It took the Germans nearly two months and armies consisting of SS units assisted by armored tanks and warplanes to defeat a few hundred poorly equipped fighting Jews. The flames that burned down the last Jewish strongholds became the lasting symbols of human and spiritual triumph against oppressive evil. Those flames also mark the complete annihilation of Polish Jewry, the largest Jewish community in eastern Europe.

Alexander Ford's Border Street was a special commemoration of the plight of the director's own people in Poland. Ford was a leading figure in the Polish cinema, and he spent the war years in the Soviet Union as the chief of the Polish army's film unit. In 1945 he was appointed director of Film Polski, the government-run film organization, and also taught film, becoming a key figure in the rise of Polish cinema in the fifties. His most famous protégé was Andrej Wajda. Ford supervised the production of Wajda's first movie, A Generation (1954); in his second film, Kanal (1957), Wajda paid homage to his mentor by demonstrating visual indebtedness to Ford's Border Street. However, as a Jew living in a Communist repressive regime with a long tradition of official and social antisemitism, Ford's position was always a precarious one. He was once denounced by Stalin himself for featuring "a Jewish instead of a class hero."[11] In 1967, following Israel's victory in the Six Day War, Ford fell victim to a new wave of antisemitism in Poland. He immigrated to Israel and in 1970 directed there The Martyr, a movie on Polish educator Janusz Korczak, who joined the children of his orphanage in the Warsaw ghetto on the transport to the extermination camp, declining an offer to save his life. Unfortunately, due to a weak story line, poor acting, and excessive sentimentality, The Martyr is a regrettable failure, even though it borrows much from the remarkable Border Street.

The title of Ford's postwar movie refers to the area between the ghetto and the city, reflecting the director's concern with the Jews and the Poles and the place of the Jews in Polish society, as well as implying a dry comment on the intolerably thin line between the centers of atrocities and the complacent bystanders' world during the war. Border Street focuses on the dismal fortunes of the residents of one crowded block, supposedly comprising a cross-section of the people of Warsaw and their actions during the war: a family of German origin collaborates with the Nazis; the members of an old Jewish tailor's family are brutally victimized; a Polish officer participates in underground activites; a half-Jewish family of an assimilated doctor is torn apart; and, as an additional special tribute to Marxism, a lower-class family maintains a resistant spirit and makes efforts to help the Jews (in reality most Poles who helped Jews belonged to the intelligentsia and higher social classes). The development of the plot parallels the gradual destruction of Polish Jewry. Antisemitic sentiments in prewar society are illustrated when a Jewish child, David, clumsily falls into a tub of water during a football game and one boy remarks that it is the first shower the boy has ever had. After the swift occupation of Poland, we see a German soldier ordering his trained dog to attack the Jewish boy. When the Nazis search private apartments for resistance members, they conduct brutal physical assaults against the Jews. The next stage in the Jewish catastrophe is deportation to the ghetto: Jews, wearing yellow stars and carrying their meager belongings are expelled from different quarters of the Polish capital.

The film's best moments present a forceful realistic picture, reinforced by the use of newsreel footage, of the Jewish predicament. In particular, the ghetto scenes show the terrible living conditions of dense overcrowding and famine. Many die of typhus, and the bereaved lament the dead, knowing that they are soon to share their fate. In order to survive, Jewish children try to smuggle food from the city, under the threats of Nazi guns and the dogs of the SS men. Others beg or try to sell their few remaining belongings while, ironically, the streets are full of random pieces of furniture abandoned by the deported Jews. The adults are forced to slave labor in order to survive. The notorious process of "selection" is demonstrated on a small scale when a German officer orders the execution of a disabled old man in a fabric factory. Another old man escapes deportation to a death camp by living inside a hidden wall. After spending many months standing stiff between two walls, and following the deportation of his wife and daughter, he loses the desire to survive as a subhuman. At the end, he wears the traditional prayer shawl, recites the *Shema*—"Hear o Israel, the Lord is our God, the Lord is One"—and, engulfed by the flames of the burning ghetto, he dies like many other Jewish martyrs, at the final word, *Ehad* (one).

The heroic revolt and the ghetto's complete liquidation make up the film's finale. Ford uses newsreel footage of the German attacks, interweaving it with the presentation of how the fighting Jews are killed one by one. Throughout the fighting, Polish citizens impassively watch the flames—a reminder of the film's ironic title. The pictures of the "curious" bystanders are contrasted with the visually impressive sequences in the sewers where doomed fighters struggle through turbid air and foul water, muddied with excrement evoking the atmosphere of hell. The concluding scenes show a few surviving fighters, including the Jewish boy, David, returning to the ghetto from their temporary shelter in the sewer to fight until the end.

Border Street's ending defies pessimism and nihilism. David's friends, Bronek, Wladek, and Jadzia—the half-Jewish girl—watch him vanishing into the sewer's fog on his way back to the dying ghetto; whereupon a commentator's voice reads: "No, little David, you will not die, for as long as there are people like you, like Bronek and Wladek, the barriers built by man against man will continue to be torn down, destroyed by those who sacrifice themselves that others may live."

Against the background of terrible and tragic events, the main action of *Border Street* develops around five children. Alexander Ford was probably influenced by the works of the postwar Italian neorealists, which often feature children in central roles. However, in Ford's film the children function as representatives of general historical forces and their relationships reflect the larger social divisions in Polish society before and during the war. Bronek, whose father is an antisemitic officer in the Polish army, mistreats David and rejects the friendship of Jadzia when he finds out her father was Jewish. Wladek, who comes from a lower-class family that has joined the resistance, fights against Freddie, the child of a collaborating Polish-German family who joined the Hitler youth movement. Eventually Freddie is killed, and Bronek, Wladek, and Jadzia stand united as the seeds of a new, "positive" Polish society. David's joining of the other Jewish fighters can be interpreted as Ford's tribute to the contemporary Jewish struggle in Israel to establish an independent state. (In 1934 Ford made the first feature-length film in Palestine, *Sabra*, in the fifties Stalin denounced him, and, as noted before, in the late sixties, when Polish antisemitism became intolerable for him, he settled in Israel.)

Like Jakubowska's *The Last Stop*, one of Ford's remarkable achievements is that the imposition of historical patterns on action and character does not result in a schematically rigid narrative. Highly moving moments include, for example, the scenes of brutalization and humiliation of David's father, the execution of Bronek's father, and the death of Jadzia's father from typhus; all of these moments are reconstructions of actual incidents, inspired by the direct war experience of those involved in the making of the film. However, the juxtaposition between the promising future of the young children and the tragedy of their parents is unbalanced because of the enormity of the latter. Thus, although the children occupy the central role in Border Street, the pathos of their private dramas is eclipsed by the powerful events of the historical background. Moreover, the narrative incorporates motifs and conventions of popular children's literature. Consequently, the main story line involves cliff-hanger children's adventures and many frivolous actions. The climax of these ill-suited thrills is an incredible last-minute rescue of little David from the ashes of the ghetto with the assistance of a German dog, the same dog that had attacked him earlier on. This part of the film demonstrates plot contrivances and happy outcomes that present a whimsical drama dissonant with the somber fate of Polish Jewry.

Unlike the makers of the two Polish films, Italian director Gillo Pontecorvo and author Franco Solinas approached the subject of the concentrationary universe without personal experience of the actual horrors. Pontecorvo, a descendant of an assimilated Jewish family, was an officer in the Communist underground in World War II. The late Franco Solinas was a prolific screenwriter with socialist convictions, whose works address tense political realities concentrating on their acute moral problems and personal existential dilemmas; his works include Pontecorvo's most well known film, The Battle of Algiers (1965), many of Costa-Gavras's movies like Z (1968), and Joseph Losey's Mr. Klein (1976). Solinas and Pontecorvo's Kapo (1959) presents an extreme example to the dubious quality of a work on the Holocaust that uncritically embraces melodramatic narrative conventions.

Kapo tells the story of Edith, a Jewish girl who collaborates in order to survive the death camps. Pontecorvo, who specialized before in documentaries and approached his first narrative work under the influence of the Italian neorealists, was committed to a truthful, naturalistic representation of the camps' world. Kapo was shot in Yugoslavia and featured Susan Strasberg, who had won critical acclaim for her characterization of Anne Frank in the successful Broadway production. In her autobiography, Strasberg relates the following on the making of Kapo: "The producers had re-created a concentration camp, authentic in all details, just outside Belgrade. When the natives saw the camp going up, they almost rioted. It was only fifteen years since the war. Large signs had to be posted: MOVIE SET. FILMING. MOVING SET."[12]

The film's first part follows Edith's experiences from her deportation until she becomes a Kapo in the camp. Early in the film, we see Edith playing baroque music on a harpsichord in an apartment in Paris adorned with paintings and artifacts. At the end of her music lesson, she rushes out to the street like a little child, happy to end her class and enjoy her freedom. But something is wrong. A group of impassive people are staring down the street in terrifying silence. The local Jews, including Edith's parents, are being loaded into trucks under the guns of German soldiers. Despite efforts by the music teacher and other bystanders to keep Edith still, she runs crying to her parents and is taken along with the other doomed victims.

Pontecorvo illustrates in the opening scene the initial phase of the genocide, the cruel uprooting of the Jews from their European societies, which usually took place while local people stood by helplessly, indifferently, or even complacently. The street pictures consist of extreme long shots of the Jews taken from their homes and herded into the trucks, and the sight of the motionless neighbors silently watching the arrest gives an uneasy theatricality to the sequence. Realistic details of confusion, interruption, or even resistance are avoided in order to show a smooth action that is more ceremonial and ritual than real, the ritual of meticulous destruction. The careful organization of the silent stony faces is a striking tableau-vivant image, emphasizing the role of the bystanders as passive onlookers rather than concerned neighbors or fellow citizens.

The next sequence presents a sharp stylistic contrast. The harpsichord music is abruptly replaced by loud, dissonant sounds and a low-angle shot follows the deportation train hurtling violently forward onto the camera. Pontecorvo refrains from showing the people inside the cattle cars, but the wild sounds and the violent image of the long snaky train rushing to its destination suggest the mounting agonies of this trip.

The first contact with the Kingdom of the Night is also, aptly, a nocturnal scene. The establishing shot shows the ramp and the arriving train from behind the barbed wire with watchtowers and Nazi guards in the middle ground of the frame. This visual exposition of the camp thus captures its essential icons—train, darkness, smoke, barbed wire, guards dressed in black, and watchtowers. Particularly impressive is the train's arrival, when a swirling cloud of locomotive smoke fills the screen, accompanied by the roaring of the train's engines, strongly connoting the infernal smoke of the crematoria and the imminent doom of the newcomers.

The arrival of the new deportees evokes the parallel scene in *The Last Stop*, concentrating on the prevailing confusion, the cries of separation, and the unendurable disorientation during the initial Nazi selection. Pontecorvo employs montage, showing many close shots of the people on the ramp, and thereby achieves remarkable effects. By focusing on individual expressions, he avoids the impersonal quality of many documentary pictures recording the plight of masses of people; at the same time, the rapid cutting from one person to another prevents excessive pathos, while the pictures of Edith, the recognizable protagonist, help define an interest in the worth of one human life.

Later that night Edith tries to take things into her own hands. After a young boy informs her of the sure death of all the newcomers, she leaves the building in a vain attempt to escape. She reaches a barrack of female prisoners. The establishing shot of this barrack is based on the famous pictures of the camps as seen by the liberating Allied soldiers. Multitudes of bodies lie in four-level bunks, hands stretching out lifelessly into the narrow hallway. The floor is covered with shoes and other objects. One of the inmates, Sophia, approaches the startled Edith, and, recognizing her ethnic identity, dryly says: "You're a Jew, tough luck!" Despite her cynicism, Sophia takes Edith to a doctor to organize her survival. In accordance with con-centration camp logic, she takes Edith's necklace as a reward for her service. In the doctor's office Sophia again demands a reward for bringing Edith. When the doctor says "tomorrow," she responds, "tomorrow, my foot," expressing the inmates' disregard for the uncertain future.

For Edith the introduction to the concentration camp universe reaches its climax in this encounter with the doctor. An authoritative, helpful, and pragmatic character, the doctor explains to her that although she has been selected for the gas chamber, she is very lucky because another prisoner has just died. He orders her to get undressed and to be ready to take on the identity of the dead prisoner, a non-Jew. Edith's moral inhibitions make her hesitate, but the doctor's calm and paternal authority convinces her that everything he does is for her sake. He explains to her the basic rules of concentration camp life, especially the meanings of the different triangles sewn on the inmates' clothes, emphasizing the danger from those assigned as Kapos. Meanwhile, he cuts her hair, tattoos her, changes her name, and literally transforms her into Nicole, prisoner #10099. The matter-of-fact talk of the doctor and the general restraint and understatement make this scene an outstanding representation of the camp's harsh reality. Gillo Pontecorvo, the cre-ator of *The Battle of Algiers*, has declared:

> The best scene I have ever done in film is that in *Kapo* when the doctor, long ac-customed to the sadness and sorrow of the camp, transforms the girl through hardness and efficiency. He changes her from someone outside of the world of the camp into a person able to survive it.[13]

After this restrained scene, Pontecorvo films the most horrific aspect of the death camp, the executions in the gas chambers. Edith watches with terror the endless processions of the deported Jews taken to their death. Pontecorvo limits what we see to Edith's point of view from behind the window of the doctor's office. Extreme long shots give a necessary moderating effect to the image of naked people being marched toward the gas chambers. The guards push and beat the nude victims; the gas chambers are in the background, and in the far distance, right above the central gas chamber, two electric poles are visible forming the shape of a cross. Pontecorvo alternates between subjective shots of the marching victims and re-action shots of Edith's shocked face. When she recognizes her parents, she ago-nizedly screams, "Papa, Papa." Her parents disappear and a new group follows them. Then the doctor appears from behind, uttering the crucial words: "You must live. Just live. Survival is what counts."

The next section of *Kapo* takes place in a labor camp and shows Edith, now Nicole, trying to survive the intolerable hardships of hunger and exhausting work. Unable to bear the cold weather, she runs to the hot soup pot. She is punished by being denied food. Her unendurable hunger impels her to steal the potato from the barrack's interpreter (Emmanuelle Riva), a highly sympathetic woman who had always tried to help Edith but who is madly indignant when she finds out about the theft of the food. Then comes a selection scene. Nicole fears her burnt hands will condemn her to death. When she faces the inspecting Nazi officer, she boldly opens her dress, exposing her naked body to distract him from looking at her hands. Her ruse works. Instead of consigning her to the selection, the SS officer chooses her for servant duty. Then, despite her friends' protests, Nicole decides to go to the Nazi's room, where she loses her virginity and her innocence.

As the mistress of the Nazi officer, Nicole begins her rise in the camp's hierarchy, ending up in the notorious role of Kapo. She has seemingly accepted the logic of the concentration camp which justifies every possible means of survival. But, in the process, she becomes a hollow person devoid of any significant interests or desire. Her relationships with her German lover are emotionless and icy. She summarizes her situation by coldly remarking to him: "I eat well, sleep well; there's not much work and no more selection. What else is there?"

The answer to Nicole's quasi-rhetorical question marks the beginning of the second half of the movie. A cut to a group of prisoners of war marched into the camp singing Russian songs implies the answer to Nicole's question—it indicates that solidarity, fighting for freedom, and Russian-inspired socialism are bases for moral regeneration. Unfortunately, the narrative switch also marks the artistic degeneration of Pontecorvo's film. Leftist propaganda and simplistic moralizing, which are so inimical to the harsh realities of the concentration camp universe, are coupled with a highly incongruous shmaltzy love affair. It begins when the Russian soldiers arrive and are tearfully hugged by the female inmates. Then Sascha (Laurent Terzieff), the most attractive soldier, and the socially isolated, now beautiful Nicole exchange one of those fateful looks, establishing at first sight a romantic bond between potential lovers. The apparent psychological basis for this love in the concentration camp is a "boy-hates-girl" situation. It gets under way when Sascha tries to stop Nicole from beating another prisoner. For challenging a representative of the camp authority he is made to suffer hideous punishment: standing naked a whole night, inches from the electrified barbed wire, he must stand still or be electrocuted, or be shot by a trigger-happy guard. The pictures of the sweaty, or rather oily, muscular, naked macho, displaying supreme physical effort, are designed to evoke admiration for a herculean superhero. The most admiring person is, to be sure, Nicole, the Kapo, who makes advances to him during the following day. Sascha works in a field which looks more like a kolkhoz than a Nazi labor camp. His muscled body with a sickle in his hands resembles that of a superlaborer on a cheap socialist poster extolling collective farms more than that of a Russian prisoner of war in the hands of the Nazis. The romantic liaison culminates in Edith's confession of her Jewish identity. Sascha responds that his parents would love her for what she is, the idea being that there is absolutely no antisemitism in socialist Russia—unlike in France or Germany.

After accomplishing the part of a pathetic lover, Edith gradually develops into a romantic match to Sascha's heroic adventures. She joins an organized uprising and takes on the crucial role of cutting off the fence's electric current. The narrative here creates a special tension when Edith finds out what the others know all along, that she has no chance to survive German retribution. The prisoners are ordered to dig a large pit in the center of the camp. Nicole, in her position as Kapo, is one of the supervisors. The inmates are ready to attack the moment she decides to cut off the electricity to the fence. After long and suspenseful hesitation, Nicole, now Edith again, does commit the suicidal act, thereby redeeming her sinful life as a Kapo. Shot by the Germans she dies as a Jewish martyr, reciting the *Shema*. The prisoners' attempted escape is all but a Pyrrhic victory as the German machine guns mow down scores of people. The incident was inspired by the actual revolt that took place in the death camp of Sobibor in October 1943. The massive bloodshed leaves Sascha alone in the midst of the pit; his face fills the screen as he utters a terrible cry of anguish in the final image of the film.

Despite the problems and shortcomings of the second half, *Kapo* deserves serious consideration for its representation and vision of the victim's predicament. The film's paramount interest is the human confrontation with extreme experience in terms of the moral implications of each individual response. Edith's ordeals present a case in which physical security stands in opposition to ethical standards. The physical and moral lines of her development parallel each other but in opposite directions. At the beginning she is physically in shambles, in the middle she lives in security and comfort, and at the end she dies. The moral strain follows her development from an intimidated and innocent young girl, to a ruthless beast collaborating with the Nazis, and finally to a true martyr. However, the postulation of a necessary contrast between morality and survival is avoided by the ironic presentation of Nicole's life as Kapo. Nicole's adjustment to the camp's reality involves the loss of personal integrity for the sake of bare physical survival. She is devoid of emotions, has lost all her friends, and her German lover means nothing to her. Nicole has become a machine, blindly following Nazi-promulgated rules and regulations, and she is nearly completely expelled from the human realm. The meeting with Sascha marks the beginning of her moral regeneration, her regaining of emotional involvement, and her return to human society. In the crucial moment before turning off the electricity to the fence, she hears the harpsichord melodies she played as a child. Thus her sacrificial act also marks the return to civilized values. Remarkably, her degeneration-regeneration career is closely associated with her consciousness of being Jewish. Edith initially manages to survive by becoming the non-Jewish Nicole. Nobody knows her background and, as a ruthless Kapo and a mistress of Nazi officers, she too evidently represses any memories of her past. Her relationship with Sascha induces her to regain her Jewish identity. Finally, in dying she utters "*Shema*," in a kind of atavistic cry exhumed from the depth of her soul and her Jewish tradition.

The impressive Hebrew prayer *Shema Yisrael* is not actually Edith's very last utterance. She dies with the words "Oh my God," a totally incongruous banality, normally expressing kitchen mishaps rather than mass murder, and a typical example of the general insensitivity of the film's second part. Trivialized plotting, absurd romance, political bias, and excessive sentimentality drastically offset the successful somber tone of the film's beginning. Even the visual style undergoes a drastic change. The reserved presentation of extreme horrors is replaced by cheap pictures of graphic violence such as brutal beatings and mass killing, significantly never shown in the first part. Also, the powerful stark literalness of the first part gives way to trite symbolism. Thus a sort of a prop, Edith's cat, is used to characterize her new position and personality. With her newly acquired black long hair, her Kapo uniform, and the black pet in her possession, Edith is identified with the dark forces in the best tradition of popular melodramas. Furthermore, the cat's name is Faust, an additional symbol to designate the one who sold her soul to the devil.

Judith Crist hailed the first part of *Kapo* as a film which "brings us a time and place of tragedy in authentic and soul-wracking detail that is almost too painful to follow." Reacting to the disastrous ending, however, Crist concludes: "we emerge to find that our emotions have been exploited mercilessly for the telling of a romantic tale that is less than trivial in contrast to the setting."[14] Crist's objection is understandable, but her diagnosis is incorrect. Pontecorvo and Solinas did not seek to exploit the extraordinary background of the Holocaust to enhance melodramatic action, but conversely, to exploit melodramatic action to upstage the historical events. Their failure stemmed primarily from the desire to tell a story with a popular narrative line which would hold the viewers' attention throughout the entire film. Pontecorvo made an honest admission.

> We made the greatest error movie people can commit—we underestimated the possibilities of the public. We forgot the fact that when you speak through any situation to eternal themes in the human condition, you always have the hope of reaching an audience. So we censored ourselves and inserted this horrible episode of a love story between the soldier and the girl. Its style was completely different from the rest of the film, and it made the section melodramatic.[15]

Border Street, *The Last Stop*, and *Kapo* demonstrate the potential or actual dangers to every narrative aiming at telling the historical tragedy: improbable plot contrivances (e.g., the German dog that had attacked little David saved him at the end), stock action (e.g., love affair, the chase), and extrinsic measure of ideology. In regard to the last point, all these films imply some form of socialist propaganda. In *Border Street*, the lower-class people are the most sympathetic characters, those who vehemently resist the Nazis and help their Jewish victims. *The Last Stop* emphasizes the resistance of the Communist women in Auschwitz; in *Kapo* the propaganda line begins with the admirable character of the doctor, who wears a red triangle (as a socialist), and culminates with the cheap symbolism associated with Sascha, the heroic Red Army soldier.

The most disturbing aspect of these films, however, is their reliance on popular and conventional narrative codes resulting in melodramatization or trivialization of the subject. But given the essential popular dimension of the narrative film, these flaws are almost inevitable—at least they are very common in cinema. We therefore need to reserve the final judgment of individual works depending on the measure of trivialization and the genuineness of the filmmaker's intention. We cannot forget that in cinema popular reception usually determines the scope of exhibition and circulation as well as the impetus for subsequent treatments of the same subject. In the case of the subject of the Holocaust, the attraction of many beholders has a special moral dimension, rooted in the need to inform the masses about the Nazi atrocities and the genocide against the Jews. The films discussed in this chapter, unlike most popular, exploitative movies, resorted to popular narrative formulas to enhance their appeal and their effect, fearing that an uncompromisingly stark presentation might lose many potential viewers. Remarkably, despite the apparent compromises, the two Polish films enjoyed favorable reviews, essentially because critics appreciated the proximity of the works and their creators to the actual horrors; *Kapo* was more severely criticized, seen by many as more derivative or even exploitative of the Holocaust than a serious attempt to cope with its dread. But indeed all three films were equally concerned with truthful depiction of the extreme conditions under Nazi terror. The authentic settings of *The Last Stop*, Ford's combination of realistic mise-en-scène, newsreel footage, and moving dramatic moments, and *Kapo*'s remarkable naturalism in its first part constitute the most impressive cinematic representations of the camps' ordeals and the genocidal process in narrative cinema. However, the uncritical adoption of popular narrative conventions offsets the works' representational power and the somberness of their historical content.

Although films can theoretically avoid the potential flaws of trivialization and propaganda, the narrative deterioration of each of the three films discussed in this chapter is not merely a lapse of good taste; rather, it is symptomatic of one of the most problematic aspects of any dramatic representation or fictional plotting of the Holocaust horrors. Most Holocaust films belong to what Robert Scholes and Robert Kellogg call the empirical historical type of narrative, which "owes it allegiance specifically to truth of fact and to the actual past rather than to a traditional version of the past. It requires for its development means of accurate measurement in time and space, and concepts of causality referable to human and natural rather than to supernatural agencies."[16] More specifically, the Holocaust film tends to be in the dramatic epic form, with an action which reflects the broader historical development of the Nazi era. It often follows the process of persecution while real historical events, such as the Kristallnacht, the outbreak of World War II, or the Warsaw ghetto uprising, function as focal points in the narrative action. Fiction films, however, are usually based on tight dramatic plot because of the ninety minutes or so conventional length and the fact that the story is presented through characters' actions with little or, more often, no presence of an observing and commenting narrator. Therefore, the accounts of the concentration camp universe which always involve depictions of shattering facts and unsettling details and painful reflections on the concrete horrors pose a special problem to those who seek to translate the historical material into a single, unified, dramatic action.

In general, the dramatic narrative is composed of the following essentials: a significant conflict whose development and resolution induce a serious reflection on and refine our perception of the human predicament; the behavior of the dramatic agents in the framework of the basic conflict whose actions involve crucial decisions that affect the progress of the narrative and bear special moral weight;

and a complete action whose narrative units relate to each other in a sequential manner, creating expectations for probable and meaningful developments whose fulfillment is achieved and dominated by an overall coherence.

The Holocaust defies each of these fundamentals of drama. The attempt to annihilate the Jews was not a significant conflict that can generate the cultivation of moral sensitivities but rather a brutal assault effecting shock and outrage. Nor was the Holocaust an ethical clash of good versus evil culminating in the defeat of the evil forces. The Nazi horrors were monstrous and satanic. The Six Million were absolutely innocent, and they posed absolutely no threat or challenge to their victimizers; their deaths were neither sacrificial, nor an act of defiance or martyrdom. Alexander Ford ends his film with hopeful notes after the heroic and desperate battle of the doomed Jews; the heroine of The Last Stop commits suicide on the Nazi gallows with a defiant speech against her killers; and in Kapo Edith regains moral stature as a result of her death for the sake of the rebelling prisoners. These stories are perhaps morally inspiring, but as truthful representations of the fate of the Nazis' victims they are sadly incongruous. Lawrence Langer wrote that in the death camps "moral choice as we know it was superfluous, and inmates were left with the futile task of redefining decency in an atmosphere that could not support it."[17] Indeed, the inhuman brutality of the Nazis achieved an extreme debasement of the victims which has denied the Jobian notions of "ennobling suffering" any application to the concentration camp universe. Steven Katz stated: "The Holocaust in its awesome magnitude was overwhelmingly evil. Murder was only one, and not the most horrible of its children. Abuse of every sort, degradation in every form, technology run riot, medical experiments of abhorent, frightening inhumanity, and finally death by truncheon, by bullet, by fire, by gas—this is the stark, terrifying world of the Holocaust, the 'Planet Auschwitz.' Phenomenologically this reality reveals darkness and abyss, despair and degeneracy."[18]

The Holocaust, then, cannot serve as a proper premise for dramatic conflict. As a subject matter for mimetic epics it also presents serious problems relating to the climax and resolution of the overall narrative. The empirical historical narratives, in their attempt to give a comprehensive view and an epic story to the events of the Nazi era, are led, by the logic of the historical chronicle, to the final phase of the extermination process. In the camps, inmates lived on the basis of day-to-day struggles for their lives, trying to survive starvation, atrocious labor, deadly diseases, or the Nazi selections. Dramatic action in prose fiction or film usually centers on the significant change of a character who gains new recognition and moral stature as a result of a series of events requiring morally important decisions. But in reality the inmates were denied any choice, nor were they able to cultivate sensitive perceptions. According to the Nazi accounts and calculations, the average inmate's existence lasted three months; those who survived the inhuman trials did so, by their own admission, thanks to the undramatic element of sheer luck and/or ruthlessness toward their fellow prisoners. Kapo and The Last Stop start with the final stage of the extermination process, creating narrative expectations that could never transcend the initial shock. After the protagonist's dearest ones are shown sent to the gas chambers and the smoke from their burning corpses is seen pouring from the chimney of the crematoria, it is simply impossible to conceive a more climactic scene to follow these pictures.

Further, in dramatic narrative, scenes always function as sources or causes for ensuing action; but to use a massive execution in the gas chamber for any conceivable narrative purpose—to forward the plot, or to develop character traits—is merely exploitative. For example, in the incomplete version of Andrej Munk's *The Passenger* (Poland, 1962) there is a highly detailed and realistic depiction of a group of Jews pushed into a gas chamber, followed by presentation of an SS man throwing the gas cans from the roof of the building. These are shocking scenes which have never been shown with so much realism and detail. But then we find that the shock of the literal content of the horrors is rather secondary within the dramatic context of the fictional narrative. For these scenes are designed to show the effect of inhuman killing on the sensitive mind of Lisa, the protagonist Nazi guard. We end up witnessing unbearable atrocities in order to understand a fictional character and her psychological development—that she is a Nazi adds even more offense—resulting in an untenable disparity between the weight of the factual sources and the dramatic needs of a specific narrative.

The essence of all narratives is the story of a human quest. Narratives are imaginative manifestations—the imaginative process may be limited to only the arrangement of real events—of the human will, which expresses itself in seeking to accomplish a mission, to attain a desired object, or to fulfill a spiritual challenge. They tell stories of human triumphs and defeats, describe the obstacles that have to be overcome, and define essential aims, goals, and stakes. The different narratives that we have, in their archetypal modes and their endless offsprings or versions, reveal in the context of their cultural background how each period or society conceives the ultimate test of the human will or defines its most profound antagonists. But whether we deal with the blind force of the Moira, or the irreconcilable contradictions of a particular system of values, or the perception of an inherent and fatalistic human flaw, what we always find in the center of each narrative is the struggle of a remarkable and representative character. As the protagonist sets out to achieve his goal, he (or she) is confronted by all kinds of obstacles, which require two types of decisions and actions, expedient and moral. The expedient actions and their ultimate results testify either to the triumphs of human resourcefulness and perseverance or to our defeating limitations in the natural world. The moral decisions concern the most critical problems of human interactions, social structures, and the relationships between man and Providence. Thus while the substance of the narrative movement is a manifestation of the human will, the core of the action in terms of the nature of the obstacles and the final goal reflect the moral universe as the context which defines the quality of the human will.

Many narratives of Holocaust movies are variations of martyrologies, for they present protagonists' deaths by overwhelming forces of evil, while, at the same time, they show that the physical defeat is a testimony to a spiritual triumph of superior values or the victory of a noble cause. Under the extraordinary circumstances of the genocide, most willfully meaningful actions were drastically limited.

The naked and disturbing truth is that the methodical killing of the Six Million left no room for meaningful sacrifices. In particular, the act of martyrdom was pathetically inadequate. Throughout history the Jews suffered endless pogroms and persecutions, their foes aiming at their faith or at the disintegration of the Jewish community as a distinct cultural group. The Final Solution, on the other hand, called for the total physical liquidation of all Jews. Thus, whereas in the past Jewish martyrs chose death over the abandonment of their identity, and their sacrifice was defined as an act for "the sanctification of the Name" (the name of God), under the Nazi threat the primary commandment was to sanctify life. Already during the war years many rabbis and community leaders came to this somber recognition and urged Jews to struggle for survival. Recently Emil Fackenheim wrote the following:

> Finally—and perhaps most devastatingly—the Holocaust did not present itself as demanding the response of martyrdom. . . . the Nazi Empire, far from repeating the Roman folly of creating Jewish martyrs, was on the contrary cunningly designed to murder Jewish martyrdom. . . . Within the Nazi universe, what mattered was only that Jews existed; as for their beliefs or their deeds, even, and indeed especially, when they were saintly or heroic, they were of no account. As for us who come after, of all things unbearable about the Holocaust, the most unbearable, and most necessary to remember and therefore to bear, are not the prayers of the martyrs or the hero's death of the fighters but rather the cry of innocence that comes to us from all those who *did not, or could not, or would not choose* heroism or martyrdom or any of the ways in which men and women throughout the ages have managed to give meaning to suffering and death. The men. The women. The children. Theirs is a cry unlike any other. He who listens can hear it still—and can conceive of no possible future world that will silence it.[19]

The conclusion is that any dramatization of the Holocaust is liable to betray its subject, for the enormity of the genocide and the Nazi atrocities cannot serve as the springboard for the presentation of the meaningful action of a few remarkable dramatic agents; rather, the very scale and magnitude of the suffering and victimization paralyze dramatic action. Indeed, in sharp contrast to the proliferation of short stories, novels, and poetry on the Holocaust, there is little Holocaust drama that is of meritorious significance. The notable examples, Rolf Hochhuth's *The Deputy* and Peter Weiss's *The Investigation*, actually demonstrate the inherent limitations of dramatic presentation to cope with historical atrocities and the subject of genocide: Hochhuth's lengthy play—more than eight hours long, because of the necessity to give an exposition of historical background that ultimately overwhelms the fictional, and dubious, action—had to be substantially cut for viable production, and Weiss's work is a theatrical reenactment of court testimonies, devoid of plotting and characterization. At the same time, literary descriptions must be distinguished from narrative dramatizations. Survivors' memoirs, eyewitness accounts, and attempted depictions of historians or novelists constitute the basic discourse of the Holocaust. But the incomparable horrors of the concentration camp universe cannot serve as a context for dramatic action that involves narrative plotting in terms of causal development, neat story closure, and realistic, psychological characterization.

Successful narrative stories on the Holocaust are possible when they focus on the peripheral dimension of the concentration camp universe, on the plight of the victims before they entered the gates of Auschwitz. In the next chapter we shall study a few outstanding Czech films that provide forceful portrayals of life and death in the Nazi hell without foregrounding gas chambers, crematoria, or even barbed wires. We shall examine alternative artistic visions of the concentration camp universe—visions that subordinate the narrative to the overall conception of a discourse conceived and designed as a profound reflection of the Holocaust trauma—bearing in mind that the special Czech perspective was the result of their experience during Hitler's era and the combination of national cultural tradition, a successful film industry, and the crucial contribution of sensitive artists.

CHAPTER III

Stylistic Approaches to the Representation of the Holocaust on the Screen: The Czech Cinema

During the Nazi era, despite western assurances and universal sympathy, Czechoslovakia was the first country to fall prey to Hitler's aggression. The crisis was triggered by Hitler's imperialistic ambitions against the Sudeten regions, which were inhabited by German-speaking Czechoslovak citizens. Threatening war and cynically exploiting the principle of self-determination, Hitler achieved his goals by obtaining British and French consent to his territorial designs against Czechoslovakia. In the early morning hours of September 30, 1938, the fate of the small, sovereign republic of Czechoslovakia was determined in a meeting of the leaders of four European powers: Great Britain, France, Germany, and Italy. The agreement signed in Munich effectively ended Czech independence, culminated a process of betrayal of a small nation by the superpowers whom the Czechs had considered to be their closest allies, and eventually turned out to be the critical prelude for World War II.

On March 13, 1939, Hitler ordered Slovak nationalists and two pro-German leaders, Monsignor Josef Tiso and Ferdinand Durcansky, to proclaim Slovak independence in the eastern regions of Czechoslovakia. On the following day the two collaborationists formed an independent state, a move used by the Germans to justify their invasion of Czechoslovakia. On March 15, 1939, the Germans occupied the country without encountering resistance, claiming its western part to be part of the Greater Reich. The provinces of Bohemia and Moravia, including the capital, Prague, were declared a protectorate, a joint, autonomous part of Germany. The people of German origin became Reich citizens, while the Czech inhabitants were designated protectorate nationals.

After the Czech army was demobilized, the Germans proved to be ruthless masters. Their policies of harsh political repression and economic exploitation stirred activities of underground resistance and continuous political unrest. Hitler decided to appoint Reinhard Heydrich, chief of the Gestapo and perhaps the cruelest of the top Nazi officials, as the Reich Protector. The rule of terror introduced by Heydrich had considerable effects, but the Nazi general was assassinated, in an action directed by the Czech government-in-exile with British aid. The German reaction unleashed a new form of cruel reprisals: the wiping out of the village of Lidice and the killing of all its male inhabitants became a special symbol of Nazi brutality in World War II.

Unlike the melodramatic pathos of the German smashing of Poland, the brutal atrocities on the Russian front, the pitiable impotence of the small countries in western Europe, and the humiliating capitulation of France, the fate of Czechoslovakia in the Nazi era demonstrates mostly the disasterous consequences of twentieth-century political intrigues and of more fundamental modern contradictions. The Czech situation during the Nazi era was outstanding because of the country's affinity to the heart of the Nazi evil, a geographical affinity which had also been political and cultural. In particular, German culture and the German language were usually adopted as the evidence of progress and refinement.[1] Hitler's rise to power and the subsequent annexation of the Czech regions generated conflicting and profoundly mixed reactions. The Czechs did not view the Germans as completely foreign invaders, as did the Poles or the French, nor did they accept the Germans as compatriots, as did the Austrians. The divisive effects of Hitler's policies, beginning with the separation of Slovakia, ran deep through Czech society, which during World War II displayed numerous examples of heroic resistance along with cases of blatant collaboration.

After the war, the Czech nation came into the grasp of the Soviet bear. In the socialist countries of eastern Europe the war was used as a theme to display the evil consequences of western capitalism and to commemorate Russia as a force of liberation from the Fascist tyranny. But the Czech predicament during the war was a great deal more complex than this simple reading of history would suggest. Questions of collaboration, national unity, resistance activities, and individual courage were examined against the backdrop of a turbulent reality. The gruesome experiences under the rule of the Germans, who were the supposed representatives of a highly civilized society, sharpened the Czech sense of the unendurable cultural contradictions inherent in their sufferings. For many Czech artists, the war was a Kafkaesque inferno come alive, a surrealistic existence in which law and order had been used to impose angst and terror.

The history of the small nation of Czechoslovakia in the heart of Europe shows a continuous endurance of pressures and assaults from the neighboring empires of Austria, Hungary, Germany, and Russia. Being powerless to stage an effective physical resistance, the Czechs have become the perennial underdogs, observing historical realities from the losers' point of view. The geographical location has led also to an intriguing position between the cultural idiosyncracies of east and west Europe, while the influence of various foreign forces has never prevented the Czechs' striving to create a genuine and authentic culture of their own. Considering the character of Czech art, critic John Simon notes its traits of bittersweet, ironic love of man, its strange blend of surrealism, humanism, and socialism, and its half-grotesque, half-plaintive melodies and rhythms.[2]

Cinema forms an important mode of artistic expression in Czechoslovakia. Czech filmmakers have made significant contributions to the development of cinema throughout the medium's short history. The Barrandov Studios near Prague, built in 1932–33, were the most advanced in central Europe and attracted many foreign productions. Their excellent facilities were coveted by the Nazis, who used them for their own purposes during the war. The golden age of the Czech cinema flourished during the 1960s. The sensational outburst of young talent and the detectable influence of the French New Wave led critics to name it "the Czech New Wave." Antonin Novak, in his book *Films and Filmmakers in Czechoslovakia*, contends that the new crop of artistic masterpieces was not indebted to foreign influences nor was it an unexpected miracle, but rather it was the result of a rich tradition, for "film art is linked by an umbilical cord with the cultural and spiritual traditions of its native country."[3] In addition, the young filmmakers had excellent training in FAMU, the distinguished film school, which provided expert guidance as well as financial security and artistic freedom during the sixties.

The artistic renaissance was facilitated by the relief from Communist tyranny and stiff dogmatism of Zhdanovism and Socialist Realism. The initial change came in 1956, as part of the Thaw or de-Stalinization which swept eastern Europe following Stalin's death, but the major breakthrough occurred in 1959–1960. The opportunity to create in a more free fashion produced high-quality cinematic art with distinct Czech characteristics. The Czech cinematic success came to an abrupt end with the Soviet tanks invading Prague in August 1968, a tragic cultural casualty of the fateful connections between film and politics.

One of the most outstanding films in the history of the Czech cinema is Alfred Radok's *Distant Journey* (1948, also known as *The Long Journey*). Alfred Radok was born in southern Bohemia to a Christian mother and a Jewish father and was brought up celebrating the holidays of both religions. He was in college at the outbreak of World War II but was unable to study under the Nazi occupation because his father was Jewish. Committed to an artistic career in theater, he lived through the war years working under various pseudonyms and hiding in Prague theaters. "Then came a work camp for Jewish Mischlings, half breeds," wrote Radok. "My father was arrested; he died in cell #3 in the Little Fortress at Terezin. Other members of my family perished in other concentration camps."[4] After the war, Radok directed mostly opera productions in Prague, and in 1947 he began to work on *Distant Journey*.

Radok's first film highlights one of the most remarkable products of Nazism in World War II. Theresienstadt, or Terezin, the "model ghetto" near Prague and a scene of many horrors, perhaps more than anything else realized the apparent devilish contrasts of the Nazi apparatus. Terezin was initially planned by Heydrich to accommodate German Jews who had been seriously wounded in World War I or who had been distinguished for war service fighting on the German side. It developed into a "model camp" for deported Jews of distinguished social stature, celebrated scientists, artists, and musicians, from all over Europe. During the war it also served as the ghetto into which Prague Jews were deported. The Nazis turned the former garrison town designed for five thousand inhabitants into a ghetto containing sixty thousand people. Despite the awesome overcrowding and the horrible living conditions of the place, the Nazis tried to present it as a "gift from the Fuehrer to the Jews," and as a proof of their considerate treatment of the Jewish victims. Indeed, the Germans managed to deceive a number of Red Cross commissions that visited Terezin concerning the real character of the place.

In *Distant Journey* Alfred Radok set out to tell the story of the Nazi persecution of the Jews by combining a narrative of individual characters with the visualization and dramatization of the major aspects of the historical terror. The film's action falls into two main parts. The first features Tony, a Gentile, and Hannah, a Jewish doctor, who fall in love and eventually get married in wartime Prague; the second part describes life in Terezin.

The film opens with documentary sequences taken from *Triumph of the Will* showing a banner with the title "This is Germany," followed by Rudolf Hess's declaration "Germany is Hitler." Virulent antisemitism is visible in the next dramatized picture of a small boy dwarfed by a huge sign behind him saying "Zid Vidi"—"Jews out."

The transition from the dark, frightened Jewish boy to a group of blond youngsters from the 1934 Nazi convention at Nuremberg creates a juxtaposition between the opposite forces in the Holocaust: the Aryan versus the Jew, the well-orchestrated machine against the helpless victim, the Fascist masses of Nazi Germany about to disregard and crush the worth of an individual human being. The profound connotations of the contrasting images lie in the following statement by the late, distinguished historian Jacob Talmon.

> From the "meta-historical" point of view, the Nazi holocaust thus transcends the dimensions of just another wave of anti-Jewish persecution, of a dire warning of where racism combined with ultra-modern technology may lead, even of a manifestation of genocide in all its horror. It assumes the character of a grandiose confrontation between the two Nietzschean moralities, of Rome and Judaea: on one side the will to imperium, power, conquest, dominion; and on the other, ethics of slaves and priests, with their ascetic values of humanity, self-restraint and mutuality; on one side the aim to bring forth superior specimens in the crucible of rivalry, struggle and war; and on the other the vision of a Theodicea, the denouement of history in reconciliation, retribution, and harmony.[5]

After the suggestive imagistic beginning, Hannah, the film's protagonist, enters the hospital where she works and finds the antisemitic slogan "Zid Vidi" written on the wall next to her name. Hannah is summoned to the director's office, and the ugly phenomenon of antisemitism is further displayed by the hideous-looking bureaucrat who fires her in compliance with the newly adopted racial regulations.

The next sequence takes place in a warehouse for confiscated Jewish property and illustrates the escalation of social antisemitism into systematic, bureaucratic persecution. Radok uses the accumulation of objects—an image which has become central in Holocaust iconography—to convey the sense of massive destruction. In the confiscation center an old Jew is driven mad by this very sense, and the madness is intensified when he notices an Iron Cross—a starkly ironic reminder of the identity of the perpetrators and the absurdity of the victimization. He wraps himself with prayer shawls and a medieval ark-curtain decorated with Jewish stars and kills himself in a frenzy. The man's funeral, a gloomy ceremonial gathering of his friends and family in the synagogue, is abruptly interrupted when a rumor about a forth-coming transport spreads through the community. In these two scenes, Radok economically presents the end of ancient Jewish culture in eastern Europe. The pictures of confiscated property demonstrate the liquidation of Jewish symbols and ritual objects, and the interrupted ceremony represents the brutal termination of the practice of religious services.

The Jews' attempts to escape the persecutions are pathetically futile. Hannah's parents decide to leave the country and try to apply for visas to South America. Their naive hope of escape is quickly shattered when they see the huge crowd of doomed Jews lining up in front of the foreign embassies. Hannah declares that she will not leave her country, where she belongs in body and soul. Tony, her boyfriend, gives her the opportunity to be even more belonging to her Gentile society. He offers to marry her, hoping that as a Gentile's wife she will not have to suffer the same ordeals as the other Jews. Their wedding takes place during the full force of the onslaught against the Jews and is carried out as a poignantly gloomy and dreary ceremony, culminating with the receipt of transport orders by Hannah's family.

Hannah's marriage grants her momentary relief: she is not to be deported with the others. But her lonely life in Prague is a continuous suffering of isolation, the result of local antisemitism and official oppression. In addition, her husband Tony and his family begin to be persecuted. Deeply agonized and totally desperate, Hannah decides to commit suicide by taking a lethal drug in her former hospital clinic. A last-minute appearance by Tony prevents Hannah from killing herself, but he cannot save her from ending up in the ghetto.

The ghetto segment of *Distant Journey* is an astounding cinematic tour de force in terms of representing the horrific conditions of the concentration camp universe. It features the first confusing moments of initiation, the constant hunger, slave labor, the fierce struggle to survive, exhausting roll calls, and the ultimate deadly selections. Without any clear narrative line, Radok composes a series of expressive pictures, brief episodes, and insightful dramatic moments to convey the ultimate horror.

The establishing shot of the ghetto's entrance is one of the numerous mem-orable images in *Distant Journey*. To the sounds of promenade music, reminiscent of Ravel's "Bolero, " the doomed quietly enter through the walls in an orderly manner; at the same time, a caravan of coffins exits by the same gate. The cere-monial movement in opposite directions illustrates the imminence of death, fore-shadowing the newcomers' end, and under the spell of haunting music and pictures, the camera enters Terezin, evoking the lines Dante found inscribed on Hell's gate:

Through me you go into the city of grief
Through me you go into the pain that is eternal
Through me you go among people lost . . .
ABANDON EVERY HOPE, YOU WHO ENTER HERE.

Inside the ghetto, long takes of slow and complex camera movement survey the brutal compilation of people and objects. The camera penetrates into the heart of the infernal world, pausing to record revealing glimpses of human tragedy, the view often obstructed by iron nets, furniture, and walls erected to accommodate the unbelievable degree of overcrowding. The intimacy of private life has been completely lost. The desperate and ruthless struggle for survival has stripped away any behavioral inhibitions. Hannah's first experience in the ghetto is an encounter with that kind of dehumanization. In the middle of the dense and by now deserted dwellings, where Hannah is looking for her family, an old man appears, hungrily looking to steal any remaining property. Hannah is shocked to witness such a stark act of criminality.

The loss of human dignity had been previously portrayed through Hannah's father and his desperate attempts to save himself from the ghetto transports to Auschwitz. While Hannah was still free in Prague, he had asked her to send to him to Terezin a black shoe polish. In his final scene, we see his broken figure marching with the other doomed deportees, trudging in the mud under heavy rain toward the awaiting trains. The most striking aspect of his appearance, though, is the newly acquired black hair that falls on his face. The viewers who shared Hannah's puzzlement at his unusual request now understand. In his pathetic attempts to survive, the former dignified businessman, with his silver hair and confident behavior, has been reduced to a grotesque figure, like an ugly clown whose makeup has been partly washed away.

Another incident shows the reduction of human beings into creatures motivated by the instinctual need for food. Hannah accidentally jostles another person, causing her to drop the potato she is carrying. The piece of food triggers a frantic chase by numerous people. In their state of unendurable hunger, the wretched inmates trample one another in an attempt to claim the potato, a thing which in the camps could easily mean the difference between life and death. The potato rolls under the skirt of a woman who freezes on the spot lest she lose it to someone stronger. Her anxiety over protecting the piece of food is tinged with the painful restraint of keeping the treasure hidden a few seconds longer. Once the crowd disappears, she devours the raw potato like a starved animal.

The physical brutality of the Nazis is demonstrated when they order the Jews to prepare the ghetto for a visit by an international commission of the Red Cross. Jews are forced to clean the streets, polish the walls, and decorate the building exteriors. This sequence culminates when an SS guard forces a kneeling woman with his jackboot and his gun to hold a bucket with her teeth, an image which, as Andre Bazin has observed, seems to have been taken from de Sade's imagination.[6] But the ultimate cynicism of the Nazis is shown through a children's chorus practicing for a musical performance. The overwhelming character of this incident and its direct impact on Radok are evident from a statement he made to an interviewer twenty-five years after the completion of his film: "There really was such a choir, you know; and when it had performed its duty for the commission, all the children, along with their choirmaster were gassed."[7]

Radok even deals with the ultimate step in the genocidal process, the physical extermination of the Jews. Following actual footage of a concentration camp showing its characteristic icons, such as barbed wire, watchtowers, barracks, and a huge heap of clothes left by the victims, the narrative returns to slave laborers in the ghetto, engaged in the construction of special buildings whose function puzzles them. The ominous signs of the operation are visible from the use of expressive contrasts of lighting and darkness in a subterranean setting. Into this setting Hannah leads a transport of terrified children from the east preparing them to take a shower. High-angle shots from the holes in the ceiling evoke the real pictures of the Nazis peeping into the gas chambers in Auschwitz. The children are extremely tense, and Hannah tries to calm them by entering the showers and testing the taps. Suddenly the children run amok and the panic passes to the workers, who announce with terror that they are building gas chambers.[8]

In the beginning of the film, the transport orders for the Jews of Prague evoked the horrors of concentration camp life. For the inhabitants of Terezin, transport orders meant death in the east, in Auschwitz. This is presumably also the end of Hannah. We see her standing alone in the middle of one of the straight streets in the former garrison town of Terezin, and the dark, lonely figure does not move as a tram approaches and passes by her, graphically "swallowing" her. The train's smoke fills the screen, and Hannah, visually and quite literally, has disappeared into the smoke.

The final sequence in *Distant Journey* involves the camp's liberation. One young woman who observes the approach of the Russian units runs through the deserted streets, shouting the message of freedom in the heart of the dreary ghetto and human desolation. Slowly and gradually people emerge from rubble and windows. One is not sure whether they are ghosts or real survivors. The young woman frenziedly hits a harp-shaped piano skeleton, and the ghostly multitude joins in a bizarre, frantic celebration. This celebration is neither the joyous end of past suffering nor the optimistic preparation for a brighter future, but rather an apt finale to the horrible story of the concentration camp universe.

The soundtrack plays an important role in *Distant Journey*. One of the infernal disparities of the Nazi world was the use of music to accompany the slave laborers and those marching into the gas chambers. Because of the abundance of talent in Terezin, the Czech ghetto is connected with a number of unforgettable music events, such as the production of an original children's opera in the ghetto and the special performance of Verdi's *Requiem* for Adolph Eichmann. Beyond the hideous incongruity associated with Eichmann enjoying a piece of beautiful music while preparing the extermination of its performers, in the Nazi world the language of the angels became indeed an instrument of the devil. Radok presents a small band of old Jews on a wagon with huge drums and cymbals. This grotesque version of a Klezmer band engages in playing for the deportees to the east. The wide-open eyes of these performers reveal that they have peeped into the abyss and know exactly the destiny of their audience and the bizarre role of their accompaniment. Their monotonous and dissonant sounds, dominated by the repeated bangs of the drum and the cymbals, render them the infernal conductors to the countless victims participating in their own funeral march.

The piano is used as a central motif to drive home the idea of disenchantment with culture, showing how high culture betrayed its fundamental humanistic promises under the spell of Nazism. During the gloomy wedding ceremony of Hannah and Tony, the background music is provided by someone practicing piano in a neighboring apartment. The distant and incongruous sounds—a special counterpoint effect produced by the annoying monotony of scales practice—constitute a reminder of the extreme gap between the victims' predicament and the rest of the Gentile population trying to maintain its normal way of life. One scene in the ghetto shows an old piano as a direct "accessory" to murder. In one roll call, a Nazi soldier brutally pushes a helpless Jew, who falls backward on the piano and is immediately killed by the impact. The ending uses the same motif again with an added meaning. The piano, or what was left of it, is used merely as an instrument to alert the remaining survivors to the imminent liberation. Bazin points out the similarity to the big gong in the climactic moments of Lang's *Metropolis*, which warned the people of the city about the disastrous flood.[9] This analogy reinforces the ambiguity of the final scene, which is a climax of madness and frenzy more than a real celebration of freedom. The piano and the values it stands for appear to be worthless against the background of Nazi atrocities. Its original function is displaced by the urgency of the new situation, and in that context hitting and breaking the musical instrument is an act of frustration and disenchantment.

This wild climax comes at the end of a film which, despite the awesomeness of its subject, is dominated by Radok's subtle style and his preference for understatement. For example, in the first part the cruel uprooting of the Jewish community in Prague and its devastation are conveyed through an image of a ball resting motionless on an empty terrace. Earlier, in the same place, the ball was being played with by a group of cheerful children. Hannah's observation—the picture is shown from her point of view—imparts an additional poignancy to this scene. She realizes the inevitable doom of young children in the engulfing horror, and her expression exhibits the suffering of a newly married young woman forced to suppress her own motherly instincts.

Radok's narrative is loosely structured to allow delving into intriguing dramatic moments which contribute little to the progress of the central action but which ·better convey the historical sources and the multiple facets of the concentration camp universe. Following the wedding ceremony, one of Hannah's relatives finds his transport order. He enters his office, whose massive desk and luxurious pieces of furniture suggest a respectable social background, sits in his armchair and lights a cigarette. His slow movements, the depressing silence, an unusual camera angle, and a graceful but also suspenseful camera movement surveying the entire room render this ostensible gesture of relaxation instead as an act of dignified despair. The camera focuses on his desk, when, all of sudden, sounds of panic are heard from the street outside, where cars stop abruptly and people are screaming. Then, in the same shot, the camera moves slowly from the burning cigarette left on the ashtray—the small pillar of smoke indicates one more victim of the Nazis—to the empty armchair, and finally to the open window with its blowing curtains.

This suicide scene illustrates Radok's aesthetic approach to death and violence. It also demonstrates his concern with the total tragedy rather than concentrating on one central action. Radok literally abandons the narrative in order to go beyond the story to history. He does not hesitate to leave the original story of Tony and Hannah unresolved. Their end is not described, nor is it referred to clearly in this work. They simply disappear from the film when the historical drama surpasses the artistic concern with the fate of individual fictional characters.

The real source of Radok's outstanding style in *Distant Journey* is implied in his following statement:

> What I wanted to say on film, and later in the theatre, probably has its origins with Hitler. My father was a Jew. I think that is important, it played an important role in my life. The name "Hitler" evokes a picture in my mind: A little girl, all sugar and spice, is handing Hitler a bunch of wild flowers. Hitler bends over her and smiles a benevolent smile. To me this image is linked with the awareness of what National Socialism meant, just because the image conceals something. I can't imagine how it would be possible to describe the war, Hitler, National Socialism, and concentration camps, without this image.[10]

Thus, while Resnais focused on the monumental disparity between the present appearance and the past reality, Radok finds a terrific incongruity in the nature of Nazism, simultaneously embodying a pleasant appearance and a monstrous essence. Aware of this outrageous disparity, Radok's distrust of external reality underlies his aesthetic approach to the concentration camp universe.

Radok's outstanding style, for all its complexity and visual marvel, never tends to excessive aestheticism at the expense of a basic grip of historical truths. The film's beginning, taken from Nazi footage with the statements "This is Germany" and "Germany is Hitler," cues us in to the political reality. The suicide scene ends with a match cut from the blowing curtains to the SS flags and pictures of Himmler and concentration camps. The image of the tortured woman in the ghetto, forced to kneel and hold a bucket in her teeth, diminishes in size on the screen and is gradually wiped out by the new image of documentary material on the Nazis and the SS. This visual device recurs many times in *Distant Journey* and illustrates the notion of a story within a story, or a story within history, reminding the spectators that the story and the individual cases Radok relates in this work should be viewed within the context of the more general and more bloody history of Germany and Europe in World War II.

Radok's overall style can be best characterized as expressionist. The incor- poration of images of expressionist painting and earlier practices of expressionist cinema is exhibited in the massive concentration of people and objects in dismal or nightmarish conditions, surveyed by long and slow camera movements; distortions of time and space achieved by unusual camera angles; the stark darkness which dominates many of the scenes; individual pictures with strong imagistic power; and the loose narrative which often displaces conventional logic by juxtaposed incongruities.

The subject of expressionism in the context of the aesthetics of horror requires a special discussion. In general, the graphic art of the Holocaust is predominantly expressionistic. In the concentration camp universe, the other modernist styles, such as futurism, surrealism, cubism, or abstract art, became thematically irrelevant or all but frivolous forms of expression which do not belong to "the other planet." Most paintings and drawings made by the victims during the war years demonstrate that expressionism offered both thematic orientation and stylistic practices to the artist-victims and survivors, whose sights and visions had been shaped by their war experience.[11]

The expressionist style flourished at the turn of the century and was rooted in the cultural malaise of the *fin de siècle*. It especially appealed to German artists and is often mistakenly identified as an exclusively German art movement. Those who see Nazism as an offspring of the entire tradition and history of German culture should acknowledge the irony implicit in the fact that expressionism became the main mode of artistic reaction taken by the Nazi victims. (The most crushing irony in that context, though, is that one of the earliest groups of expressionism in Germany had organized near Munich and was called the Dachau School, a name which today few would fail to associate with the first concentration camp built by the Nazis.) When the Nazis came to power, they banned the expressionist style as decadent and sickening and suppressed it completely in Germany. Instead they tried to foster art deco, whose aesthetics is visible in numerous Nazi posters and in the images of *Triumph of the Will*.

The fathers of modern expressionism were the Dutch Vincent van Gogh, the Norwegian Eduard Munch, and the Belgian James Ensor. Their works indulged in tragic themes of spiritual agony, existentialist anxiety, demonism, madness, and pervasive morbidity. When van Gogh painted a pair of ragged shoes to convey human misery, the image was revolutionary, introducing a new icon into modern culture. During the war, shoes became a main source of obsession for the camps' inmates. The shoe is a motif in Primo Levi's *Survival in Auschwitz:* "And do not think that shoes form a factor of secondary importance in the life of the Lager," Levi tells us. "Death begins with the shoes; for most of us, they show themselves to be instruments of torture, which, after a few hours of marching, cause painful sores which become fatally infected."[12] Likewise, in the Czech film *Diamonds of the Night*, which is based on the autobiographical book of author/survivor Arnost Lustig, the protagonist is tortured by a hurting shoe, and director Jan Nemec often focuses on the foot and the shoe as silent emblems for the misery of those caught in the predicament of relentless persecution.[13]

But the main influence on Holocaust art is traced to "the kind of approach which, descending from Munch, depended on the angst filled human figure."[14] This kind of expressionism is haunted by a compelling grim vision. The paintings are often dominated by dark colors or thick, black strokes (e.g., Rouault), distorted forms of both nature and the human figure (e.g., Soutine), expressing horror, disorientation, and chaos. In expressionist paintings, agonized facial expressions convey a reaction to a general state of affairs rather than a particular behavior in one passable moment. Indeed, usually the portraits lack realistic individuality. For the Holocaust painters, this style gave them an opportunity to project the totality of their misery. In the vein of Munch's famous painting "The Scream," many pictures on the Holocaust are entitled "Despair," "Scream," or "Longing."[15] The expressionists' interest in abstract qualities and general human conditions fits the Holocaust experience of massive, almost anonymous suffering. In the early stages, the artist saw in the eyes of a child, the bending back of an old man, the powerlessness of a helpless mother, the sorrowful state shared by many others. In the end, the loss of physical individuality was quite literal as the living skeletons showed only bald heads, bones, and skin, and the remains of the dead, heaps of unidentifiable, emaciated corpses.

But when we come to think about the unparalleled trials of the concentrationary universe, the basic question emerges again: Can art represent the extreme horrors of the Holocaust? The artists of the Holocaust have provided compelling and horrific pictures of their contemporary setting. They have also demonstrated a form of spiritual resistance against the Nazi oppression and a moving testimony to the endurance of man's creative faculties. Thus, the aesthetic evaluation of their work is often eclipsed by considerations of their historical predicament and personal plight. Robert Hughes offers a highly intriguing opinion about the possibilities of plastic art to express the unspeakable. In his book *The Shock of the New*, he describes and analyzes modern artists and art movements. Although he never refers to any specific work on the Holocaust, he appropriately deals with the issue in his chapter on expressionism, entitled "The View from the Edge."

> The event which revealed that painting could no longer deal cathartically with modern horrors was the Holocaust . . . after Auschwitz, Expressionist distortion of the human body in art seemed to many sensitive minds to have no future—in fact, to be little more than an impertinence or an intrusion, a gloss on what the Nazis had done, on a vast industrial scale, to real bodies. Reality had so far outstripped art that painting was speechless. What could rival the testimony of the photograph?[16]

The prominent art critic reinforces our previously pronounced position on the unmatched power of the photograph to transmit the Nazi horrors. The triumph of Radok's work is that his expressionism is cinematic and fundamentally photographic. Cinematic expressionism was born in Germany in 1919 under the strong influence of expressionist painting and theater. Radok's style in *Distant Journey* is, however, as Bazin has noted, more in the style of Fritz Lang's *Metropolis* than the seminal *The Cabinet of Dr. Caligari*.[17] The great force of Radok's art lies in the employment of a certain degree of stylization to create a visual texture to enhance the impression of nightmarish reality without ruining the basic realistic effect of photographic verisimilitude. His film maintains a certain degree of realism by avoiding the excessive artificiality of the image created by means of heavy makeup, studio sets of distorted and painted background, and unrealistic contrasts of black and white. Radok also avoids the artificial theatricality or stylization of the performances found in many early expressionist films, including *Metropolis*. Radok also displays a high degree of good taste by avoiding explicit graphic horror and visual gore. The film's acclaimed expressionism is ultimately rooted in the realistic impulse to re-create faithfully the authentic conditions in Terezin. And unlike most other works of expressionism, Radok's excells in touching on the rich variety of human experience and the nuances of individual tragedies in the camp.

Distant Journey, with its multiple layers of subjects and styles, is a miraculous cinematic tour de force—and unfortunately a neglected masterpiece. As Josef Skvorecky has declared: "It was a tragically premature and anachronistic work of art."[18] The film can be fairly compared to *Citizen Kane* and, further paralleling Welles, it was Radok's first film. In 1950, when the film was shown in the United States, Bosley Crowther called it "The most brilliant, the most powerful and horrifying film on the Nazis' persecution of Jews," and a poll at the year's end ranked it as the best foreign language film.[19] Robert Hatch found the story confusing but admitted that *Distant Journey* "is moving, frightening, macabre, and penetrating to a degree matched by none of the factual pictures on the subject."[20] And Crowther wrote in the *New York Times*: "The faint of heart, however curious, are advised to see it at their own risk."[21]

It is perhaps more interesting to read Andre Bazin's reaction to the film style. Bazin is known as a major spokesman for realist theories of the cinema, an influential critic who viewed cinema's essence as lying in its ability to reproduce truthful images of reality. Bazin was specifically against expressionism in cinema, especially as embodied in *The Cabinet of Dr. Caligari*. On *Distant Journey* Bazin wrote:

> The astonishing thing is that here [in *Distant Journey*] the most questionable traits of expressionism paradoxically regain a profound justification. . . . All the features of those [classic expressionist] works which could be considered outdated appear here very logical, [achieving] the most necessary [style of] representation for the reality of nightmares. Out of internal and in a certain way metaphysical fidelity to the universe of the concentrationary ghetto, the film, unwittingly, no doubt, evokes the world of Kafka, and, more strangely, that of de Sade.[22]

For many other critics, the depiction of extreme sufferings and the systematic exposition of increasingly greater horrors evoke Dante's *Inferno*. In general, Holocaust literature abounds in allusions to Dante's *Inferno*. Upon entering Auschwitz, Primo Levi stated categorically and perhaps also instinctively: "This is Hell." He later includes direct references to Dante's work by quoting whole verses from the *Inferno*. Peter Weiss's compelling drama *The Investigation* imitates the structure of Dante's work. In his *The Holocaust as the Literary Imagination*, Langer finds allusions to Dante's *Inferno* in scores of books on the Holocaust. Alfred Radok, like Alain Resnais, invokes the notion of inferno with no explicit reference to Dante's work. The depiction of massive punishment and suffering, climaxing in scenes of frantic madness, seems to fit the medieval imagination of hell. The comparison with Dante is also established in terms of the method of exposition. Dante, accompanied by his mentor Virgil, provides a comprehensive and gradual survey of the inferno. Radok and his camera systematically expose the different facets of the concentration camp universe, moving progressively into the darkest areas, and, like Dante, highlight scenes of individual tragedies without betraying the human dimension of the inhuman suffering.

While the analogy to hell is a convenient source for artistic imagination, it raises some problems regarding its accuracy or adequacy. Obviously the inhabitants of hell are sinners, whereas the victims of the Nazi atrocities were innocent. But here I will limit my comments to the stylistic implications of that analogy. The Christian hell, which found its grand expression in Dante's *Inferno*, was transcendent to human experience, and its conceptualization was universally acknowledged by Christian believers. The Holocaust, by contrast, has been unique and too concrete. The artist's task is to express incomparable examples of human experiences and to convey that the Holocaust was an unprecedented hell taking place on earth. That means that while making the allusions to the mythical hell, the artist feels compelled to emphasize the reality of the described events. Peter Weiss resorted to court testimonies focusing on dry facts of specific incidents, reported practices, and much accurate numerical data expressed in a deliberately factual and emotionless language. In *Distant Journey*, Radok incorporated documentary pictures and direct references to Nazi Germany to remind the viewers of the historical context, which, along with authentic settings and keen dramatization, resulted in an astounding reflection of the Holocaust reality.

Distant Journey also occupies a special place in the development of Czech film. Josef Skvorecky, in his personal history of Czech cinema, describes the impact of Radok's work on the sixties.

Radok's first film *The Long Journey* (1949) was so much of a revelation to all of us as were the films of Vera Chytilova, Milos Forman or Jan Nemec fourteen years later. It was a tragically premature and anachronistic work of art. It dealt with the fate of the Jews in the Third Reich; as far as artistic influences are concerned one might perhaps find traces of German expressionism. I am not aware of any comparable work created at that time in world cinematography . . . the socialist-realist critics said that the film reflected "only" humanitarian philosophy. It possessed as little "class approach" as the Nuremberg Laws. It was simply not comparable to anything else produced at that time. The appropriate official places exploded: the film was labeled "existential" and "formalistic." After a very brief run, it was withdrawn from public showing and for almost two decades was locked away in the Barrandov vault.[23]

It is not surprising that one of the first movies that heralded the Czech New Wave in the early sixties was also on Terezin, Zbynek Brynych's *Transport from Paradise* (1962). Arnost Lustig wrote the script, based on his book *Night and Hope*, a collection of autobiographical stories on life and death in Terezin. The screenplay features no protagonist; it follows the fate and human conduct of many characters in the crucial twenty-four-hour period which involved the preparations for the visit of the Red Cross commission and the massive deportation the day after.

The film's ironic title signifies the filmmakers' focus on the surrealistic double function of the original Terezin, a model town "presented to the Jews as a gift from the Fuehrer," and a stopover on the way to extermination in Auschwitz. Brynych's handling of this outstanding combination is nicely described by Novak: "Everything about this town is both real and unreal. This artificially created world, abnormal in spite of every semblance of normality, represents a trauma organized with absolutely inhuman thoroughness. A phantom town, the streets are crowded with people looking at show windows, sitting about on park benches. But look any one of them in the eyes and you will see death. Death is the only certainty existing in this world of hallucinations, where every second is a second snatched from annihilation. Death in this phantom town is called Transport."[24]

The beginning features the peculiar aspect of Terezin, the monstrous incongruity between the Nazi desire to maintain the appearance of normal if not pleasant reality, as contrasted with the pall of terror, hunger, and death that lay underneath the artificial serenity. Brynych and Lustig focus on one of the most notorious episodes associated with the Nazi special plans for Terezin, the production of a propaganda movie on the ghetto entitled *Hitler Presents a Town to the Jews*. Joseph Goebbels appointed Kurt Gerron to prepare the Nazi work. Gerron had left Germany in 1933, after a successful career as an actor and a filmmaker. He settled in Holland, where he ran a literary cabaret, frequently ridiculing Hitler from the nightclub stage. After the Nazi occupation he was allowed to work in a Jewish theater for Jewish audiences in Amsterdam under strict German supervision. In 1944, he was shipped to Terezin, where he was forced to make the Nazi propaganda film. Herbert Luft has described the project:

For this film the commander of Theresienstadt ordered the muddy streets and alleys of the ghetto city cleared of debris and rubble. The town was scrubbed and disinfected. The sick and injured were removed from sight. The streets were lined with patriotic banners. Swastikas flapped against flagpoles. Inmates had to have curtains on the windows of their pitiful shanties. Exteriors of the vermin-infested medieval buildings were adorned with flowers. For the first time in years, Theresienstadt was fully lit. While the stage was being set for the film, clean clothing was issued to all the inmates who were to participate in the main scene in the marked square—a huge banquet with waltz tunes provided by the camp band.

When *Hitler Presents a Town to the Jews* was completed, the banquet food was collected by the Kapos and punishment given to those who had dared to touch it: even the children who might have eaten some candy and cookies. Kurt Gerron was promptly sent to die in the extermination center of Oswiescim.[25]

Transport from Paradise begins with a film-within-a-film sequence, featuring Gerron preparing the Nazi propaganda movie. Unlike other neomodernist works which use the film-within-a-film as a device to ponder philosophically and often playfully about the border line between illusion and reality, for Brynych, exposing the depressing reality and highlighting the unique aspects of Terezin are the main concerns in *Transport from Paradise*. When a group of people are choreographed before Gerron's camera to declare that they are "happy in Theresienstadt," the impassive voices and the dry monotonous recitations leave no doubt about the forced nature and falsity of such declarations. The surrealistic atmosphere is provided by a group of young inmates whose incongruous appearance is marked by their fancy costumes and playful postures to the unseen camera, rendering them like a bunch of modern urban dandies. The only girl in the group, Lisa, adds a special poignancy to the scene. Dancing in a light dress, she genuinely enjoys the unexpected momentary relief from the ruthless Nazi oppression, a brief interlude which allows her to express her youthful charm.

In addition to the propaganda movie, and closely associated with it, the preparations for the Red Cross visit in Terezin were another demonstration of the Nazis' demonic strategies of deception (whose ultimate symbol is, indeed, the *Arbeit Macht Frei* sign on the gates of the death camps). Just as the Warsaw ghetto uprising became the epitome of the brutal annihilation of the Jews of eastern Europe and their hopeless predicament during the war, the Red Cross visit in Terezin signified more than anything else the pathetic tragedy of the Jews of central Europe who fell prey to their own illusions about German culture and the deceptive devices of the Nazis. *Transport from Paradise*, like *Distant Journey*, avoids the dramatization of the Red Cross visit, for the emphasis is put on the depiction of the victims and the victimizers. The Nazi evil is featured through the sadistic practices of an SS major, commander of the local German forces, and through the limitless arrogance of the German general who visits the ghetto to assure its readiness for the international commission. The general also conducts a special transport of the sick and the elderly in order to eliminate them from the scene as part of the preparations for the Red Cross visit.

In the transport scene, Brynych and his cinematographer, Jan Curik, achieve a remarkable degree of verisimilitude. Throughout the sequence there is no melodrama, no attempt to impose meanings or suggest explanations, nor even the sense of moral indignation. Amidst masses of people in a courtyard and the constant shouting of numbers in German, the camera moves slowly in all directions. At one point, it all looks like an ordinary, busy train station; people pick up their suitcases, numbers are announced, and the people prepare to go. One critic observes that "when Curik's camera surveys the scene in the courtyard where new arrivals are being registered, we are tempted to think that this sequence was actually made for a contemporary newsreel."[26] But it is this apparent normalcy of the situation and the amoral efficiency of the Nazi bureaucracy that highlight the undercurrent threat and an unambiguous mood of impending disaster. A tilt of the camera discloses the white tag, indicating its wearer has been selected for the transport. As the camera moves closer, the human faces display deep confusion and resignation, while the Germans appear alert, pragmatic, and efficient. The inhuman Nazi herding of human beings tolerates no deviations. When an old man accidentally moves in the wrong direction, he is brutally removed from the group to be given "special treatment." This striking scene ends with a huge pile of now ownerless, numbered suitcases and the announcement "Transport is ready."

The film's middle part focuses exclusively on the victims. It takes place during a night filled with the tense expectation of the transport of two thousand people scheduled for the following day. We see a boy writing his last letter to his parents (temporarily spared because one of them is Gentile), a young couple engaging in dreams of a bright future, and a gigolo-type character yielding to the seduction of an older married woman. These little episodes reveal resignation, despair, and the painful recognition of inevitable tragic endings, but they also manage to underscore noble gestures of friendship, devotion, mutual understanding, and love. The central act features Lisa, who agreed to have sex with a group of youngsters before their deportation to the east. Lisa's action is sacrificial and even heroic, for she has refused to make love to the deputy chairman, an act which could have saved her from the next transport. Instead she chose to spend the last night with her male pals. By means of understatement and graphic restraint, Brynych repudiates any potential pornographic charge. Nor is there any sense of these characters mindlessly enjoying the present because tomorrow doesn't matter. In the dimly lit dwelling, one plays a wistful melody on his guitar, and the camera focuses on the boys' tense expressions before and after they go to Lisa. The entire sequence is highly emotional and poignant. It also illustrates the reversal of natural order in the concentration camp. The adolescents' sexual act is an initiation to life, signifying both newly gained maturity and reproductivity; in this scene, however, it is motivated by the characters' knowledge of their imminent death.

The final phase of the picture focuses on the transport roll call. It takes place outside the ghetto in a muddy open field where the entire ghetto population is lined up in gigantic rows. Repeated melancholy whistles of the waiting train form an ominous reminder of the purpose of this roll call. The names of those selected are called out and the Jews are forced to run and stumble through mud and puddles. Once again, like the first transport scene, the verisimilitude is striking. Skvorecky's reference to it as an unforgettable scene is echoed by Bosley Crowther: "Running frantically (as they are compelled to) down the sodden, human aisles, to no other sound except the harsh calls, the splash of the running feet and an occasional shrieking whistle of the waiting train—presents a scene that is not to be forgotten."[27]

Transport from Paradise demonstrates an outstanding combination of stark realism, with poignant lyricism of individual human dramas, and surrealistic impressions of Nazi horrors. However, in many dramatic moments of potentially sensational scenes of excessive violence or sentimentality, Brynych often chooses to show the reaction of a minor bystander present at the scene. Thus, when the SS major tortures an old Jew in the middle of an empty street, the camera steadily focuses on the reaction of the major's driver, Sergeant Binde. By showing many scenes from Binde's point of view, Brynych achieves a special distancing effect, for usually viewers cannot identify with the tough-looking, Nazi-uniformed sergeant. Binde, however, is a conscientious German who loathes the brutality of his fellow countrymen, and in his own way attempts to support the victims. He lets a resistance member escape, and during a roll call ignores the absence of another resistance fighter whom his commander is determined to capture. At the same time, Binde remains passive and prefers to obey orders rather than directly clash with his superiors. His compassionate attitude is ironic because those he tries to help by shutting his eyes or saving them from torture are eventually caught and killed.

Another example of diverting the focus from the core of the action occurs during the night before the big transport. A young loving couple sits on the stairs planning a brighter future of homely happiness. It is a common dramatic device to present hopeful moments before an impending disaster, designed usually to increase the pathos of an unhappy ending (even though in this film the small talk of Lustig's script appears especially truthful, simple, and moving). However, throughout the scene, the young couple remains in the dark with their backs to the camera. Brynych focuses instead on Vagus, the young gigolo, a truly poignant detail, for Vagus himself is an orphan who had always had the desire to attain some domestic happiness. Vagus, unlike Binde, makes a sacrificial act—in the roll call the following day he voluntarily joins the transport in place of his engaged friend.

The systematic killing of millions of people led many to argue that the massive destruction was facilitated by the victims' failure to stage any resistance; according to a popularized and degrading version of this position, the victims went to their death like sheep to the slaughter. Brynych and Lustig struggle with the notion of "sheep to the slaughter." In the beginning we see a flock of sheep in the street, an unlikely image in Terezin, inserted into the sequence to symbolize the capitulation to the arrogant Nazi general. In response to the general's question, one of his assistants remarks that "they come from Lidice." The reference to the Czech village demolished by the Nazis after the assassination of Heydrich also evokes one of the most well-known heroic acts of resistance during World War II. Later on, during the humiliating roll call and the following arrangements for deportation, we hear characters protesting "never again like sheep." But despite the indignant tone of this statement and the ironic reference to the sheep from Lidice, *Transport from Paradise* is in no way a condemnation of Jewish inaction and passivity.

The film features the existence of resistance in Terezin. Beneath Nazi ads there are posters screaming "Death to Fascism." The underground also prints information on the fate of the Jews in Europe and the development of the war, especially the upcoming defeat of Germany. When the Nazis discover the secret printing shop in the ghetto, the elderly widow Feinerova caught there pleads with the benign German soldier Binde to shoot her rather than let her be interrogated and tortured to reveal the other members of the resistance. (Binde, who tries to help the resistance members, ends up shooting the old woman, and thereby he demonstrates his fateful membership in the network of evil.) A more daring heroism is displayed by the chairman of the Jewish council, modeled after the legendary Jacob Adelstein, who refuses to sign a list of two thousand names selected for transport to the east because "There is gas there where you are sending these people." He is ordered to the bunker for "special treatment." Finally, he himself is sent with the transport, but not without first defying his oppressors: "You will lose the war. History teaches us tyranny always goes under."

The resistance in Terezin could not alter historical events. The actual impact of the resistance there was minimal due to the level of impotence to which the Jews were reduced. Its presence attested to spiritual resistance and individual dignity. Spiritual courage is required to acknowledge the true nature of the Final Solution. And while the Jews have no power to organize and fight back, the reaction becomes essentially personal; the adoption of codes of behavior displaying noble altruistic assistance to others and defiance of the Nazi ideology indicates high morality, an existential commitment to human dignity, and renunciation of passive suffering, rather than a viable option to enhance the prospects of survival. The portrayal of complex characters denied any glamorizing melodramatic roles is a major achievement of the film's acclaimed realism. Until *Transport from Paradise*, most of the eastern European films on World War II were what Antonin Liehm called a kind of western,[28] showing a clear-cut moral conflict with both good guys and bad guys bigger than life, in accordance with conventional cinematic, melodramatic connotations that one finds in classic Hollywood westerns. By contrast, Brynych and Lustig show true-to-life characters, reminding us, in Novak's words, that "there were far more of those who did not fight but whose actions, suffering and anxiety provided an incentive to fighting humanity."[29] Mira and Antonin Liehm consider the obsession with resistance, or the lack of resistance, as essentially didactic: "For some this is a signal to revolt, and the cry 'Never again like sheep!' sounds loud and clear from the screen as a message for the present and the future."[30]

Transport from Paradise also marks a distinct deviation from the former dominance of Socialist Realism in the Czech cinema. Its stylistic complexities and thematic attitudes were a breakthrough, signifying the new age of modernism in Czech cinema. The radical change in style, foreshadowed in the work of Alfred Radok in *Distant Journey*, was observed by Antonin Liehm, who noted "the camera freely altering both time and narration: documentary reconstruction, sheer lyricism and philosophical mediation coexisted side by side in a new unity of style."[31] Despite the surrealistic effects, the film retains its realistic force. After all, its loose narrative is based on true historical episodes, and it focuses on stories of real individuals and incidents taken from Arnost Lustig's personal experiences as an inmate in the ghetto. The film was based on documentary reconstructions. It was shot on location in Terezin, with thousands of extras transforming the place into the way it had appeared during World War II, which, like Pontecorvo's concentration camp re-created in Yugoslavia for *Kapo*, frightened many local people who were unaware it was being used for a film project. Even the car used by the arrogant German general was authenic: it was the same Mercedes used by Eichmann when he visited Terezin. *Transport from Paradise* also incorporates information taken from actual records of the administrative procedure deployed by the Third Reich. For example, after the Jews have been evacuated to prepare the big transport to the east, the Nazi major receives the following report from a shouting guard: "Total inhabitants of the ghetto 62,353 dirty Jews. 59,984 have passed out of the ghetto, 192 are insane, 2,156 are ill, 21 dirty Jews died on the march." In summary, Brynych's mise-en-scène and his special utilization of documentary sources can be labeled "fantastic realism" with a striking surrealistic effect. As one critic observed, while to Radok "Terezin was a town in which the most fantastic things were real . . . where Brynych is concerned, the fact itself is fantastic enough."[32]

Brynych's second film on the Holocaust was *The Fifth Horseman Is Fear* (1965), based on Hana Belohradska's novella *Without Beauty, Without a Collar*. As the film's title indicates, Brynych concentrates on the terror perpetrated by the Nazis against the victims and the bystanders. The main plot concerns Braun, a Jewish doctor in Prague, who treats a wounded resistance fighter and pays with his life for this heroic deed. Brynych transformed the original story of honor and heroism into a penetrating study of human reaction to the Nazi menace, against a striking visual exposition of the apocalyptic life in Nazi-occupied Prague. In fact, the emphasis on expressive visual representation tends to overwhelm narrative clarity; therefore our discussion of the film requires a specially detailed presentation of the story line.

The plot is composed of three distinct parts. The beginning shows Braun working in a synagogue that has been turned into a confiscation warehouse. The former doctor, forced to serve as a cataloguer, finds himself cooperating with the Nazi persecution of the Jews by assisting in the process of confiscating Jewish property. When a fellow worker appeals to him to fight back because "everything is against us," Braun turns him down, claiming, "I'm a realist. I don't deserve to become involved with more than I have to."

It is, of course, fear which prevents Braun from taking any action to alter his situation. The centrality of this theme is especially illustrated in his daily journeys from work to home. Doctor Braun, a bearded figure in black overcoat and black hat, scurries from one street corner to another, fearfully looking over his shoulders all the time. The narrow lanes, the ill-lit yards, and the mysterious backwaters of old Prague are a landscape of terror. The persecuted Jew resides in a small room on the top floor of an apartment building. He has no relations with his neighbors; they know nothing about his life, and evidently prefer to ignore his existence. Sensing his presence is a burden, Braun tries to hide from his neighbors. In his bare room, an old violin is his sole piece of property and also his only companion. The depressing emptiness of his home is sharply contrasted with the abundance of items in the warehouse, but it correlates to his physical predicament as well as the current drifting of his soul. A marvelous image of his long black coat hanging on the bare walls, which has an uncanny resemblance to a human figure, reflects the shadowy status to which he has been reduced.

The drastic change in Braun's life occurs when one of his neighbors, a hard-working butcher, begs him to operate on a wounded resistance member who has found shelter in their building. The doctor's initial rejection is followed by more tortured reflections and hesitations. Realizing that the life of another person is in his hands he cries, "Why me? Why should I do it?" Although the enormous risk involved haunts him, Braun, the antihero, spurns the notion of heroic martyrdom. "Who cares about death," he asks himself, "as long as it's not your own let others die." But ultimately, the dramatization of Braun's hesitation helps to define the importance and moral weight of his final decision. He approaches the wounded man in fear and trembling, his hands literally shaking, before he regains control over himself and extracts the bullet from the fighter's body.

After completing the operation, Braun faces another, more dangerous challenge. He responds to the butcher's plea to go out and obtain morphine necessary for the fighter's survival. Braun's quest for morphine begins an odyssey into the nightmare of the Nazi occupation. His first stop is in a brothel where his older sister works as a cleaning woman. The scene begins with an amazing sequence of a score of naked women washing themselves slowly to the strains of enchanting baroque music. The camera surveys their naked bodies, mostly in medium shots, showing parts of the human bodies in chiaroscuro lighting. As the girls bend to rub their skin, their postures are gentle, conveying humility, frailty, weakness, and resignation. The alternating reaction shots of Braun's startled face are used to avoid pornographic exploitation. The overall effect is that of a ritualistic preparation, for the brutalization which follows renders the girls sacrificial victims. The stylistic contrast between the shower sequence and the following aggressive sexual abuse also recalls one of the most terrible contrasts of the concentration camp universe, the use of showers, associated with the acts of cleanliness and purification, to accomplish the mass murder of innocent and unsuspecting victims. Nevertheless, the attempted metaphorization of the gas chambers into a forced prostitutes' shower room fails because the enormity of the real death factories is incomparable. In a departure from Brynych's usual style, characterized by slow pace, a cool visual approach, and understatement, this scene exposes the violence and brutality of the Nazi soldiers as they storm the helpless, naked girls. (The scene was inserted into the movie because Italian producer Carlo Ponti insisted on adding nudity and sex to assure the film's financial success in the west.)[33]

Doctor Braun's next stop is at a nightclub, where he goes to meet one of his former colleagues. The club, called Desperation Bar, is a place for people to escape their predicament with drinks and music. Nobody pays attention to the man who enters with newspapers announcing that new regulations have just been issued. They prefer to drink, dance, and sing folk songs. The music often changes abruptly to a more monotonous nondiegetic melody, and the bizarre atmosphere is underscored when we see people laughing, dancing, and enjoying themselves without actually hearing them on the soundtrack. One woman keeps laughing nervously and incomprehensibly at Braun's face. When he ignores her she breaks a glass and steps into the center of the bar, interrupting a billiard game to present herself in a slow, solo dance. As everybody in the room is staring at her, two big male nurses in white enter the bar and grab her away. However, in this fantastic sequence, the real human tragedy is not ignored. It is supplied by Doctor Wiener, Braun's friend, who tries to drown his deep despair in drinks. His situation is especially poignant since earlier, in his apartment, Braun had witnessed Wiener's furniture being confiscated. Wiener asks in pain about his wife, and Braun's answer is evasive for he cannot tell his friend that his wife has just tried to commit suicide.

The themes of madness and detachment from reality are developed in the next sequence. Braun's final stop is at an asylum for mental patients, where the inmates have lost all contact with external reality. Braun is especially moved when

he identifies the woman who was earlier taken from Desperation Bar. The exhausting and traumatic effects of the infernal odyssey are visible on Braun's face,
and his story about the need for morphine classifies him as a potentially new patient.
Wiener's note to the hospital doctor finally clarifies his identity, and Braun receives
the morphine with the hospital doctor's impassive remark: "We have twenty Jewish
suicides a day, but most of them we try to save. But you want morphine? There
you are."

The third and final part of *The Fifth Horseman Is Fear* becomes the story of
the house and its tenants. The action revolves around the police visits to capture
the underground fighter. During the first visit, the Gestapo searches inside the
apartments while Braun slowly and laboriously carries the wounded man up through
the building. The tenants see him but refuse to offer any help. Terrified at his
daring act, they fear possible reprisals against all the occupants of the building.
One neighbor who is an affluent lawyer is particularly disturbed when Braun takes
momentary shelter in his apartment; he offers the Jewish doctor anything to leave
the apartment at once, including—crushing irony—morphine.

The police leave empty-handed, but return the following day after being
anonymously informed about Doctor Braun by one of the tenants. This time the
tenants are herded into the cellar as the police await the doctor. Mutual suspicions
and intolerable tension engulf the neighbors. Braun finally arrives, having managed
to secure the fighter's safety, and he appears defiant and triumphant. "You won't
find anyone there," he taunts the police commissioner, "He left last night. I can't
tell you his name or why he's wounded. I'm a doctor. I used to be a doctor. Now
in fact I am one." Suddenly he swallows a poisonous capsule and instantly dies.

The tenants are then forced to file past Doctor Braun's body. The guilt-ridden
people are unable to look upon the corpse, except for a mad woman who pauses
to close the dead man's eyes. As the tenants go upstairs the commissioner holds
them, witheringly questioning them as to who phoned the police that morning.
There is no answer.

In dealing with the bystanders' conduct during the Nazi rule, Brynych presents
the tenants as a cross section of European society: a rich lawyer, an old music
teacher, a petty clerk serving the government, a lower-class butcher, an eccentric
old lady who keeps rabbits, and a young attractive maid. Skillfully and economically, Brynych reveals the lifestyle in each apartment, showing the individual
activities and domestic problems of this representative group. Especially important
is the role of the lawyer's son, a young boy who matures during the course of the
drama, gaining new understanding of the harsh realities around him. In the beginning there is a brief sequence illustrating this pattern of personal development.
When the boy first sees the underground fighter fall off his bicycle, he laughs—
presumably believing the man is drunk. When the man falls a second time he
laughs again. The third time, as he realizes the rider is wounded and trying to
make it into the building, a look of horror comes over his face. The last sequence
involving the tenants' reactions to oppression and humiliation is seen primarily
through the eyes of the child. Although he is not a dramatic agent taking part in
the unfolding action, he is an innocent observer with whom we can identify, and,

like him, we, the viewers, undergo the same process of recognition and understanding.

In spite of the film's visual and stylistic complexity, the thematic concerns of *The Fifth Horseman Is Fear* are apparently fairly simple. Essentially, "the film is about courage and honor," writes Renata Adler, "very much in the old style physical courage, moral honor—the sacrifice of one life for another and in the name of that historical optimism that is at the heart of faith and morality."[34] The Jewish doctor is the positive, exemplary figure, contrasted with the other tenants who share with him the same apartment building. With the exception of the mildly sympathetic butcher (a necessary tribute to the proletariat in a socialist country), who originally pleaded with him to perform the operation and then to go out and obtain the morphine, Braun's neighbors comprise a bunch of cowards, collaborators, informers, and unstable characters. The escapist behavior of the multitude of Jewish victims seems equally reprehensible. Braun, who has shared the same anxieties, appears at the end as a true hero, proud of his accomplishments and accepting his death with the reassuring knowledge that he has made his contribution to the overthrow of Nazism. He dies like a classical martyr, defying the tyrant-commissioner and the forces of evil the Nazi agent represents. From the staircase he looks down at the police commissioner, stating, with a slight grin of victory, that he ensured the fighter's safety. When he dies we recall the answer the boy was given when he inquired about the definition of a hero: "a hero is one who dies in pain as opposed to one who lives in pain."

The Fifth Horseman avoids excessive melodramatic sentimentality thanks to Brynych's talent at understatement and the conception of the central character. Braun is actually the opposite of the attractive, crusading doctor-figure of popular novels and Hollywood movies. He is not even a surgeon, but trained to lab work only, and the text implies that he was partly motivated to take on the dangerous task in order to prove to himself that he could do the work of a surgeon (after the operation he cannot suppress a grin of self-satisfaction, and his final words to the commissioner emphasize his triumph at the reclaimed identity of doctor). Throughout the film, Brynych focuses on his lack of resolution and physical strength, including numerous reaction shots to indicate that the protagonist is mostly affected by the situations rather than initiating or creating them. Clearly, Braun is an antihero, a sort of unremarkable everyman; however, these traits underscore the moral implications of his story and its universal significance.

Apart from his skillful use of understatement, Brynych is, above all, the master of expressive mise-en-scène. Indeed, his concentration on images comes at the expense of narrative pace and clarity. One critic observed that "everything in this film takes place in an atmosphere of intense anxiety, both the interior and exterior scenes seeming like something out of a nightmare."[35] The stark black-and-white photography of the desolate streets of the Jewish ghetto, the fantastic atmosphere in Desperation Bar, and the hallucinatory pictures of the mental asylum set up the nightmarish mood. Brynych deals with horrors by mingling visual illustrations of Kafkaesque angst (e.g., the setting of old Prague and Braun's fearful scurrying in its narrow alleys) along with Dantesque hellish visions. The film's triptych structure, and in particular the middle section, in which the brothel, Desperation Bar, and the Jewish Asylum constitute a series of infernal "regions," has led some critics to claim that many parts "owe much more to Dante than to Kafka."[36]

But the film also exhibits its indebtedness to specific works on the Holocaust. One striking image in *The Fifth Horseman Is Fear* was inspired by a memorable sentence from Tadeusz Borowski's book *This Way for the Gas, Ladies and Gentlemen* (1948). From the top of his gloomy barren room, Braun peeps outside; two images in particular seem to haunt him—a large chimney, and a group of people playing soccer in the distance below. The black smoke is a reminder of the fate of the Nazi victims, while the soccer game shows the terrible incongruity of the Holocaust reality, juxtaposing the normal lifestyle of victimizers and bystanders with the enormity of the victims' suffering, an incongruity eternalized by Borowski's incredible statement: "Between two throw ins in a soccer game, right behind my back, three thousand people had been put to death."[37]

Another tour de force of visual representation is displayed in the first scene, described by John Simon:

> I was particularly struck by the opening sequence, showing a synagogue converted into a warehouse for confiscated Jewish property. While harsh voices are loudly sorting out banned books, the hero, who like other Jews, is in charge of outfitting the despoilers with desired articles, wanders through this awful kingdom of furniture, roomful after roomful of a single item like clocks or radios. Each object is neatly labeled with the name of someone already dead or in a death camp—each object is a cenotaph. The wide screen fills up with these ghostly things that, bizarrely agglomerate, assume nightmare configurations. Braun traverses the chambers of this necropolis until he collapses on top of one of an army of large, black, batlike pianos. One of these is being tuned: while we see a stop-shot of Braun crumpled over a piano, a triadic progression of notes climbs higher with ghoulish insistence. Despair could not become more archetypal.[38]

The historical source for this sequence is another peculiar aspect of the Czech experience during the Holocaust. As the Nazis were deporting the Jews from 153 local communities in Bohemia and Moravia, they confiscated their possessions that had historical and artistic value. The Germans devised a special museum in Prague that would function as a pathological "research" of the "lost race" and as a propaganda "institute" justifying to the world the "Final Solution to the Jewish question." A small staff of Jewish librarians and art historians temporarily were spared from death and served as curators under the Nazis. Only one of them, Hana Volvokova, survived, and she called the hideous project the "Noah's ark" of Czech Jewish culture. By war's end the collection of Judaica filled eight historic sites and more than fifty warehouses throughout the city. (The museum that the Nazis envisioned as a bizarre mockery of Judaism has turned out to be the basis for an impressive collection of Judaica in central Europe. Thousands of artifacts were preserved by the Czech authorities after the war, and in 1983–84 an exhibition from the State Jewish Museum in Prague toured cities in America under the title "The Precious Legacy: Judaic Treasures from the Czechoslovak State Collections.")

The numerous objects left behind by the Jews—an excruciating testimony to the scale of human devastation and the countless victims—are *The Fifth Horseman Is Fear*'s point of departure. In a way, *The Fifth Horseman* begins where *Transport* ended. Brynych's later film continues and develops many of the ideas present in the first work. Historically, Terezin was a stop for the Prague Jews on the way to Auschwitz. But Brynych's Prague presents a later stage in the destructive process. The empty streets indicate that most of the Jewish population has already been deported and exterminated. Those left behind appear to be in a more desperate situation than the inhabitants of Terezin in *Transport from Paradise*. The paralyzing effect of fear denies even the little freedom to act and to resist which was available in the ghetto. Whereas in *Transport from Paradise* Lustig illustrated Nazi atrocities by relating various dramatic moments and situations based on real incidents, *The Fifth Horseman Is Fear*, with the strong apocalyptic connotations of its title, abandons any attempt to detail historical events to convey the ultimate terror of the Nazi phenomenon.

Remarkably, even though *Transport from Paradise* and *Distant Journey* deal with the same subject, it is *The Fifth Horseman Is Fear* which is directly and heavily influenced by Radok's work. The scene in the confiscation center and the motif of the piano in the context of the concentration camp universe exemplify Brynych's incorporation of visual quotations, metaphors, and motifs taken from Radok's masterpiece. Novak points out that in *The Fifth Horseman Is Fear*, "Brynych again uses modern techniques (arrangement, a roving camera, documentary film methods), [but] he does it in order to come closer to Radok . . . he has found that the idiom best suited to him is the idiom of expressionism, revived by modern means."[39] Brynych's expressionism, like Radok's, avoids the excessively grotesque as well as distortion and exaggeration, displaying rather a remarkable grasp of the nuances of human behavior. The main difference between the two Czech artists is that Radok conveyed madness through drums and trumpets and the frantic behavior of the victims, whereas Brynych shows the reduction of victims to unwilling and unwitting puppets trying to escape reality through detachment and distance.

The Fifth Horseman Is Fear is a remarkable film, for it deals with the Holocaust with the precise equilibrium of expressive visual images and narrative action, limiting the latter to an economical morality tale. One should point out, however, that for the average viewer, conditioned to follow a clear narrative line (although the film's narrative is in no way complex), the emphasis on mise-en-scène and the horrific appearance of the Nazi terrors are disorienting. Renata Adler, however, considered Brynych's work as one of the best films of 1968. She wrote in *The New York Times*: "*The Fifth Horseman Is Fear* . . . is so beautifully and thoughtfully made—well-written and acted, shot with perfect economy and care—that one is almost surprised at the end to be very much moved by the substance of it. . . . Zbynek Brynych . . . becomes with this movie quite simply one of the best directors we have."[40]

In contrast with the pervasive passivity caused by the paralyzing effect of fear as shown in *The Fifth Horseman*, the next Czech film in our discussion exhibits the frantic struggle to survive, sparked by the terror of Nazi apprehension. It is interesting to note that while escape dramas are popular stories, providing a thrilling framework of a chase drama, the celebration of human endurance, ingenuity, and usually a final courageous triumph, they are not common in Holocaust literature for the simple reason that very few people actually managed to escape the concentration camps. The Nazis' disregard for human life nearly perfected the mechanism of entrapment and destruction, and their utilization of methods of starvation, slave labor, and random, arbitrary killing made their grip on their victims virtually absolute. The few who were saved from the death camps attribute their survival to mere chance or blind fate.

The escape of Arnost Lustig came near the end of the war when the Nazi machine was collapsing. Even so, his escape was an exceptional occurrence, caused by an air attack on the wrong train, and it succeeded by sheer luck. The book he has written on these events, Darkness Casts No Shadow, lacks all the glamorizing devices usually applied to the theme of the man on the run.[41] It systematically reverses the conventional elements of supreme physical effort, determination, concentration on the act of survival, and resourcefulness into an account of extreme fatigue, deep confusion, mental anguish, and disorientation. Based on Lustig's book, Jan Nemec directed Diamonds of the Night (1964), a film on the plight of two youngsters who escape from a deportation train and struggle to reach their home in Prague.

The film begins with the two boys, alone in an unknown forest, exhausted and hungry, trying to make their way home to security and freedom. Their natural background illustrates the film's title; as John Simon observed: "The dews of the nocturnal forest catching stray moon beams and the faces of the boys glistening with determination in the soul-devouring darkness—these are diamonds of the night."[42] The central action is triggered when they reach the outskirts of a small village and attempt to take food from a farmer woman in an isolated cottage. Realizing the danger of being discovered and denounced, they want to kill her but, after long hesitation, they leave her unharmed. The woman reports their presence, and the old men of the village take the opportunity to help the Germans by conducting a manhunt. The youngsters are captured and taken to the mayor of the village to have their fate decided. At the end, the bunch of feeble old men order the boys to move out of the village at gun point, staging a mock execution. After the unbearable torture of the mock execution, the terrified boys head back to the forest to continue their ordeals.

Jan Nemec's direction presents a complex and powerful surrealistic work. He focuses on two areas: the personal and subjective experience of the tortured boys and the exposition of their nightmarish environment. Nemec's style is outstanding, for he dispenses with some basic elements of conventional dramatic action. The dialogue is minimal—there are only six sentences within the film's seventy-one minutes. The narrative line is ambiguous, and there is no sense of dramatic buildup. Most of the film consists of the boys' attempts to escape from the forest, and the long takes of hand-held subjective camera movement express the endlessness and futility of their efforts. As the youngsters run, the camera runs with them, becoming dizzy when they do, ducking and hiding, and resting when they do. The depressing monotony of their predicament is further emphasized through the lack of vocal sounds other than heavy breathing.

The depiction of their present ordeals is interwoven with the younger boy's visions and fantasies. These comprise and combine brief recollections of the deportation train and the beginning of their escape; vague, distorted, subjective perceptions of the external world; and longer sequences of flashforwards, fantasizing the end of their journey in Prague. Pictures of empty streets, gloomy buildings, cemeteries, empty staircases, and sealed doors convey the fear of finding that their parents and all their relatives have perished in the Holocaust. Thus the flashforwards express the fears of the present rather than creating an expectation of future developments. Likewise, the pictures of past experiences do not have the character of reminiscence; rather, they dramatize impulses emanating from the ongoing situation of the two fugitives. Thus the past and present , the present and hallucinations, all become one—one continuous stream of consciousness, but also a very palpable reality, real for all its nightmarish effect.

The complex pattern of the film's combination of subjective visions and objective narrative is manifest in the memorable confrontation scene between the young boy and the farm woman. The youngster's unendurable hunger is conveyed through his long contemplation of a loaf of bread. He expects the woman to give him food but also realizes that leaving her alive will threaten their chances for safe escape. The farm woman looks back at the staring boy, her face reflecting calm and determination. The silence is breathtaking as we expect each side to make the first move. Suddenly the boy rushes at the woman and clubs her to death. But in the next shot she appears as before, staring at the boy calmly and resolutely. Once we recognize the attack as a subjective fantasy, the act of murder happens again, as if this time it has really happened. By the third repetition, we understand the pattern of the protagonist's mind. The repressed rage of persecution and hunger, together with the consideration of the woman as a real threat to their survival, results in an intense desire to kill her. At the same time, seeing a live human being in her natural domestic environment and associating her position with the benevolent archetype of a food-supplying mother figure prevent the boy from committing murder. The alternation of murder, domestic pictures, and the actual tense encounter between the two characters creates a narrative ambiguity which is resolved only later when we realize that the manhunt was initiated by the woman's act of informing.

The boys' ordeals in the forest involve mostly running through woods and underbrush. The oppression of the Kindom of the Night is cosmic, as the unknown forest proves to be a source of exhausting confusion and harsh trials while nature offers none of its resources to meet the boys' needs for food or shelter. Nevertheless, the core of evil is located in the human realm. The film's climax shows the old villagers participating in a festivity while the two boys stand facing a wall awaiting their end. The final sequence displays the uncanny transformation of old men from rabbit hunters to head hunters, and the apparently normal German grandfathers become murderous beasts, while the fleeing boys become the hunted game. Simon considered this scene "as powerful as anything ever filmed," and discussed it as follows: "Powerful in its ultra-Bruegelian manner is the macabre orgy of the almost visibly decomposing greybeards. They sing foolish German songs about St. Peter in heaven as they stuff and stupefy themselves and dance about precariously before the young boys, whom they starve and will deliver to their deaths. This scene is such a head-on collision of outrageous comedy with absolute gruesomeness that whatever sense there may be in life falls apart before our stunned eyes."[43]

In contrast with its moral thrust and thematic straightforwardness, Nemec's work features a complex form which is indebted to several cinematic influences. Critics have compared its handling of narrative to Resnais's *Last Year at Marienbad* and the interspersion of personal fantasies with objective dramatic development to Robert Enrico's *Incident at Owl Creek*. Nemec was also consciously influenced by the work of Robert Bresson, who attempted to penetrate the inner life of his characters, deemphasizing external action. But the two most important sources for *Diamonds of the Night* are undoubtedly the works of Jean Renoir and Luis Buñuel. Renoir's *Rules of the Game* (1939) provides the antecedent for Nemec's manhunt sequence. Renoir included a hunting episode as an example of European decadence on the threshold of World War II. The sequence is striking for its depiction of the senselessness and vanity of the upper classes who derive dubious pleasure from the slaughter of defenseless animals. In *Diamonds of the Night*, the moral indignation is more apparent—for the human vice is a given active force.

The adventures of the two fugitives also recall the escape section in Renoir's classic *Grand Illusion* (1937). But once again, the predicament of Nemec's characters is radically harsher. In Renoir's film, the exterior setting of mountains and forests projects a sense of nature promising salvation. On the narrative level, when one of the French fugitives twists his leg, the injury is a dramatic obstacle—overcome by endurance and courage. By contrast, Nemec's protagonist suffers from a bad shoe and swollen foot which, apart form their association with a central icon of the victim's experience in the Nazi camps, function as a continuous source of frustration and torture. Finally, in contrast with the informing woman from *Diamonds of the Night*, the German woman whom the two French fugitives encounter is kind, friendly, and eventually falls in love with the central character. In summary, the comparison with Renoir's vision shows that the reality of war, terror, and persecution is too brutal for a Renoir's poetics with its lyrical and philosophical elegy to the decline of culture and society. In 1937 Renoir sought to demonstrate how human kindness, benevolence, and love can transcend national boundaries and triumph over political conflicts. After 1945 such ideas look pathetically, or rather tragically, naive.[44]

The other major source of *Diamonds of the Night* is the art of Luis Buñuel. The presentation of the ugly old men, mixing grotesque ritual festivity with ominous signs of erupting evil, is visually inspired by the "Last Supper" sequence from Buñuel's *Viridiana*. But in terms of the relentless concentration on mental states and the exposition of hallucinations, daydreams, fantasies, and nightmares, the basic model for Nemec's work is the classic surrealist film *Andalusian Dog*. The image of the ants covering the boy's hands, and he lies in exhaustion on the forest ground, is a cinematic quotation, indicating the direct connection between the two films. Nemec follows this with the even more horrifying picture of ants climbing over the boy's face. Extreme fatigue prevents him from resisting, so that the ultimate effect is that of a corpse being devoured by worms. The intriguing difference between Nemec's image and Buñuel and Dali's work is that this part of *Diamonds of the Night* is an objective depiction of the boys' predicament. In other words, unlike the earlier surrealistic works, the metaphorical image has become quite literal, demonstrating what Alvin Rosenfeld describes as one of the central characteristics of the aesthetics of Holocaust art. Because "annihilation overleapt the bounds of metaphor and was enacted on earth," the concretization of metaphor and the literal rather than figurative use of language become characteristic of the genre. [45]

The final film in this section was made by two veteran directors who did not share the New Wave modernist aesthetics. Jan Kadar and Elmer Klos's *The Shop on Main Street* (1965, based on Ladislav Grossman's book and screenplay) is also rooted in a different historical experience, namely the history of Slovakia during the war as opposed to the Czech Protectorates of Bohemia and Moravia. After the annexation of the Czech provinces, Slovakia was declared an independent state with Father Jozef Tiso, a Catholic priest, as prime minister, and a right-wing Catholic nationalist group, the Hlinka People's party, as the only legal party. In Slovakia, which was poorer and less industrialized than the Czech provinces of Bohemia and Moravia, there lived 90,000 Jews in small towns and villages, engaging mostly in retail trade and handicrafts while maintaining strong ties to traditional Jewish culture. In September 1940, the Slovak government enacted anti-Jewish laws, while the Hlinka Guard and Slovak volunteers to the SS were assigned the responsibility of carrying out the antisemitic policies. Deportations of Slovak Jews began in March 1942 and within a period of five months some 58,000 men, women, and children were deported, mostly to Auschwitz. At war's end only 15,000 Slovak Jews survived, while their cultural tradition, as was the case with all the Jewish communities in eastern Europe, was completely wiped out.

The story of *The Shop on Main Street* features Tono Brtko (Josef Kroner), a humble carpenter in a small Slovakian town, who becomes fatefully entangled in the Holocaust horrors. The crucial change in Tono's life occurs when his brother-in-law, Marcus, the head of the local Fascist militia, appoints him Aryan controller of a shop owned by an old Jewish woman, Rosalie Lautmann (Ida Kaminska). Provoked by his wife's greed, Tono accepted the offer, which would allow him to expropriate the shop and its profits. A tragicomic twist in the plot occurs when Tono finds out that Lautmann's shop is a pathetically unprofitable business, and that the old lady lives from contributions of the small local Jewish community. Tono is deeply upset and ready to challenge the brother-in-law who fooled him so mercilessly. But such a move is not in line with Tono's simple character, which normally keeps him away from actual clashes. When Kochar, a dignified antifascist fisherman, suggests that the Jewish community might be persuaded to contribute extra money for the Aryan controller, Tono hesitates, as this is unlawful—it is typical of him that "Aryan control" is less disturbing for him because it is legalized than is a truly exploitative situation which conflicts with his basic morals. But Kochar explains that it is necessary to conceal Lautmann's condition from the authorities lest they instantly dispense with her. Rosalie Lautmann is half deaf and so old that she is unaware of her own problems. Kochar had always arranged the contribution for her without her knowledge. Now, in order not to offend her feelings, Tono is presented by Kochar as Mrs. Lautmann's new assistant.

The new arrangement holds nicely, even though Tono's wife continually presses him to bring more money from the old Jewess, whereas Rosalie is unsatisfied with the clumsy "assistant" who doesn't even know that shops never open on Sabbath. But she still gets to like him, prepares good meals for him, and, in return, Tono, a carpenter by profession, fixes her apartment's furniture. Gradually, Tono's social status improves. His wife has new clothing, and on Sundays he dresses up to go to church. Afterwards he parades the main street alongside the respectable Marcus.

Meanwhile, the Fascists' control of the small town becomes more gripping and more threatening. The rise of their sinister power is reflected in the growing pyramid-monument, a bombastic project supervised by Tono's brother-in-law. When it is completed, the Fascists, joined by many local folks, celebrate with a nocturnal festivity of dancing, drinking, and music. The title on the tower says, "Life for God, Liberty for the Nation," and the Slovak double cross is placed on its top. The black-uniformed officer delivers a Hitlerite, pseudo-Teutonic speech which, like many speeches in the Third Reich, is pregnant with catastrophic consequences, for the call to drive out the night is followed by the statement "We'll drive out the Yids," an act scheduled for the following day.

The Jews are summoned to the town square, where both the tower and Lautmann's shop are located. In the shop, Tono realizes that of all the Jews, Rosalie is the only one who has not received an official deportation order, and that he must report her to the authorities. Kochar's fate haunts him. The old man had been publicly humiliated and tortured and finally executed as a "white Jew," one who, according to Marcus, is worse than a Jew because he helps the Jews.

The last part of The Shop on Main Street is a dramatic tour de force, showing the ongoing deportation process on the town square and focusing on Tono's mental anguish and the drama within the shop. The deportation process is seen from Tono's point of view, so that the long shots of the doomed deportees result in a remarkable restraint of the visual presentation. The Jews are herded into the square, and the constant calling of names in alphabetical order becomes the most striking aspect of the scene. Names, names, names: they all stand for actual Holocaust victims, as we are in fact reminded when we hear the names of Grossman, presumably the parents of the author of The Shop on Main Street.

The agonizing process alternates with the dilemma torturing Tono in the shop. For the first time in his life, Tono encounters a situation requiring him to make a life or death decision. The burden of this decision, his fear of punishment, and his reluctance to dispense with the old lady drive him mad. Rosalie, completely oblivious to the harsh realities outside, fails to understand his odd behavior. But when he becomes too aggressive, it finally penetrates her mind; uttering one word—

"Pogrom!"—she goes into her bedroom, covers herself with a prayer shawl, and begins reciting prayers. Tono follows her, trying to push her out, but her dignified resignation stops him. Finishing her prayers, Rosalie is prepared to go outside and join her fellow Jews. But the Jews have already been boarded into the trucks and Tono fears that her appearance now would certainly condemn him, or else he sees a chance to save her. Rosalie, however, is not inclined to listen to this erratic man any more. She wants to go out, and this forces Tono to push her into a closet, which he locks to secure her safety. When the deportation act is over, Tono, exhausted and resigned, opens the closet to announce to Rosalie that she is safe now. Horrified, he discovers that his brusque treatment of her has killed the fragile woman. Silently, Tono finishes a bottle of brandy, sends his dog outside the shop, closes the shutters and the doors, takes a small chair and a rope, and commits suicide. In the few seconds before he expires, he fantasizes happier times when he and Rosalie stroll the town's central park on a sunny day dressed in holiday costumes like an idyllic retired couple.

The Shop on Main Street is essentially the story of an average community in central Europe. The pictures of the small town project an aura of nostalgia and sentimentality. The soundtrack enhances these feelings through the tunes of sweet melodic marches with distinct Slavic strains, played by the local brass orchestra in the town's park on Sundays. With the rise of Nazism, an external brutal force disrupts the idyll. The ominous presence of sinister forces and imminent threat is marked by recurrent nondiegetic string sounds of a fast-paced but incomplete musical theme. Other period songs represent the dichotomous worlds of the Fascists with their crude revelries, the local folk songs of simpletons like Tono, and an old record of Jewish music, Rosalie's husband's favorite tune.

In this seemingly benign, provincial town, most people accept the new political reality simply because they do not grasp its full meaning and have never been involved in any similar turbulent situation. When the Fascists decide to build a monument in the center of town, the political vanity is not disturbing enough to overshadow the opportunity of more jobs. Likewise, the anti-Jewish policies, although insidious, for a while go unnoticed. Even the vulgar antisemitism of Tono's wife is the expression of crude social prejudices rather than venomous racial hatred. The Jews form a distinct ethnic and religious group, harmoniously coexisting with their Christian neighbors. They freely interact in commerce and business, and the neighboring families often develop genuinely close and friendly relationships. When Tono greets Mr. Rosenfield at the beginning of the film, someone comes to him and whispers something in his ear, presumably reminding him of the new racial laws. Still, most people do business with the Jews and prefer to ignore the new rules.

Marcus and Kochar represent prototypes of conflicting moral tendencies. Marcus is the bullying head of the local Fascist group, proud of his flashy uniform and position of authority, who apart from executing Nazi policies is busy fostering personal interests. Kochar is a respectable old man, profoundly antifascist, who helps the Jews, especially Rosalie Lautmann. But the portrayal of these two characters is realistic and not demonic or simplistic-melodramatic. Marcus has a sense of humor, is sociable, and can be very friendly. He is essentially a little bureaucrat who craftily exploits the new conditions to gain power and wealth, but is neither a Nazi fanatic nor an avowed antisemite. His foil, Kochar, is also not a paragon of virtue, possessing cunning that helps him manipulate Tono, and a burden of personal indebtedness to Rosalie Lautmann because during World War I her husband was killed while saving Kochar's life. Nevertheless, his uncompromising and ceaseless assistance to Lautmann and his association with the Jewish community signify very brave behavior and ultimately cost him his life.

While Marcus is the major villain in the drama, Tono's wife, Evelina, is the most unsympathetic character. Her excessive provincial vulgarity eludes Tono, who even tolerates her unabashed admiration of powerful Marcus. Her extreme greed prompts Tono to accept the Aryanizer's role. Her disregard for Jews is mixed with her mindless antisemitic belief in hidden Jewish fortunes, which she wants her husband to find for themselves. But as the driving force behind the attempted exploitation of Rosalie's property, she represents the prevailing form of societal antisemitism, rooted in greed and petty envy of the Jews, which, in its own way, fueled the implementation of the Final Solution.

Paralleling the Kochar/Marcus contrast, Evelina is the foil to her husband Tono. As Judith Crist described him, "His lack of vice is his virtue."[46] Tono is the typical bystander, characterized as one who is primarily interested in his own physical comfort. His favorite activity is soaking his feet in a bowl of water while smoking a cigarette. Tono is a churchgoer who has a big cross in his own house and who always humbly crosses himself when passing by priests.[47] He is a friendly character with no evil prejudices who greets with equal respect the Jews he meets in the main street. His humbleness and simplicity make him feel intimidated by Marcus's flashy authority. Likewise, his dislike of Marcus has nothing to do with politics. He resents his brother-in-law because the latter swindled him and took over their wives' fortune.

In the historical situation described in The Shop on Main Street, Tono is both a victim and a victimizer. Tono's major flaw is rooted in his attempt to escape moral responsibility. But Tono's attitudes were all too common during World War II, as people everywhere concerned themselves with personal comfort or safety and ignored the erupting evil of Nazism, although the failure to resist Nazism was often followed by actual complicity. In short, the prototypical bystander exemplified by Tono is not a sinner or a villain but an ordinary person whose passive weakness is a character flaw leading to tragic consequences. Indeed, it is Tono's lack of vice which leads him to an unendurable choice. The tragic dilemma in the climax of the story revolves around his treatment of Rosalie Lautmann. The choice between hiding Rosalie or giving her away reflects the conflict between the impulse of his good conscience on the one hand and the fear of Fascist punishment on the other. Tono's tragic predicament renders his damnation unaviodable, but his fall prompts fear and pity in the viewer. Tono's suicide is, in fact, presented as an impressive moment, a sudden spiritual awakening vis-à-vis final physical defeat.

While the central action in The Shop on Main Street is tragic, the work as a whole is a tragicomedy. The comic level stems from Tono's character, who, like most other modern heroes, differs from the classical tragic figures in his lowly social status and his commonplace personality. The disparity between Tono's excessive simplicity and the grave historical predicament is a source of many comic gags. In the beginning, Tono sees a military train crossing near his house and wonders how many ships the British sank, or the Germans, supposedly not knowing, or even caring, about the difference between them. In the immediate environment of his small town, Tono is a loser—jobless and poor. His closest friend is his little dog, which highlights Tono's status as an underdog. Finally, Tono's comic character is unambiguously defined through his conscious evocations of Charlie Chaplin—his oversized clothes, cane, and hat, his Chaplinesque imitation of Hitler—and in one of the numerous mirror shots in this film, which serve to highlight the process of the protaganist's self-reflexiveness, Tono realizes that he looks like Charlie Chaplin.

The action of *The Shop on Main Street* moves from the light and the comic to the somber and the tragic. However, unlike the dramatic modern tragicomedy that mingles the classical modes to celebrate paradoxes, contradictions, and the absurd, Kadar and Klos's film presents a moralistic tale displaying the tragic consequences of human failure to cope with the existence of evil. The basic realistic mode of presentation serves a genuine interest in human fate, and this realism, plus the unequivocal pervasive humanism, accounts for the effectiveness of *The Shop on Main Street*.

The core of the film's humanism lies in the role of the old Jewish woman. Jan Kadar entitled his statement on the film "Not the Six Million, But the One,"[48] indicating his intention to concentrate the drama on a palpable case of one human being instead of trying to deal with the fate of the millions, an attempt that is liable to be metaphorical, allegorical, or abstract. Rosalie Lautmann is a representative of the old Jewish culture that had been preserved for nearly a thousand years in small villages in central and eastern Europe and that was completely annihilated by Hitler's twelve-year Reich. Her traditional religious practices and her favorite old Yiddish songs make her part of a past world. Further, her seclusion from reality, conditioned by her age and near deafness, renders her as a Jew willfully living in a private ghetto and almost irresponsibly ignorant of the threatening historical forces. But the great triumph of *The Shop on Main Street* is that when the old lady, who is all but an archaeological relic with one foot in the grave, finally dies we feel excruciating pain over the loss of an individual human life.

It is Lautmann's frailty, benign traditionalism, simple domestic concerns, and supreme innocence—supported by the extraordinary performance of the great Yiddish actress Ida Kaminska—which create a memorably sympathetic character. In fact, her simplicity and innocence make her a perfect match for Tono. Initially, there is an uneasy misunderstanding between them. Tono is impatient with the incomprehensible old lady and Lautmann is suspicious of her strange "assistant." The significant differences between the two characters show them to be worlds apart. First, the difference of sex that yields no attraction because of the big age gap; then Tono is a devout Christian and Rosalie is an orthodox Jew; finally, Rosalie is a middle-class shop owner and Tono is a proletarian—a significant difference when it appears in a film made in a socialist country. The miracle of the story, however, is that despite all these differences, the Aryan controller and the Jewish victim develop a unique and warm relationship. Eventually, the human bond between them is presented as no less than a surrogate marriage. For Rosalie, Tono takes on the role of her deceased husband. She has him listen to an old record, her husband's favorite song; she goes out to the market to buy a goose and prepare her special dish for him—something she had not done since her husband's death. The identification is completed when she urges Tono to wear her husband's suit and is visibly happy with his appearance. Tono makes Lautmann's place his home. He fixes the old furniture, eats there, and freely enters Rosalie's bedroom. When he had a big fight with his wife—significantly caused by her derogatory remarks on the old Jewess—he goes immediately to sleep in Rosalie's place as if she were his mistress. The best illustration of Rosalie and Tono as a pair of lovers appears in two dream sequences when Tono fantasizes better times and a happy ending to their suffering. He envisages them strolling in the park, hand in hand, like a romantic couple in an idyllic, small-town setting.

The surrogate marriage which develops between the central characters in *The Shop on Main Street* is also a brilliant, and possible calculated, inversion of some unfortunate dramatic conventions in narrative works on the Holocaust. Many Holocaust films tend to exploit the sensational aspects of the historical tragedy to provide exciting forms of narrative entertainment. The most common pattern focuses on the plight of a young Jewish woman seen with pain and compassion through the eyes of a loving Gentile. This formula is intended, first and foremost, to exploit the potentialities of romantic melodrama, adding thereby an attractive popular spice to an essentially depressing story. The negative aspect of this approach, manifested in numerous films, is that the romantic story subordinates the historical drama and the Jewish girl functions primarily as an erotic symbol, an especially desirable sexual object against the backdrop of a thrilling danger, as, for example, *Judith*, (U.S., 1965), *Morituri* (U.S., 1965), *The Rape* (Greece, 1964), *Stars* (Bulgaria, 1958). In East European films, when the Jewish girl is not killed the love story is a means to demonstrate her conversion to socialism and complete identification with the specific national country (e.g., *Landscape After the Battle* [Poland, 1970], *Hell River* [Yugoslavia, 1975]).

The Shop on Main Street was praised for its "intense realism," authenticity, and highly moving simplicity. The key to the film's successful simplicity is indeed the unabashed adoption of a realistic approach to the subject matter. Realism in this context means faithfulness to the physical appearance of empirical reality, the logical organization of events according to clear cause-effect relationships, and the introduction of well-defined characters vis-à-vis a specific social milieu. The characters possess distinct psychological personalities and display a variety of emotional responses in different concrete situations. The emphasis in realistic works thus falls on the human drama, and in film the characters are usually shown in the center of the frame, against the background of a recognizable, natural setting. The styles and techniques employed to achieve realistic presentations are indiscernible, for the prime concern is with the subject matter and not with formal manifestation.

The Shop on Main Street was shot in Sabinov, using its local population as extras. Sabinov, a small town in northeastern Czechoslovakia, is, according to Kadar, "a town which has not changed much in appearance since the days of the Slovak state."[49] The story focuses on the main square, where Lautmann's shop and the new pyramid are located, and which is also the setting of the last deportation scene. We also see the city park with the local orchestra, the main street, the marketplace, the bar, the barbershop, and scores of other places that give a nearly complete exposition of the physical and social background. The characters operating within this setting are also representatives of the entire population, including brief but remarkable appearances of a Hassidic Jew, a friendly Gentile neighbor, a Jewish boy who escapes deportation, in addition to the gallery of central characters who interact with one another. The naturalistic presentation of the protagonist covers different moments of his daily life: going to work, eating dinner, resting, soaking his feet and smoking a cigarette, preparing to go to bed with his wife, waking up, getting drunk, getting silly, being fooled, and trying to reflect over his predicament. In short, *The Shop on Main Street* features empirical and recognizable reality and concentrates on individualized characters in a specific detailed setting. These are essentially the characteristics of nineteenth-century realism in the novel and the drama, even though the tragicomic character of Tono is more in line with modernist antiheroes.

The humanistic realism of *The Shop on Main Street* can be contrasted with the modernist, sophisticated works of thoughtful auteurs who consider the moral dichotomy of the Holocaust artistically uninspiring, or, even worse, a challenge to be met by a novel, complex approach to the subject. Whether one deals with Nazi demonism, the banality of evil, existential angst, cultural decadence, moral bankruptcy, or inhumanity and dehumanization, the modernist clinical approach is often devoid of necessary compassion for the victims and moral indignation in the face of the criminal enormity. By contrast, *The Shop on Main Street* exalts basic humanistic values. First and foremost, the moving death of Rosalie Lautmann conveys the invaluable worth of one individual human life. In the same vein, the film also never loses its grip on the basic meanings of good and evil. The use of black and white is consistent with the idea of moral dichotomy. The former bright idyllic life has been shattered by the dark forces of the black-uniformed Fascists who celebrate their triumphs in night rites. Lautmann, the pure innocent victim, is dressed in white, and Kochar, who associates with the Jews, is called a "white Jew." A white stork which appears in the opening shot becomes a recurrent motif of serenity, freedom, and the promise of life's continuation, an elusive ideal under the Nazi terror. Other animals figure predominantly in this work to underscore the Nazi assault on natural life. Tono's dog symbolizes free, instinctual vitality, which is contrasted with the tormenting moral dilemmas of the human society. Another motif which serves to contrast with healthy, animal life is the tower built by the Nazis, an anachronistic pyramid, artificial and impractical, expressing only the vanity of its creators. In sum, though, the stylistic devices involving the use of special motifs and expressive as well as significant black-and-white photography are fairly subtle against the backdrop of a highly realistic re-creation of a wartime town reality.

The superb performances of Josef Kroner and Ida Kaminska, enacting the haunting drama of a Gentile and a Jew confronting the terror of genocidal laws, make a significant contribution to the quality of the film. One memorable image of the two outstanding performers dominates the final dream sequence, when Tono and Rosalie enjoy happy moments together in time unreal. This romantic fantasy is in the eyes of many "an obvious sentimental softening of the picture's intense reality."[50] Kadar and Klos did not consider it a compromising ending, but a rejection of excessive pessimism or even nihilism that might be concluded from the tragic story. According to Crowther, Kadar declared that the effect of the illusionary ending "does provide him—and, he assumes, his countryman—the balm of spiritual uplift and hope that the horrible injustices committed against innocent people may bring some realization of the need of brotherhood."[51] Judith Crist also praised the edifying aspects of the grim story:

> Genocide is a concept of such enormity, its twentieth century manifestation so bestial in its details, that the imagination shrinks from its depiction. But in The Shop on Main Street we are able to see it at last in comprehensive and comprehensible terms, with a simplicity and humanism that are soul-searing, an honesty and integrity that are unforgettable. A company of Czech filmmakers has omitted the beasts with the whips and the barbed wire, the emaciated corpses and the fragmented survivors. They have presented to us the tragedy not only of the millions who died but of the millions who stood witness to their murder in terms of a handful and epitomized it in a couple—a doltish, dim-witted carpenter and an elderly, doddering shopkeeper—a foolish, well-intentioned young man and a sweet harmless old lady.[52]

The thematic concerns of the Czech Holocaust films display a curious combination of existentialist ideas, which in the sixties gained popularity in the west, and socialist ideals of east European societies such as solidarity, loyalty, and idealistic sacrifice. Their treatment of history reflects David W. Paul's observation that "in East European films, history becomes more than just an evocation of the past. It is a manner of discourse, in which the portrayal of past events is a medium through which the filmmaker speaks to the audience of today about realities that concern them."[53] Indeed the modern Czech films served as subversive statements vis-à-vis the Communist repression of their society. Either way, while the combination of existentialism with subversive socialism yielded serious narratives dealing with critical moral issues, this thematic approach is inadequate to represent the unique human predicament in the concentration camp universe, for the extreme and disorienting horrors of the Nazi world are simply beyond an inherently triumphant discourse whose central concepts are courage, idealism, moral choices, and humanism. However, the most important contribution of the Czech cinema to the study of Holocaust representation lies in the exhibition of different stylistic approaches to mise-en-scène.

Indeed, what is most remarkable about the five Czech films discussed in this chapter is that they display a striking variety of artistic styles. Radok's expressionism, Brynych's fantastic realism, Nemec's surrealism, and Klos and Kadar's naturalism are the results of searches for the adequate cinematic texture to portray the horrors

of World War II. They reflect Rosenfeld's postulation of the possibilities of Holocaust literature in the light of the singularity of the historical events.

> Implicit in this rejection of analogous or antecedent example is the necessity to begin
> all over again, to place whatever understanding or representation of the Holocaust
> may be possible within its own terms. Just what these may be will vary from novelist
> to novelist, but the task for the writer would seem to involve either some form of
> fictional realism, in which the charge will be to re-create what life and death were
> like in almost naturalistic terms, or some form of surrealism, in which the Holocaust
> is transmuted into more abstract visions of agony, absurdity, or mythic suffering.[54]

However, there is always the danger that the adoption of "more abstract visions
of agony" might obscure the unsettling details of the historical enormity. *Diamonds
of the Night* is a case in point.

Arnost Lustig has praised Nemec's direction, for "he accentuates the story's
lack of reliance on the usually stressed horrors of war. The presence of armed
German soldiers is minimal; there are no interrogations, camps or guards."[55] In
fact, there are very few—and these almost insignificant—clues about historical
sources. The film never explains that the two boys are persecuted Jews, and aside
from one inconspicuous swastika in the mayor's office, the antagonists can scarcely
be identified as pro-Nazi elements. Lustig told me that the original book was so
well-known in Czechoslovakia that it could be assumed that the Czech viewers
were aware of the historical context. However, Czech critics Antonin and Mira
Liehm define *Diamonds of the Night* as "an almost abstract vision of young people
persecuted by a hostile world with which they strive in vain to establish contact."[56]

In the case of *The Fifth Horseman Is Fear*, the process of abstraction was related
by Josef Skvorecky:

> The novel [Hana Belohradska's *Without Beauty, Without a Collar*] submits a realistic
> portrait of a Jewish family, in a country which was forced to follow the Nuremberg
> laws. The original scenario written by Belohradska and Brynych, was also realistic.
> They situated it in Prague, with typical Czech and Nazi characters. Then Brynych got
> an idea, and with the help of Ester Krumbachova, he rewrote the scenario, eliminating
> all historically realistic elements. The representatives of the totalitarian regime in the
> film did not wear Nazi uniforms, the city is not Prague, and the impunity of the Nazi
> public notices is exaggerated into a paradoxical grotesque. (By timely denunciation
> you are assuring your own security.) Rather than achieving a simple condemnation of
> Nazism, they managed to create a parable: a legend that attacks the disease called
> Fascism.[57]

Although Brynych never tries to conceal or downplay the identity of the victims
as Jews, his work still lacks the expression of a genuine concern with the Jewish
tragedy. His Jews never pray to their God, nor do they engage in any discussion
of a special Jewish interest. In making *Transport from Paradise* it was Lustig who
insisted that most of the Jewish roles were played by handsome Czech actors. But

the young dandies in *Transport* look like contemporary youths, just as the patrons of Desperation Bar strike us as a gathering of effete Czech bourgeoise.

Both *Transport from Paradise* and *The Fifth Horseman Is Fear*, in look as well as content, present allegorical microcosms, focusing essentially on issues of human behavior in extreme situations. Albert Camus's *The Plague* can be considered the literary model for *Transport from Paradise* and also is a clue to the understanding of Brynych's spiritual background. The philosophy espoused and expressed in Brynych's art is modernist existentialism. The main elements of this existentialist art include an extreme situation engulfing the characters, an emphasis on individual reactions and on the moral implications of their stands, and the individual hero is defined vis-à-vis the pressures of an alienated world. One of the major themes of existentialism dominant in Brynych's work is that of self-deception (*mauvais foi*), demonstrated through the concern with various forms of escapism. Both Brynych and Nemec focus on existentialist entities, examining the human response to an extreme situation without exploring the historical context and the unique nature of Nazism.

But in Nemec's work we find that the abstract characterization of the two protagonists in *Diamonds* demonstrates the inherent limitations of this approach. In spite of the numerous subjective shots, the emphasis on states of mind and the avoidance of dramatic development render the characters as abstract as the film's thematic concerns. We know almost nothing about the protagonists in terms of their background, ethical values, relationships with others, and visions of themselves and the world. Consequently we can barely identify with them. In *Diamonds of the Night* we are impressed by the filmmaker's skill, the surrealistic images, expressive camera work, and allusions to and quotations from earlier cinematic sources, so that the film's excessive aestheticism seems to be achieved at the expense of its human drama. Novak observed: "Nemec is trying to make us share the very anxiety and loneliness tormenting the minds of the two boys. The connection is broken only where, intoxicated with his opportunities or overdoing his efforts to achieve the deserved effect, he too blatantly reveals the mechaniques of his methods, and arousing mere curiosity."[58]

The Shop on Main Street cannot match the virtuosity and stylistic sophistication of the other films, but with the exception of *Distant Journey*, compared with the other sixties movies it presents a more honest treatment of the historical drama. Kadar and Klos's humanistic realism is a moving homage to the victims of the Holocaust. The final judgment on the film's realistic approach can be supported by the following: "What is more real in our universe than a man's life?" Camus had once asked, adding, "and how can we hope to preserve it better than in a realistic film?"[59]

While the Holocaust does not rule out stylistic diversity for its expression, there is always the danger that the adoption of one style would fail to acknowledge "the necessity to begin all over again," as Rosenfeld put it.[60] More specifically, formal artistic conventions are often tied to metaphysical premises which threaten to force themselves on the historical material, thereby betraying its unique reality. Even the acclaimed naturalism of Klos and Kadar shows its indebtedness to nine-

teenth-century determinism that considered physical environment as a crucial factor in determining human behavior. In *The Shop on Main Street* there is an excessive
concern with realistic details that supposedly form the keys to characters' motives
and reactions. During the climactic deportation scene Tono drinks a whole bottle
of brandy. He is almost driven insane by the excruciating dilemma whether or not
to inform on Rosalie Lautmann. The attempt to further explain his erratic behavior
by the alcohol consumption is evidently redundant and inappropriate, for the
burden of the moral choice itself in such an extreme situation is definitely sufficient
to induce tremendous mental turbulence. Ironically, then, while Nemec presents
nearly abstract existential entities without any details of human individualization,
Klos and Kadar provide too many details that might obscure the weight and moral
meaning of the individual's decisions. *Distant Journey* was condemned as existentialist and formalist, but it is Alfred Radok who appears to have acknowledged the
limitations of excessive stylization and modernist indulgence in semi-abstract notions of horror, persecution, inhumanity, and angst. In addition to foregrounding
the issue of antisemitism, Radok uses documentary footage, extrinsic to the unity
of the fictional narrative, however crucial in establishing unambiguously the singular character of its true historical background, while utilizing ingeniously the
arsenal of cinema art to offer a penetrating and comprehensive picture of the
concentration camp universe.

In summary, any artistic treatment is liable to resort to some conventions of
expression and to contain some extrinsic metaphysical premises. In a similar vein,
one cannot stretch too far the assertion about the Holocaust's uniqueness, for
without any comparable notions or even analogies we would not be able to cope
with it in any human discourse. (Even in *Night and Fog*, the concern with the
memory of the past can be traced to the influence of Bergsonian and Proustian
philosophies.) Thus, while "the necessity to begin all over again" is an unattainable
objective, acknowledging the Holocaust's uniqueness has to be a guiding force,
perhaps a primary impulse rather than a formulated program. The most regrettable
cases of distortion occur when the Holocaust is used to enhance some conventional
wisdom or to fit different human situations. On the other hand, the most successful
Holocaust works ensure that the references to the truthful historical horrors demonstrate their singularity and challenge any metaphysical compromises with ready-
made structures of thought and neat explanations.

CHAPTER IV

The Hollywood Film and
the Presentation of
the Jewish Catastrophe

The inhumanity and unspeakable atrocities of Auschwitz and other death camps assign to the Holocaust a critical universal significance. But the attempt to grasp universal meanings must not involve the overlooking of the crucial details that made the Holocaust such an extraordinary event. One of the most critical issues regarding truthful accounts of the Third Reich and the Final Solution is the presentation of the Jews as the main and ultimate targets of the Nazi atrocities. Without question, millions of non-Jewish victims were exterminated during the war, but the six million Jews (no less than two-thirds of European Jewry) who perished, along with the complete annihilation of the rich Jewish culture of eastern Europe, do not represent merely a quantitative difference from the other victims. The Nazi assault against the Jews was total—all Jews, including the most innocent women and children, were marked for death. The death factories of Auschwitz and other camps were built to facilitate the systematic liquidation of the Jews. The Jews posed absolutely no threat to the Third Reich and their extermination could not be rationalized in pragmatic terms. This point is not intended to diminish the enormity of the Nazi killings of, for example, the Slavs to create *Lebensraum*—living space— for the Third Reich, but to emphasize the demonic and unique aspect of Nazi antisemitism, which saw the Jews' very existence as the cardinal sin. In the course of World War II, the extermination of the Jews became a matter of top priority for Nazi Germany. Unlike the other apocalyptic programs of the Third Reich, the Final Solution was to be achieved immediately, and, where the Jews were concerned, conflicting considerations such as economic disadvantages or the burden on the military machine never stopped the extermination process. Historically, then, the persecution of the Jews in its intention, execution, and scale of accomplishment was unprecedented. The fact that the target of annihilation was a people who had helped establish the foundations of western civilization and had continually made significant contributions to its development ought to startle every sensitive mind.

If we want to learn about the Holocaust and to draw some kind of lesson from it, we must first come to terms with its unsettling facts. The refusal to acknowledge that the perpetrators of the incomparable crime were Germans and that the main victims were Jews means ignoring the crucial facts of history, thereby blocking any avenues toward the possibility of comprehending this monstrous tragedy. The view that Nazism was the expression of man's vilest instincts and Jews the unlucky scapegoats is a narrow reduction of the reality of the Third Reich in human history, limited to the rather banal conclusion that mankind embodies forces of evil threatening to inflict misery on other human beings. It becomes even worse when authors seek to distort the identity of victims and victimizers in the name of an abstract vision of mankind which believes in interchangeability of the roles. Peter Weiss, author of *The Investigation*, does not mention the word "Jew" once in his otherwise powerful work. He has stated: "I see Auschwitz as a scientific instrument that could have been used by anyone to exterminate anyone. For that matter, given a different deal, the Jews could have been on the side of the Nazis. They too could have been the exterminators."[1] This radical view is far from being a bold, original position vis-à-vis the Nazi terror. Indeed, it is the opposite of that, a cowardly, escapist retreat into the abstract formulas of universal patterns to avoid the harsh truth. The scandalous interchangeability theory is an easy way to displace moral burden and guilt, adding offense to the enormous crime of the Holocaust. For, as Rosenfeld puts it, "to generalize or universalize the victims of the Holocaust is not only to profane their memories but to exonerate their executioners."[2]

The study of cinematic treatments of the Holocaust Jews throws light on the nature and magnitude of the problem of accurate presentation. In dealing with identity of the Jews, cinema faces a special problem rooted in its generic conventions and essential features. The portrayal of the Jew in cinema, like the portrayal of other ethnic characters on the screen, always leaves much to be desired. One clear reason is the status of many films as popular manifestations of prevailing social attitudes which lead to the conception of a minority character in stereotypical terms. In addition, given the economy of dialogue in film and the relatively fast development of the dramatic narrative, there is a fundamental limitation in regard to character depth and complexity. Hence cinema, like drama, features prototypes or archetypes. Specifically the problematics of presenting Jewish characters in the context of Jewish experience such as the Holocaust is twofold: if the prototype is manifestly Jewish, he or she might turn out to be a stereotype, usually with derogatory implications; on the other hand, if the central character is an archetype individual of universal significance, the Jewish dimension of his or her identity is usually deemphasized and lost. For example, the heroic fighter Marta Weiss in *The Last Stop* is identifiable as Jewish because we see the Jewish star sewn on her clothes; but in her relationships with others and in her own stated attitudes she displays no Jewish concerns at all. On the other hand, David in *Border Street* comes from an orthodox Jewish family and his father is in the garment business (a tailor); David is a little dark boy, considerably weaker than his Gentile blond friends, in short, an unflattering stereotype of a Jew in Poland.

The sharp problematics involved in the treatment of the Jewish identity of the Nazi victims is best illustrated in Hollywood films. The stories and the characters of Hollywood films project well-defined ideological attitudes, although they avoid the appearance of propaganda bombardment by implying that their content is entertainment. The undisputed universal appeal of Hollywood tells us that its ideological positions have widespread following or great influence, hence the con-centration on Hollywood cinema is also rooted in the urgency to disclose its premises and warn against its distortions. Finally, it is the fact, perhaps even more impor-tantly the myth, of the strong Jewish presence in the American film industry that requires a special historical account of Hollywood films on the Jewish persecution during World War II.

During the first seven years of the Third Reich, even after the outbreak of World War II, Hollywood was extremely cautious in its handling of Nazi Germany. The studios punctiliously abided by Article X of the Production Code, which stated: "The history, institution, prominent people and citizenry of all nations shall be represented fairly. No picture shall be produced that tends to incite bigotry or hatred among peoples of differing races, religions or national origins."[3] This kind of indiscriminate evenhandedness was designed to secure the universal appeal of Hollywood movies and their financial success all over the world. In addition, the studios' adopted neutrality toward Nazi Germany was politically and socially a comfortable position. It complied with the official neutrality of the Roosevelt administration and avoided political problems that might arise out of angry reactions from the German government. In the United States millions of Americans of German origin, including prominent personalities like Charles Lindbergh, displayed unequivocal support for Nazi Germany, while the public at large was indifferent to the persecution of the Jews.

American Jews and their supporters, acknowledging the existence of antise-mitic tendencies in western societies, preferred to keep a low profile in order to divert attention from Nazi assertions that the Jews would provoke a world war. Indeed a wartime document called Government Information Manual for the Motion Picture Industry included the following warning: "There are still groups in this country who are thinking only in terms of their particular group. Some citizens have not been made aware of the fact that this is a people's war, not a group war."[4] Obviously what we have here is the expression of impatience with the Jews and their grievous concerns at that time. Moreover, such nasty attitudes played right into the hands of Hitler and his genocide program in their intention to suppress any foregrounding of the Holocaust. Hitler was quite explicit about his intentions against the Jews. On January 30, 1939, addressing the Reichstag in a famous speech on the anniversary of his accession to power, Hitler declared:

And one more thing I like now to state on this day memorable perhaps not only for us Germans. I have often been a prophet in my life and was generally laughed at.

During my struggle for power, the Jews primarily received with laughter my prophecies that I would someday assume the leadership of the state and thereby of the entire Volk and then, among other things, achieve a solution of the Jewish problem. I suppose that meanwhile the then resounding laughter of Jewry in Germany is now choking in their throats. Today I will be a prophet again: if international finance Jewry within Europe and abroad should succeed once more in plunging the peoples into a World War, then the consequences will be not the Bolshevization of the world and therewith a victory of Jewry, but on the contrary, the destruction of the Jewish race in Europe.[5]

In spite of the heinous record of Nazi Germany on human rights and Hitler's explicit threats against the Jews, the first seven years of the Third Reich passed without any significant cinematic work in the west which examined the manifest Nazi evils. The case of MGM's *Three Comrades* (1937) illustrates the kind of sociopolitical pressures faced by the early attempts to expose Nazism on the screen. F. Scott Fitzgerald and Edward E. Paramore wrote the script, based on Erich Maria Remarque's novel, which describes the ordeals of three German veterans of the First World War in the period of the Weimar Republic through the rise of Hitler as the dominant force in German society. Fitzgerald's efforts to chronicle the rise of Nazism with all its bias and threats were frustrated by the revisions of producer Joseph L. Mankiewicz, who sought to blunt the political denunciations, and director Frank Borzage, who shifted the emphasis to the story's romantic content. A contemporary report in *Time* magazine described the fate of the attempt to present "a corrosive arraignment of Nazi Germany."

They [Fitzgerald and Paramore] wrote a scene in which a poor Jew proclaimed his love for Germany, another in which a rich Jew refrained from cheating three young gentiles, a scene in which famed books, including Remarque's, were burned by Nazis. Hays office censorship left none of these scenes in the finished picture. Much political content is removed by a camera shot of a blowing newspaper dated October, 1920, still more by removal of all definite party labels. What is left is a love story. . . . [6]

The project itself involved other intriguing stages with regard to the representation of Nazism. Louis B. Meyer, in one of Hollywood's more groveling exercises to appease all sides, invited a representative of the Nazi government to attend a private screening and discuss any potential objections to the film. Expectedly the German demanded various cuts but Mankiewicz refused. Then Meyer called in Joseph Breen of the Hays office to propose a compromise. Breen suggested that the film be slightly altered to indicate the rise not of Nazism but of Communism.[7]

When Hollywood finally gained the courage to repudiate Nazism, it was in a film based on an actual fifth-column spy trial that warned the American public against the Nazi threat to American democracy. *Confessions of a Nazi Spy*, released in April 1939 (Warner Brothers, Director Anatole Litvak; starring Edward G. Robinson and Paul Lucas), was the first Hollywood anti-Nazi film. Jack Warner reported on the attempts of other producers to dissuade him from making the picture in a revealing statement about the atmosphere of that time.

'Look Jack,' one studio owner told me, 'a lot of us are still booking pictures in Germany, and taking money out of there. We're not at war with Germany, you're going to hurt some of our own people there.' 'Hurt what,' I said angrily, 'their pocketbooks? Listen, these murdering bastards killed our man in Germany because he wouldn't heil Hitler. The silver skirts and the Bundists and all the rest of these hoods are marching in Los Angeles right now. There are high school kids with swastikas on their sleeves a few blocks from our studios. Is that what you want in exchange for some crummy royalties out of Germany? I'm going to finish this picture, and Hitler and Goebbels can scream all they want.'[8]

Jack Warner's self-aggrandizing memoir glosses over his own reprehensible timidness regarding Jewish themes. Indeed, unlike other contemporary spy melo-dramas, *Confessions of a Nazi Spy* labeled the villains by their real names, calling Hitler "Hitler," and Germans "Germans," a tendency manifested in the film title, which includes the word "Nazi." But the word "Jew" is never mentioned, even when the dramatic situation requires explicit reference to the targets of the Nazis' hatred. Thus, when Edward G. Robinson, in the role of the F.B.I. investigator, examines the files of the local Nazi organization, he notices the practice of verifying genealogical origins. His reaction says nothing about the attempt to Americanize the Nuremberg laws. Robinson raises his thick eyebrows and utters with a knowing smile, "three and four generations," in a moment of heavy-handed, deliberate evasion. Even more surprising is the fact that the fanatic Nazis in this film are not characterized as Jew-haters, even though their actual supporters in the American street were outspoken about their antisemitic attitudes.

Confessions of a Nazi Spy was an anti-Nazi film limited to the context of American political life. Anti-German movies were released only as late as June 1940. In that month, MGM released Frank Borzage's *The Mortal Storm*, the first Hollywood movie to attack and condemn the Nazi regime in Germany explicitly and unequivocally. The swift Nazi reaction to the film confirmed Hollywood's fears: all MGM movies were banned in Germany and its occupied territories throughout Europe.

Frank Borzage's adaptation of Phyllis Bottome's best-selling novel featured James Stewart, Margaret Sullavan, and Frank Morgan in a story about the trans-formation of Germany into a Nazi state and the persecution of innocent people by the fanatic and brutal Storm Troopers.

The Mortal Storm opens with a prologue of grey sky filled with clouds in a whirlwind and a bombastic narration on primitive man's search for shelter against the wind and rain and the forces of lightning and thunder, suggesting the idea that human violence is analogous to violence in nature. Apart from illustrating the title, the visual prologue significantly recalls the beginning of *Triumph of the Will*. Then the narrator declares: "The tale we are about to tell is of the Mortal Storm in which man finds himself today. Again he is crying: 'I must kill my fellow man.' Our story asks: How soon will man find wisdom in his heart and build the lasting shelter against his fears?"

The drama that follows is set in Germany in 1933, during the Nazis' rise to power, focusing on the rather mundane themes of family unity and a love affair. The head of the family, Professor Roth (Frank Morgan), is a non-Aryan scientist whose two step-sons become Nazi Storm Troopers. Despite his universal fame, Roth is fired from his university position and booed by his students for professing scientific theories contradictory to Nazi ideologies. His daughter, Freya (Margaret Sullavan), is having a love affair with one of his students, Martin (James Stewart), who turns out to be the romantic fighter resisting Nazi evil. The professor is eventually taken to concentration camp, where he dies. The daughter tries to escape Germany with Martin's assistance. After a thrilling chase on the snowy mountains with amusing skiing virtuosity, Freya is shot by Nazi troopers commanded by Fritz, her former fiancé, and she dies in Martin's arms. The film ends with shadowy pictures of Freya's grieving brothers and shots of the professor's snowy deserted house, a solemn visual testimony to the destructive effects of Nazism. A concluding image of the snow on the ground is accompanied by the narrator's voice-over comment: "Go out into the darkness and put your hand into the hand of God."

John Belto, in his study of Frank Borzage, holds the cosmic evocation of this film in high esteem. "The film's cloud-filled prologue and snow-filled conclusion look away from the lesser reality of specific characters and events towards a greater, more abstract reality of the divine presence that animates the natural world and gives meaning to its inhabitants."[9] Referring to the opening sequence, Belto declares: "More important, however, than the narrator's melodramatic words are the cosmic images that accompany them, for they convey a feeling for the presence of unknown, super-natural forces at work in the universe. As a result of the prologue, these unseen forces, more than the characters and melodrama that follow, become the subject of Borzage's film."[10]

Belto attempts to invest the frame images with an overriding metaphysical content. But the popular story, the contrived melodrama replete with moments of romantic love and family conflicts against the background of political turmoil, the thrilling actions, and the performances of superstars James Stewart and Margaret Sullavan would hardly yield to Belto's reading. Actually, the film is based on a fairly simplistic and highly contrived plot, a kind of romantic adventure with the historical drama serving as an exciting background; the turbulent historical events are responsible for several complications in the narrative, but not for its dramatic crises and climax.

Moreover, *The Mortal Storm* is dominated by underlying ideological strains which reveal the filmmakers' misreading of the unfolding historical drama. Strikingly the word "Jew" is not mentioned even once in the film. Many critics refer to *The Mortal Storm* as a film about a Jewish professor, ignoring the fact that the film pusillanimously avoids stating Roth's real ethnicity and presents him only as a "non-Aryan." In that respect the movie consistently distorts Bottome's novel, in which the doctor is clearly Jewish, Freya, his daughter, the story's protagonist, is half-Jewish and often reflects on her social predicament, while considerable attention is paid to the anti-Jewish policies of Nazi Germany. By contrast, the

Russian movie *Professor Mamlock* (1937), whose main plot is similar to *The Mortal Storm*—the protagonist is a distinguished doctor, the family disintegrates because of politics, a love affair is shattered by Nazi brutality—not only points out the Jewish identity of the central character but actually highlights it in a powerful scene when Mamlock is paraded through the streets with the word "Jude" written on his white medical apron.[11] Moreover, while Mamlock is persecuted solely because of his race, Professor Roth is presented as taking an active position against the Nazis out of faithfulness to scientific truth. In other words, Borzage's film depicts the Nazis as essentially the enemies of science and truth. Ironically, to use the Holocaust to make such a point is actually to do so at the expense of the truth. Thus, in the film's book-burning scene, Nazi students throw books into the bonfire, shouting that they are burning Heine for his sentimentality and Einstein for his false theories, rather than because these authors were Jewish.

The stubborn refusal even to acknowledge the place of antisemitism in Nazi Germany is complemented by the uncritical espousal of a Christian doctrine of sin, punishment, and redemption as being the moral lesson to be drawn from the incidence of Nazism. Frame images of the cloudy sky in the prologue and the snowy ground in the epilogue symbolize the notion of a Fall. Hollywood generally refrains from expressing blatantly religious doctrines, but the function of the Christian church as a redemptive power is unmistakable in the final chase, when pealing church bells from across the border promise freedom and salvation. In the climactic moment, as Freya lies dying in his arms, Martin assures her, "We can hear the church bells," a line that indicates where Freya's soul is about to find eternal rest. Thus, Borzage's refusal to address the real, concrete issues of the times and to pinpoint the real causes of Nazism and the true identity of its victims may suggest, to John Belto, a movement "from the *lesser* reality of specific characters and events towards a *greater*, more abstract reality of the divine presence" (emphasis mine).[12] But what we actually have in *The Mortal Storm* is a Christian morality tale, making appeals to "love" rather than resistance—delivered by Professor Roth himself after his imprisonment!—and turning the "non-Aryan" heroine into a Christian martyr who finds eternal shelter in the bosom of the church. There is no metaphysical mystery in this "great reality" of divine presence—it is simply and blatantly the call of Christendom, offering salvation to the Jewish victims of the Nazis by Christianizing them.

In the years 1940–1945, Hollywood produced five hundred narrative movies on the war and war-related themes, out of a total of seventeen hundred feature films.[13] In examining this harvest, we find striking avoidance of any explicit presentation of the Jewish catastrophe during the course of the war. Chaplin's movie *The Great Dictator* (1940) was a remarkable exception. Hollywood (which the Nazis had claimed was dominated by Jewish interests) paid abundant tribute to the sufferings of other peoples during the war. The compassion for other allies may be seen in more than one hundred movies.[14] The Czechs, in particular, received a great deal of attention with such movies as *Escape* (Mervyn LeRoy, 1940), and *Hangmen Also Die* (Fritz Lang, 1943). Other major productions paid tribute to the sufferings of the British (*Mrs. Miniver*, William Wyler, 1942) and the tragedy of

France (*Casablanca*, Michael Curtiz, 1942). Even Russia and China received homage, in *The North Star* (Lewis Milestone, 1943), *Song of Russia* (G. Ratoff, 1944), *China* (John Farrow, 1943), and *Dragon Seed* (J. Conway and H. S. Bucquet, 1944). Hollywood was evidently deeply moved by the plight of the German victims of the Nazi party and produced numerous movies on the poor, decent Germans or on the brave resistance fighters as in *Underground* (Vincent Sherman, 1941) and *Hitler's Children* (Edward Dmytryk, 1943). In 1943, two important films were released on the Norwegian predicament, *The Moon is Down* (Irving Pichel) and Lewis Milestone's *Edge of Darkness*. Milestone's film concluded with the rhetorical statement: "If there's anybody who has doubts why this war needs to be fought, let him look to Norway," suggesting that Hollywood saw the suffering of occupied Norway as a convincing pretext to fight the war, while it completely ignored the contemporaneous, systematic extermination of European Jewry.

The lack of any reference to the Holocaust and the absence of recognizable Jews in films that require their presence were not overlooked by contemporary critics. Elliot Paul and Luis Quintanilla commented on it in their personal accounts of Hollywood conventions and their application to biblical stories, *With a Hays Nonny Nonny* (1941). They suggested that if Hollywood had filmed the biblical story of Esther it would have been transformed into a tale of Nazi oppresson of the Czechs: "It would be bad for the public to get the idea the Nazis are persecuting Jews. . . . In the eyes of the producers, it is even worse to show a Jew in clover than one in the soup up to his eyes. The solution is not to show him at all. He becomes a Czech or some kind of Central European the 40,000,000 [movie-goersl can view impersonally."[15]

Perhaps to ensure that the few Jews who do appear on the screen are sympathetically accepted by the forty million, a new convention emerged, that being to show the Jew in Christian terms. *Address Unknown*, the only Hollywood war movie in which Jews are not limited to marginal, supporting roles, features a Jewish actress who is persecuted by the Nazis in Germany. The implausibility of a Jew performing in the heart of the Nazi hell did not occur to the producers, who apparently regarded Nazi antisemitism as a form of social prejudice and ignored its genocidal policies. For the Jewish actress is arrested and eventually killed only after she boldly refuses to comply with the Nazis' demand to remove some offensive lines from a play. And what are these lines for which the Jewess sacrifices her life? They are the famous New Testament verses "Blessed are the meek, for they shall inherit the earth; blessed are the peasants, for they shall be called the children of God." In another film which is somewhat more specific in its treatment of Nazi antisemitism, *Tomorrow the World*, a Jewish woman suffers from the fanatical hatred of a young Nazi boy who is brought to America by his uncle, the Jewess's fiancé. However, the Jewish woman becomes a model of Christian behavior, for her extraordinary tolerance and forgiveness, in the words of Lester Friedman, "recommends a 'turn the other cheek' philosophy."[16]

Why, then, did Hollywood, in its recurrent attempts to expose the vices of fascism, neglect to point out Hitler's irrational war against the Jews, which was, in the eyes of the Nazi dictator, a significant, if not the most important, objective of his sinister goals? The answer to this question is to be found in American politics and Hollywood's involvement in them at that time.

Hollywood's ties with political realities were indeed more than a spontaneous expression of patriotic feelings. Less than two weeks after the attack on Pearl Harbor, President Roosevelt appointed Lowell Mellett to the task of coordinator of motion picture affairs for the government. The letter of appointment included the recommendation that he "consult with and advise motion picture producers of ways and means in which they can usefully serve the National Defense effort."[17]

Several works have been written on the policy of the Roosevelt administration toward the problems of the Jews in the crucial years before and during the war, and they all disclose a shameful chapter in the history of American foreign policy. Prior to the attack on Pearl Harbor, United States officials tried to preserve neutrality at all costs, that is to say, at all moral costs. Pressure on and discouragement of the early antifascist films present one kind of evidence for that policy. Official neutrality was also indicated by the showing of foreign documentaries based on current events, both those made by the Allies and those by the Axis countries. Along with two British productions, The Lion Has Wings (1940) and London Can Take It (1940), the Germans were allowed to bring their cause to the American public with Baptism of Fire (1940), an account of the attack on Poland, and Victory in the West (1941), a dramatization of the collapse of France and the triumphal march of Fascism.[18] It ought to be noted that Fritz Hippler, the director of these two films, made in between them Der Ewige Jude (The Eternal Jew), the incredibly vicious antisemitic "documentary" which is referred to by many as "perhaps the most hideous three-quarters-of an-hour in film history," and "certainly the 'hate' picture of all time."[19]

In the face of the Nazi aggression against the Jews and in the light of even more unimaginable atrocities, the border line between American neutrality and hypocrisy was very thin. In the first stages of the Jewish persecutions in Germany, the United States refused to respond to the refugee problem. The immigration laws (based on national origin quotas) were not amended to meet the need of German Jewry; indeed, the State Department actually undermined fulfillment of the quota by failing to approve sufficient visa applicants from Germany. The American policy enabled other nations to justify fully the closing of their doors. In July 1938, Roosevelt initiated a conference at Evian, France, to deal with the refugee problem. But both the United States and Great Britain, the chief sponsors of the event, were reluctant to take any significant action to aid the Jewish refugees. The result was, as historian Helen Fine observed, that "interested and disinterested spectators saw the Evian conference as an exercise in Anglo-American collaborative hypocrisy."[20] This episode became a show of the indecisiveness and inaction of the western democratic states which offered no sanctuary for millions of Jews who wished to flee from Europe, and thus encouraged Hitler to pursue his own ends. The Nazis reported extensively on the results of the conference and saw in it the justification and the triumph of their policy toward the Jews.[21]

During the climactic stages of the Final Solution, when the Nazis were systematically liquidating the Jews, the United States continued to ignore the appeals of the victims. In General Eisenhower's warning to the Germans to abstain from exterminating prisoners still alive in Auschwitz and other camps, references to Jews were deleted from the final version. Why Allied planes did not bomb the rail lines leading to Auschwitz or the crematoria in the death camps remains a painful and controversial question. In 1939, Roosevelt himself failed to see why Jews should be considered political refugees and he avoided any mention of Jewish war victims until 1944. Helen Fine, in her essay "Socio-Political Responses during the Holocaust," adds the following information:

> Official denial, disbelief and dispassion were the prelude to later resignation. In order to maintain such detachment later, it was necessary to obscure the visibility of the genocide then being committed. Thus, the State Department in August, 1942, refused to relay reports to Rabbi Stephen Wise (President of the American Jewish Congress) from the World Jewish Congress representative in Switzerland regarding detection of the plan for the "Final Solution," claiming insufficient documentation. Furthermore, the State Department informed its Swiss representative not to accept any more messages of that type from the World Jewish Congress' Swiss representative, Gerhard Riegner.[22]

To be sure, the official policy of the United States regarding the Jewish issue was never criticized; rather, it was generally supported by the American public. Before the attack on Pearl Harbor and Germany's declaration of war against the United States, many Americans approved of isolationism, fearing the danger of financial losses in antagonizing Hitler and losing the German markets; at the same time strong pro-German factions such as the German American Bund were highly active in promoting support for Germany, and such influential figures as Charles Lindbergh, Father Coughlin, and Henry Ford publicly demonstrated supported for the Axis powers and also engaged in spreading antisemitism in America. Xenophobia was first justified by the Depression and high unemployment, and when America became involved in the war against Germany, keeping refugees out was legitimized as self-protection against Nazi agents. In addition, antisemitism was widespread and growing as a phenomenon in America of 1933–1945. Fine writes: "Public opinion polls taken before and during the War testify to the constant willingness of a significant portion of the public to blame the Jews for their troubles. One sign of the low status of Jews was the finding that in 1944 more of those sampled would have excluded Jews from entering the country than would have excluded any other group mentioned by the interviewer, excepting only the Germans and Japanese."[23]

The Jews themselves were not entirely guiltless in the American failure to save Jewish lives from the Europeon hell. Since Hitler never concealed German animosity toward Roosevelt, the Jews took it for granted that the enemy of their enemy was their friend, and they failed to appreciate the consequences of the president's inaction. Another Jewish fear was that the prominence of Jewish problems would justify, in the eyes of the American people, Hitler's claims that the world war was brought about because of the Jews. Above all, American antisemitism instigated a docile accommodative behavior: fear of assertions that Jewish interests were in conflict with national interests caused many Jews to express loyalty and conformity with national interests and to abstain from open criticism of the official policy. Finally rivalry, antagonism, and jealousy paralyzed the effectiveness of any possible unified Jewish standpoint.

The case of the wartime pageant *We Will Never Die* exhibits a dramatic example of the failure of American Jews to unify in their appeal to public opinion for an action on behalf of the European Jewry. *We Will Never Die* was prepared as a special presentation at Madison Square Garden to commemorate the murdered Jews in Nazi Europe. A number of outstanding creators collaborated on the production. Featuring Edward G. Robinson and Paul Muni as the narrators, the script was written by Ben Hecht, Kurt Weil composed an original score for it, Moss Hart directed, and Billy Rose produced the whole event. David Wyman described the show.

> The pageant was performed against a backdrop dominated by two forty-foot tablets engraved with the Ten Commandments. Suspended over them was an illuminated Star of David. In the darkened hall, the stark scenes, dramatized by sharp beams of light and contrasting shadows, concentrated on three themes; Jewish contribution to civilization from Moses to Einstein; the role of the Jews in the Allied armed forces; and a vision of the postwar peace conference at which groups of Jewish dead told of their extinction at the hands of the Nazis and pleaded, "Remember Us". . . . the pageant's final passages dealt pointedly with the inertia and silence of the non-Jewish world: The corpse of a people lies on the steps of civilization. Behold it. Here it is! And no voice is heard to cry halt the slaughter, no government speaks to bid the murder of human millions end.
> The ninety-minute memorial closed with the choir and twenty aged refugee rabbis singing the Kaddish for the dead Jews of Europe.[24]

Described by Eleanor Roosevelt as "one of the most impressive and moving pageants I have ever seen,"[25] *We Will Never Die* was presented in dozens of American cities. The first performance in New York set an attendance record for the Madison Square Garden with a crowd of forty thousand spectators. In New York and other major cities the event was also broadcast by radio. The Washington performance included the presence of six Supreme Court justices, members of the cabinet, some three hundred senators and congressmen, numerous military officials, and foreign diplomats. Eleanor Roosevelt summarized the program's impact in her "My Day" column: "No one who heard each group come forward and give the story of what had happened to it at the hands of the ruthless German military, will ever forget those haunting words: 'Remember Us.' "[26]

Despite the acclaim that *We Will Never Die* won throughout the United States, the show won little support from the established American Jewish leadership. The pageant was presented by the committee for a Jewish Army, an offspring of the revisionist-Zionist movement, which, through the actions of the political activist Hillel Kook (better known at that time as Peter Bergson) and the public appeals of the celebrated Ben Hecht, displayed relentless efforts to aid the Jews of Europe by arousing American public opinion. Unfortunately, for most of the established

American leadership, the revisionists, including the Bergson group, were viewed as "interlopers who had intruded into areas of action that were the province of the established Jewish organizations." Eventually the political rivalry stifled the program, as described by David Wyman:

> The American Jewish Congress and other Jewish organizations managed to block the Bergsonites. Pressures on prominent sponsors and telephone and letter campaigns vilifying the CJA (the Committee for a Jewish Army) led many, if not most, local backers to withdraw their support. In Baltimore, Buffalo, Kingston (New York), and Gary (Indiana), the American Jewish Congress and allied groups intervened locally and brought the process to a halt. Plans to take "We Will Never Die" to several other cities similarly came to nothing. The consequence of this bitter conflict, as one observer pointed out, was that "the most powerful single weapon yet produced to awaken the conscience of America" was stopped in its tracks.[27]

In summary, given all these factors—the official policy of the United States, American public opinion, and the behavior of the Jews—it becomes clear why Hollywood, always responsive to the public mood, closely tied with the government in wartime, and employing relatively many Jewish personnel, chose to avoid highlighting the Holocaust.

Charles Chaplin stands out as a remarkable exception, and in making *The Great Dictator* he demonstrated admirable pursuit of his goal in spite of widespread opposition. In *The Great Dictator* Chaplin plays a double role, the Jewish barber who endures Nazi persecutions, and the character which gives the film its title. While the first role becomes the source of pathos and compassion, the figure of the great dictator gave Chaplin the opportunity to fight Hitler with Chaplin's own special weapon, the weapon of humor. Chaplin invested two million dollars of his own money in the film, and being a co-owner of United Artists, he was able to free himself from the general concensus and restraints of Hollywood. It is interesting to note that Chaplin was not Jewish—a fact which paradoxically helps to explain his explicit presentation of the persecution of a Jewish barber by the Nazis. As a non-Jew, Chaplin had no equivocations in his determination to complete his film and to present it to the American public, although some adverse criticism also insisted that Charlie Chaplin was a Jew and his film was transparently Jewish propaganda. However, Chaplin's ridicule of the German leader stirred an international uproar. In Ireland, for example, the prime minister banned the film and the state's censors even prohibited ads in Dublin newspapers encouraging the Irish to see the film in Belfast. [28] *Time* magazine reports on the film's fate in several Latin American countries:

> Promptly banned in Brazil, it was shown in Mexico City under a police guard. In Buenos Aires, two days after Christmas, Mayor Carlos Alberto Puerredon (a British sympathizer, member of the anti-axis Accion Argentina) announced that *The Great Dictator* was banned in Argentina by request of the Italian Ambassador. Loud was the outcry from the film exhibitors, labor men, party leaders, but the Argentine government stood firm. Meanwhile, across the muddy estuary of the Plata, progressive Uruguay

quietly passed *The Great Dictator*. Two big river boats were refitted to handle mobs of Portenos (citizens of Buenos Aires) who made the two-hour trip across the Plata to see the picture. . . . Some 100,000 Argentines were expected to see the picture in Uruguay.[29]

Charles Chaplin described the reaction of the highest officials in the United States:

I was called to meet President Roosevelt, at whose request we sent the film to the White House. When I was ushered into his private study, he greeted me, saying, "Sit down, Charlie; your picture is giving us a lot of trouble in Argentine." This was his only comment about it. A friend of mine later summed it up saying: "You were received at the White House, but not embraced."[30]

Hollywood's failure to give apt coverage of the Jewish catastrophe, seen in the context of reprehensible official policy and public opinion, is all but part and parcel of the dark chapter of the Holocaust in western history. Across the Atlantic Ocean, Great Britain, the self-proclaimed leader of the free world, struggled in its own way against Nazi ideology. British authorities, based on their experience in World War I, developed an extensive apparatus of propaganda to achieve morale-boosting for home audiences and as a psychological weapon against the Germans. The cinematic medium had a central role in the English-inspired propaganda through both documentaries and fiction work, although more efforts and resources were invested in the documentaries.

The story of the British film industry during World War II was quite similar to that of Hollywood in the United States in terms of its slow and late recognition of the Nazi evil and its expression on the screen. *Pastor Hall* (1940, John and Roy Boulting, based on Ernest Toller's play) was, according to Roger Manvell, "the first true and serious statement about the deprivation of the freedom of the German people by Hitler to be made in British feature film."[31] The story is based on the experiences of Pastor Niemoller, whose preaching against the Nazi regime inside Germany brought about his imprisonment in a concentration camp. Manvell writes: "What he says in his church attempted to confront audiences with the true meaning of Nazism."[32] That the true meaning of Nazi evil was mostly felt by another religious group, the Jews, was generally ignored by British filmmakers.

Toward the end of the war, the first and only British film appeared that featured a Jew as its protagonist. This was Mr. *Emmanuel* (1944, directed by Harold French), based on a popular novel by Louis Golding. Ironically, the British-made Mr. *Emmanuel*, released at the end of 1944 and describing the lot of Jews in Germany in 1938, was thought so revolutionary that it was publicized in America with such slogans as "a daring picture on a daring subject" and "have you got the nerve to see this picture?"[33]

The British had generally a positive record of treating minorities within their jurisdiction, and Mr. *Emmanuel* seeks to demonstrate that the Jews too were able to enjoy British benevolence. The story involves a young refugee child who arrives in England from Germany after his Jewish father has been killed by the Nazis. When his non-Jewish mother's letters cease to reach him, he grows desperate out of concern for her fate and attempts to commit suicide. Mr. Emmanuel, an old man who has just retired from his civil service job, promises the young boy that he will go to Germany to find out what happened to the mother. In Germany, Emmanuel is arrested by the police and accused of taking part in an international plot against the Nazi regime. Emmanuel endures Gestapo interrogations, refusing to admit to the false charges. He is eventually saved from prison when his friend's daughter, a Jewish singer who is, paradoxically, the mistress of a high-ranking Nazi officer, convinces her lover to free Emmanuel. The Jewess also gives Emmanuel the address of the young boy's mother, the objective of the old man's trip to Germany. When Emmanuel arrives at the house, he discovers that the mother has married an SS man who had told her that her son had died. The husband appears in the middle of the confrontation between Emmanuel and the woman and forces her to choose between connections with her Jewish past and the opportunity to become part of the "new social system" of Germany. The anguished mother decides to forget her son and throws his pictures into the fireplace. Emmanuel returns to England and tells the boy that his mother is dead.

Mr. Emmanuel presents some of the terrors characteristic of life in Germany under Hitler. Foreigners are not welcome in the new ultranationalistic atmosphere; German Jews live in constant fear of the police, and Emmanuel's relentless inquiries about the address of a woman who has gone away and was known to have been married to a Jew surrounds him with a wall of suspicion and distrust. Popular antisemitism is illustrated by the reaction of one person who, upon realizing Emmanuel's Jewish identity, slams a window in his face; the destruction of one Jewish individual by the Nazis is exemplified by the case of an old man, a street peddler who used to be a distinguished professor and had once taught in Oxford. The prison in which Emmanuel is confined is populated by mostly Jewish prisoners who are tortured until they admit to the false charges brought against them. They are either beaten to death or taken out to a busy firing squad.

Amidst all this brutal reality, Emmanuel is a Christ-like figure in his righteousness and innocence—theological allusions are present in his name, which is the Hebrew name the Prophet Isaiah assigned to the Messiah. Emmanuel is so unaware of the horrific social order in Germany that he innocently goes straight to the Gestapo to ask about the woman for whom he is searching. He is naively happy when he learns that the police will visit him soon, unsuspecting that they will come during the night to arrest him. In the prison, Emmanuel's character changes somewhat: the revelation of the scale of the Nazi cruelty makes him more realistic, less naive, and courageously protective of his own ideals.

The extreme kindness of Mr. Emmanuel appears to underscore the evil of the Nazis in a typically melodramatic manner which contrasts good and bad. But, in addition, Emmanuel's supreme innocence is presented as an unwise political orientation. Emmanuel is punished for his ignorance of the fate of the Jews in Germany by going through an ordeal in prison. The film also contains an ironic comment on the general ignorance of the English public. At the end of the film, the school principal is happy to see Emmanuel back in England and welcomes him with fairly mindless remarks: "How good to see you. I hope your experience was not too frightful."

Throughout the film, Mr. Emmanuel, however, stresses his British nationality and is very proud of it. The English scenes of the film underscore this trend by presenting an extremely benign—even idealistic and certainly flattering—picture of life in England: friendliness, generosity, cultural manners, and strong desire to assist others—for example, the non-Jewish Cooper family adopts three refugee children, and Mr. Cooper volunteers to go to Germany to look for the mother instead of old Emmanuel. In the beginning, Emmanuel appears against the background of *Ha Tikva* music—the melody of the national anthem of the Jewish state of Israel. We learn that Emmanuel has a son in Palestine, and that after his retirement, Emmanuel plans to visit him, but only for three months. The film inspires a message that the Jews of England do not need Jewish sovereignty in the promised land, a standpoint which conforms to official attitudes at the time that Palestine was a British mandate and the rise of an independent Jewish state conflicted with British interests with the Arabs.

Thus, Emmanuel is a non-Zionist, patriotic British figure: he was born in Russia but lived most of his life in England. One object especially symbolizes Emmanuel's English pride: the passport that becomes a central image in the movie. When warned that it is dangerous to be a Jew in Germany, Emmanuel expresses great faith in the protection of the British passport. At the German border, a close-up of the passport shows Anthony Eden's signature under the statement which guarantees full protection for the carrier of the passport by the British government. Emmanuel insists on getting his passport back when the police hold it to check his identity. After his sudden apprehension by the SS, Emmanuel declares that he is a British subject, whereupon the SS officer slaps Emmanuel with his passport. This act is one which the spectators of the film in England during the war would have considered a grave national insult—certainly something more offensive than the persecution of the Jews.

Emmanuel is saved from the hands of the SS by the intervention of his friend's daughter, a Jewish singer who performs for the Nazis and attends their fancy balls; she tells her Nazi lover that she must help Emmanuel because he was like a father to her. When the German tries to deemphasize the value of the "case" by saying that the accused is "only" a Jew, the young woman replies, "We in England don't look at Jews this way." Thus the film again emphasizes English self-esteem, and the Jewish singer conveys the impression that she helps Emmanuel as a fellow British citizen and not as a fellow Jew.

The young boy on whose behalf Emmanuel went to Germany gradually acquires English manners and customs. When Emmanuel returns to England, the once lonely, depressed child has become a vivacious lad with many friends and scarcely a trace of a foreign accent. After Emmanuel tells him that his mother is dead, the boy casually joins his friends in a soccer game—a psychologically implausible reaction which seems to illustrate the film's main idea that "British is best."

Some historical facts show that during the war British conduct toward the

Jews was more favorable than that in other countries in the world. Helen Fine indicates that British protests against the treatment of Jews in Germany were voiced soon after the outbreak of the war when the previous policy of inaction and appeasement was over, and that unlike American foreign policy, whose ignoring of the Jewish problems reflected widespread antisemitism, the British showed more awareness concerning the misfortunes of European Jewry. For example, a poll from 1943 showed that a vast majority of the British would have supported action to assist any war refugees who could get away.[34] Bernard Wasserstein's *Britain and the Jews of Europe, 1939–1945* is an in-depth study of British wartime policy regarding the Jews. Wasserstein shows that in spite of the fact that other countries treated the Jews far worse, Britain's record was also unimpressive. For instance, Britain admitted 50,000 Jewish refugees who left Germany between 1933 and 1939, and allowed 53,000 to enter Palestine, compared with a total of 57,000 Jews who were accepted in the United States. But British authorities did not ease the immigration barriers significantly to save more refugees and were particularly hard on those who wanted to go to Palestine. One of the well-known consequences of this policy was the case of the *Struma*, a ship loaded with refugees which was not allowed to continue on its way to Palestine and finally sank in the Sea of Marmara outside Istanbul's harbor, resulting in the death of 767 men, women, and children. Such incidents and others proved that the British could not boast of their record on the Jewish question during the war even though it appeared superficially to be better than that of other countries.

That *Mr. Emmanuel* was the sole British-made film on the Holocaust is an indication that the British did not concern themselves unduly with the problems of the Jews. The self-admiring view of the Englishmen in *Mr. Emmanuel* was a morale-boosting act based on reassertion of desirable moral convictions rather than a reflection of the reality of the British attitude toward the Jews during the war. Bernard Wasserstein's words on British conduct at that period could equally apply to American policy and even to the whole reaction of the free civilized world to the fate of the Jews in the time of the Holocaust. Wasserstein wrote:

> The Jews, in their most desperate and dependent hour, looked in particular to Britain for some gesture of concern as a token of her adhesion to the values for which she waged war. The men chiefly responsible for sending the *Struma* to her doom were the sort who would probably have played the part of the Good Samaritan if their neighbor had fallen among thieves. But the agony of European Jewry was enacted in a separate moral arena, a grim twilight world where their conventional ethical code did not apply.[35]

The end of the war found the entire world shocked by the atrocities of the war, especially after the discovery of the Nazi concentration camps and the dimensions of the Final Solution, the effects of the atomic bombs in Hiroshima and Nagasaki, and even the Russian brutality in eastern Germany. The general public wished to forget the horrors of war; creative minds who dwelt on the Holocaust were paralyzed to the point of silence. Yet, as the war-torn countries were licking their wounds, reflection on the war experience gradually developed and concentrated on the specific national problems of each society. This period—before Stalinism, McCarthyism, and commercialism stifled free artistic expression—is characterized by the desire to explore current social conditions and respond to immediate realities sincerely and openly. The first postwar years also witnessed a certain renaissance of cinematic development. Italian directors Luchino Visconti, Vittorio De Sica, and especially Roberto Rossellini with his War Trilogy heralded the style of neorealism by refining new, more realistic modes of filmic expression. Within this context, a number of outstanding works on the Holocaust were accomplished, such as *Distant Journey*, *The Last Stop*, and *Border Street*. On the American scene, however, there was a distinct movement away from subjects of the war reality.

From 1944 onward, Hollywood decreased significantly the number of films dealing with war. The expectation of rapid victory caused the studios to abandon projected war movies, fearing that in the aftermath audiences would be repelled by recollections of the horrifying past. The end of the war presented new social difficulties such as the readjustment of the veterans, which had also some bearing on the issues of the rights and status of minority groups in American society. In 1947, two films were made on antisemitism in America: *Crossfire* and *Gentlemen's Agreement*. Edward Dmytryk, the director of *Crossfire*, told me in a private conversation that he was essentially concerned with the ugly phenomenon in his own society, and he denied that the film had anything to do with the Holocaust. Film critics and historians have a different opinion: Judith Crist writes the following in the concluding pages of *The Films of World War II*:

> When the full story of the Nazi liquidation of Europe's Jewish population became known with the liberation of the death camps, Hollywood responded with such films as *Crossfire* and *Gentleman's Agreement*, which dealt with the problems and injustices caused by anti-Semitism.[36]

Crossfire is notable for being the first moving picture made in the United States that explicitly addressed the problem of antisemitism in America. In essence, the movie is a murder melodrama in which the police try to find and catch the killer of a Jew from among four demobilized soldiers, one of whom had committed the crime out of fanatic, racist impulses. In this suspenseful story, the issue of racial persecution rarely enters the foreground of the drama. The social background and the atmosphere focus on the exploits of veterans of the war who upon returning home experience boredom, frustration, and despair. Still, the idea of antisemitism and its immoral implications play a crucial role in the development of the plot. The existence of such a phenomenon is the key clue that enables the inspector to disclose the identity of the murderer.

However, to gain evidence substantial enough to arrest the killer, one of the soldiers needs to be convinced to cooperate with the police. The inspector's account of the evil of antisemitism and racism in general mentions the recent incidence of monumental Jewish suffering, but he fails to persuade the young soldier, who responds to the policeman: "How do I know? Maybe you are a Jew, too!" At this point, the inspector tells him the story of an old man in nineteenth-century America who was beaten to death solely because he was a Catholic from Ireland, concluding with a powerful revelation that the victim was his own grandfather. The soldier, affected by this story, reverses his position and leads to the capture of the murderer. This scene was probably not simply on the analogous consequences of prejudice— a dubious approach in the Holocaust aftermath—but it rather rests on the conviction that for the American audience it is indeed more plausible that the veteran would be more sympathetic toward the Irish inspector than toward cooperating with a Jew.

In the short time that the Jew appears on the screen, he is portrayed quite stereotypically. He is identified first by name, Joseph Samuels—the racist soldier declares: "You know, these guys called Samuels have even funnier names." In physical appearance Samuels stands in contrast with the tall, handsome veterans of the war: he is middle-aged, balding, short, and has a round face and an unathletic body. In a *Commentary* article, "The Film Drama as a Social Force," Elliot E. Cohen adds: "As a matter of fact, he is, come alive, a composite of many of the anti-Semitic stereotypes of the Jew—soft-handed, flashily dressed, suave, artistic, intellectual, moralizing, comfortably berthed in a cushy bachelor apartment during a war, with a bosomy Gentile mistress, self-assured, pushing in where he is not wanted."[37] Apparently, the filmmakers' intention was to show that the Jews, although they look and behave differently than the Gentiles, are no worse people or citizens. Thus, following the killer's claim that Samuels never served in the army because "he looked like this," a document is shown in full close-up stating that Joseph Samuels was discharged from the army after he was injured in Okinawa in 1945.

Crossfire was a major production of the RKO studio, starring Robert Young, Robert Mitchum, and Robert Ryan. It was made in one of the popular styles of that period known as *film noir*, a style of film usually based on suspenseful stories of murders and intrigue, focusing on the dark aspects of human nature, and shot in strong lighting contrasts that bring out effectively the impact of shadows and darkness (hence, the name "*noir*"). The movie turned out to be a commercial success, especially gratifying for the filmmakers, who saw it, in Edward Dmytryk's words, as "a triumph for those of us who believed messages could be delivered by someone other than Western Union."

Even more successful was a second film made in the same year on the theme of antisemitism, Elia Kazan's *Gentleman's Agreement*, which won the Oscar for best film and many other prizes. Gregory Peck plays the role of a journalist who is assigned to write a series on antisemitism in the United States. Willing to experience the phenomenon firsthand, he decides to declare himself a Jew. His first test of the existence of discrimination is conducted by writing two kinds of letters to schools, jobs, and clubs; one is signed "Green" and the other—"Greenberg." Ironically, his secretary is able to provide him with a vivid example of discrimination; only after she had Americanized her name did she get the job in the liberal magazine which assigned him to this task.

Unlike *Crossfire*, which treated the theme of antisemitism within the narrow framework of a murder intrigue, *Gentleman's Agreement* tackles various manifestations of the social malaise. Green's mother's physician expresses some nasty remarks on Jewish doctors; a neighbor tries to mark off the name "Greenberg" from the mailbox; a friendly person whom he meets at a party takes it for granted that, being a Jew, he was not a G.I.; a "restricted" hotel refuses to admit him; and his child is beaten up by his friends who call him "dirty Jew." Some subtler negative attitudes are even expressed by the protagonist's fiancée. When she sees the boy after he was hurt by the other children, she instinctively comforts him: "But that's not true! You're not a Jew any more than I am." Through other similar examples the movie points a finger also at those, usually upper-middle-class people, who fail to generate actual opposition to the incidence of antisemitism. But in all, Kazan's film touches on the most familiar manifestations of social prejudice. In a contemporary review, Bosley Crowther criticized the protagonist's naivete: "Assuming that he is a journalist of some perception and scope, his imagination should have fathomed most of these sudden shocks long since."[38]

Gentleman's Agreement is basically a melodrama on an American hero, a young journalist who seeks truth and justice and at the end has fulfilled his mission and won the beautiful lady. The movie ends with strong optimistic tones, emphasizing a happy end which is imposed on the story: the writer has a good story, his Jewish friend gets a good job in California, the sick mother is assured she will live long to see the improvement of society, and the young man holds in his arms his beloved beauty. Despite all the cheap melodramatic effects, or perhaps because of them, the film was a great success at its time. Remarkably, this major production came from Twentieth Century Fox, the only major Hollywood studio headed by a Gentile (Darryl F. Zanuck)—just as all those at RKO who had key roles in the making of *Crossfire*, producers, writers, and the director, were also Gentile. The American Jewish Committee was still haunted by the experience of the Holocaust years and attempted in vain to halt the production of both *Gentleman's Agreement* and *Crossfire*. Eventually, though, the films had popular appeal and won critical acclaim, mostly for their tackling of a previously tabooed subject.

In addition, both *Crossfire* and *Gentleman's Agreement* stimulated serious research concerning the issues of antisemitism and social prejudice. To list some: Elliot Cohen, criticizing in *Commentary* the stereotypical portrayal of the Jew in *Crossfire* and in *Gentleman's Agreement*, questioned the validity of cinema to serve as a social force. Film producer Dore Schary tried to refute the critique on the basis of the positive response by the audience to the films. Reports prepared by the Audience Research Institute showed that the incidence of antisemitism decreased by fourteen percent among people who saw *Crossfire*. Similar results were found by Irwin L. Rosen, who published them in an article in the *Journal of Psychology*, "The Effects of *Gentleman's Agreement* on Attitudes toward Jews."[39] More important, a year after the publication of the book and the release of Zanuck and Kazan's movie, the United States Supreme Court cited the equal protection clause of the fourteenth amendment of the American constitution in regard to a case of real estate business which involved restrictive covenants (or gentlemen's agreements); the Court ruled against the practice of judicial enforcement of gentlemen's agreements.[40]

Viewed today, the two films look extremely naive and even phony in their overall optimistic structure. Further, with regard to the issue of antisemitism, their message is spurious and even dubious. Crossfire suggests that it is wrong to hate Jews, but at the same time it presents them as different people, and the presentation actually conforms to many derogatory stereotypical views. The lesson of Kazan and Peck's movie was best summarized by one spectator who declared: "Henceforth I'm always going to be good to Jewish people because you can never tell when they will turn out to be Gentiles." But when they were released, Crossfire and Gentleman's Agreement were considered artistically successful and were received with positive and encouraging public reaction. Their popularity aroused the anticipation of many a critic that the American cinema was on its way to a new type of socially oriented dramas, or even that the two films would inaugurate a new genre dealing specifically with the harms and dangers of racist attitudes. The fact of the matter was that for many years no other movies were made on the plight of the Jews in American society, although the impetus of the two films on antisemitism encouraged the production of several films dealing with anti-Black prejudice, for example Lost Boundaries (1949) and Pinky (1949). H. H. Wollenberg wrote at the end of 1949 an article on "The Jewish Theme in Contemporary Cinema," in which be briefly analyzed the causes for the short-lived interest in social problems:

> Those in control of film business, with rare exceptions, consider it wisest to play for safety. Controversial subjects, in times like these, mean greater risk at the box office. And what subject concerned with the real issues of human society and contemporary life would not turn out to be 'controversial' these days, at least, in one or another of the world's market? The Un-American Activities' trials in Washington have certainly been taken as a warning by the executives of the most important studios commercially in the world, and outside Hollywood as well. . . . The almost inevitable effects of the 'witch hunt' were clearly seen at the time by some British film critics. One of them, Stephen Watts, while reviewing Elia Kazan's Gentleman's Agreement last summer, predicted that this was a subject which would not be coming again from Hollywood for the time being. As a matter of fact, even before Gentleman's Agreement, America's Jewish problem was brought to the screen by Crossfire, and significantly its makers were among the foremost 'un-Americans.'[41]

Thus, the United States, which fought against the Nazis for democracy, freedom, and individual rights, as Hollywood war movies taught us, shortly after the war exercised serious restrictions on freedom of expression. McCarthy's targets were not necessarily Jewish or "pro-Jewish" filmmakers or films, but "liberals" or socially conscious themes that involved criticism of the American way of life. Kazan's involvement in the McCarthy trials and Dmytryk's six-month jail term presented vivid examples which discouraged further treatments of the subject of antisemitism in American movies.

During the nineteen fifties, Hollywood embarked on a drastically different approach toward the German nation and its immediate past. A variety of political, social, and psychological reasons caused the changes. The Cold War and the new fear of Communism eclipsed the memories of the Nazi menace. Moreover, Germany (or at least West Germany) was now perceived as an ally in the confrontation with the Soviet Union. The elimination of political hostilities led to new attitudes toward the German people. Filmmakers began to emphasize the sufferings they had experienced under Hitler and later at the hands of their enemies—particularly the Russians. In Hollywood's retrospective view of the war, the Germans appeared as the defeated underdogs, deserving of equal compassion as the Nazi victims were in the wartime movies.

Regarding the military experience, the most common message in the fifties was that war is hell. There are no real heroes, and the few who do exist encounter a system of military oppression and dehumanization. Armies consist mostly of immoral and inconsiderate soldiers and commanders. The battlefield, far from ennobling, is a catalyst of corruption and the manifestation of base emotions. And the military predicament is universal; horror and suffering are shared by the two sides, while the few brave individuals can also be on either side.

The first postwar film which portrayed a Nazi in an unambiguous, positive way was *The Desert Fox* (1951), on the career of the most well-known German military commander in World War II, Field Marshal Rommel. Based on the book of the same title by British Brigadier Desmond Young, who fought against Rommel and was captured by the Afrika Korps, the film presents Rommel as a master tactician, a chivalrous soldier, a believer in his country's cause and in Hitler, until Der Fuehrer made Germany's ruin certain. Rommel then joined the conspiracy responsible for the *attentat* of July 1944, and for doing so was forced by the Nazis to commit suicide. John Mariani points out that "at film's end, Rommel becomes a martyr, and, the producers suggested, it was our loss because Nazis like Rommel might have helped Patton roll over the Russian steppes after getting rid of Hitler."[42] The critic of *Films in Review* praised the film calling "the celebration of a German general's virtues in an American motion picture . . . a reasonable, even laudable, incident in our foreign policy," and adding that "all students of World War II . . . will be pleased by the amount of documented history *The Desert Fox* contains."[43] Thirty years later we have come to identify these students of World War II for whom *The Desert Fox* would have a special appeal. They are known as the revisionist school, whose arguments range from a denial of the existence of death camps to a complete exoneration of the perpetrators of the Nazi atrocities. British revisionist David Irving has recently tried to absolve Hitler from any direct complicity in the Final Solution and authored an extremely sympathetic portrayal of Rommel's life.[44] Irving's outrageous views are fully compatible with the presentation of Rommel in *The Desert Fox*, in which he is featured as a man of great integrity, objecting to having to command a futile, suicidal war, which ultimately leads him to participate in the Generals' plot to assassinate Hitler.

It is that alleged last episode in Rommel's life which becomes the focus of the narrative, eliciting respect for the man's judgment, admiration for his determination and courage to participate in the action, and finally a great deal of compassion and pathos when his tragic death befalls him. To be sure, all this dramatic material could have an adequate basis for an honest moving film—had it been based on facts. When serious historians recently checked the Rommel legend, they exposed the story that Hollywood eagerly adopted and helped to spread. Rommel, quite simply, had never participated in the plot against Hitler and had always remained loyal to the Nazi state.[45]

One distinguished critic who was clearly outraged by the positive portrayal of a formerly formidable enemy of the free world was Bosley Crowther, who observed "a strange disregard for the principles and the sensibilities of those who suffered and bled in the cause of defeating German aggression in World War II." He also pointed out that the filmmakers "have used all the tricks in the book to portray a military figure of great courage, generosity, and humanity. Not only have they got James Mason to play the heroic role in full knowledge that Mr. Mason is a master of the soulful, misunderstood type, but they have larded this portrait of the general with all the recognized attributes of goodness on the screen."[46]

In response to other positive reviews of *The Desert Fox*, Crowther devoted a second article to taking issue with the film's message. He reminds his readers that the true Rommel was the German commander presented in the British documentary *Desert Victory*, shown in the same New York movie theater less than nine years before *The Desert Fox*. Unable to challenge the facts, Crowther complains: "One might argue that Rommel *was* considerate of his men, that he *did* conceive a grave distrust of Hitler and that he truly loved his wife—wherefore the facts as presented in this picture are substantially true. But why should these facts be so ordered and played that great sympathy, respect and even idolization for a general who fought for Hitler (and then turned coat) should be aroused?"[47]

Crowther's passionate arguments were a voice in the wilderness. The sociopolitical factors and the prevailing mood of the time led to what Crowther defined in an understatement as the "overriding of moral judgment and good taste—a lapse to which Hollywood nabobs are as prone as anyone else."[48]

The salient characteristics of the war movies of the fifties—diffusing the antagonism between former enemies, American self-flagellation, blind condemnation of war and its anonymous engineers, and sympathy with defeated enemies—are all crystallized in the major production *The Young Lions* (1958). The adaptation of Irwin Shaw's best seller (published in 1948—Hollywood's treatment of one of a number of postwar novels which had gained critical and marketing success) was directed by Edward Dmytryk, with an all-star cast including Marlon Brando, Dean Martin, Montgomery Clift, and Maximilian Schell in his first role in an American film.

The epic drama follows the careers of three men during World War II: Christian, a young German officer, Noah, a Jewish recruit, and Michael, a popular show business entertainer. The plot covers the six crucial years of 1939–1945 and spreads over three continents, following the major stages of the war. The narrative skips around from one character to the next as the personalities and motivations of each are established as a result of the changes that the war forces upon them. Christian

(Marlon Brando) is a ski instructor who naively believes that Hitler can provide him with opportunities for social advancement and restore German national honor. When the war breaks out he is first assigned to serve in France, where, as an army lieutenant, he leads his forces to early victory. The German defeat in North Africa marks a turning point for him. He is wounded there, and, back in Germany, he witnesses the devastating effects of Allied bombardments. Returning to the front in France, his convoy is air-raided and he loses himself in the woods, where he ultimately encounters the other two major characters.

Noah Ackerman (Montgomery Clift) is a halting, rather pathetic American Jew. He falls in love at first sight with Hope Plowman, a Christian girl from New England whose father initially expresses objections to the outsider Jew but later gives his blessing to the wedding. In the film version of the novel, Noah, at first, plays the classical Wandering Jew, homeless and rootless. Here is a revealing account of the way Clift prepared the role: "He decided that because Noah Ackerman was an underdog, he would look not only Semitic, but dreadfully Semitic. He changed the shape of his nose with putty, and put wax behind his ears so they would stick out. He starved eleven pounds off a torso that was already emaciated. The slouch and other mannerisms did the rest."[49] In the course of the movie Noah gradually gains social acceptability by proving his worth as an honorable member of society and is ultimately salvaged by the Christian Plowman, whose name signifies ties with the land and rootedness. Much of the action, though, revolves around Noah's military career. After his recruitment into the U.S. Army, he is victimized by antisemitic soldiers and officers. Stoically and heroically Noah defends himself by displaying such physical prowess and endurance as to gain him the respect of his fellow soldiers. Alan Spiegel's analysis of this process highlights the religious overtones of Noah's figure:

> When Clift entered army boot camp, he could only gain the respect of bigots . . . by allowing them to beat him up repeatedly and consummately until the outlines of his saintly archetype, the Christlike Suffering Servant, rose up from its ancient depths below the agonized visual surface. The Man of Constant Sorrows (Isaiah 53: "He was oppressed and he was afflicted, yet he opened not his mouth") merges with the mythic aspect of the Victimized Jew, a tolerant stranger lost amid his intolerant neighbors, who in his neutered sexuality, indefatigable passivity, and almost bottomless gluttony for punishment, never seems to have lost favor with the public or producers (e.g., *Ship of Fools*, 1965; *Cabaret*, 1972).[50]

Dean Martin played the role of Michael Whitacre, a Broadway star who for simple egotistical reasons prefers to stay out of the war, even though his beloved girlfriend does not approve of his unabashed lack of patriotism. He develops special friendly relations with Noah, whom he first meets in the recruiting office. In the military camp, he defies the corrupt commander in order to help his Jewish friend escape antisemitic persecution, and he passes up the opportunity to use high-level connections to get out of the army. Even so, he manages to spend most of the war years away from the battlefields, until his temperament fails him in a clash with a

British officer in London, for which he is assigned to Noah's unit at the front. In sharp contrast to the novel, in which Michael is the most reflective and the most sensitive character, as one perceptive critic noted, "Mr. Martin plays a Broadway showman pulled into the army against his will as if he were lonesome for Jerry Lewis and didn't know exactly what to do."[51]

This observation characterizes the way Dmytryk's film reduced Irwin Shaw's original, powerful novel to a cheap melodrama, overemphasizing love affairs and exciting war situations and exploiting the attractiveness of big-name actors while subordinating complex dramatic roles to popular cinematic images. One scene toward the end of the film, however, demonstrates an entirely different style. It takes place in a concentration camp in the north of France and in the woods adjacent to it.

In the book, the concentration camp is no more than what literary critic Sidra Ezrahi calls "a stage prop,"[52] initially presented by Shaw as "an ordinary Army camp."[53] For the film, the actual presence of *l'univers concentrationnaire* provides the setting for the dramatic climax, involving the only clash between the three main characters, and it also highlights the theme of inhumanity in war situations and the horrible consequences of antisemitism.

The camp sequence consists of two parts. The first involves Christian's experience. Christian has been wounded during the bombing of his convoy, and, having seen the devastation of Germany, he has become completely disillusioned and resigned. From a distance he sees barbed wire, a watchtower, and the prisoners' barracks. Closer to the gate he sees a sign reading Konzentrationslager Nackerholtz. Christian enters the commander's office looking for food. Having eaten, he remains to hear the commander's revealing monologue, complaining about the practical problems of his duties.

The speech is an attempt at providing a concise verbal introduction to the reality of the death camps. While Christian is eating, the commander speaks in a dry, matter-of-fact tone: "A concentration camp is not a picnic. Believe me, with all the gas chambers, doctors with all their experiments . . . I had an extermination quota of 1,500 people a day, Jews, Poles, Russians, political prisoners, and I had only 216 men to do it." Christian stops eating, unbelieving, and the captain continues with expressed amazement: "In Auschwitz they killed 20,000 a day. (Interrupted by a phone call.) They want me to kill every man, woman, and child— 6,000 people, before the Americans get here. (To the phone.) I don't care what happened in Buchenwald." Christian leaves the camp disgusted and speechless.

The visual exposition of the camp interior is brief and powerful, presented in the second part of the sequence, when the Americans enter the camp. The Allied soldiers first see the gallows and then the execution square. Against a background of dramatic music mingling sounds of triumph and suspense, the soldiers advance to the prisoners' buildings in what has become a recurrent scene in cinema—the first encounter between the liberating soldiers and the camps' victims. The focus is on the soldiers' reactions. After one of them breaks down the barrack door, the camera shows his horrified face, while other stunned soldiers move into the frame and fill the screen with expressions of shock. The pictures of the barrack's interior and its inmates are modeled after the actual photos of living skeletons stacked in three-decker bunks. Some in the foreground stare emptily, hands and arms falling outside the wooden shelves. One Musselman crosses into the center of the frame, like a ghost arising out of the dead to stare at the living.

The whole sequence was shot in a real concentration camp near Strassburg which the French maintained as a memorial, and some of the people shown were themselves inmates of the same camp during the war. The person who crosses the screen with a Musselman's expression was one who, according to Edward Dmytryk, never recovered from his past traumas.[54]

The dramatic action concludes in the woods adjacent to the camp. Ironically, Christian, having just destroyed his gun in an outburst of wrath following his encounter with the camp's atrocities, is killed by Michael. Noah subsequently declares his faith in a better world to be run by the "Greens"—Captain Green is an American commander who has shown compassion and efficiency in the aftermath of the camp's liberation; he had especially distinguished himself by permitting a rabbi to conduct religious services and when, in response to the local mayor's antisemitic objections, he declared his readiness to shoot to kill anyone intervening with the Jews' ceremonies. At the very end of the film we see Noah returning to his pregnant wife in Vermont with a joyous expectation of reunion with his family and the promise of a better future. This ending is another expression of Hollywood's incurable optimism. On the simple narrative level, the good guys are rewarded; both Noah and Michael survive the war on the triumphant side, while Christian, who was tragically on the wrong side, ends in a pathetic death.

Unlike James Jones and Herman Wouk, who considered the films *From Here to Eternity* and *The Caine Mutiny* to be merely poor artistic adaptations of their original works, Irwin Shaw actually felt that the cinematic version of *The Young Lions* totally subverted the original thrust of his novel. In the book, Shaw had sought to expose the way war brutality affects the individual and also to demonstrate one of the worst diseases of our civilization—antisemitism. Michael is Shaw's protagonist, a sensitive and reflective character; through his thoughts the author conveyed his observations on human nature and social institutions. In the transition from novel to film, the filmmakers rendered the American, Dean Martin, as an essentially opportunistic, unsophisticated character overshadowed by the admirable German officer, Christian.

In particular, the film's conclusion is a travesty in terms of both its metaphysical connotations and its social implications. In Shaw's work, Christian Diestl is never shocked to learn about the concentration camp universe. He is there when, after the SS have left the camp and the Americans are expected at any moment, the prisoners stage a revolt. He escapes from the camp by cold-bloodedly killing his host, the camp commander; he also murders a few more inmates before he flees. When Noah and Michael tackle him, Christian manages to kill Noah with the gleeful shout "Another one killed!" before he is finally shot by Michael.

Marlon Brando used his own prestige and influence to alter the original character of the German soldier to that of an extremely kind, emotional, and benevolent young hero. Brando, in justifying his own interpretation of the role of the Nazi, asked Shaw: "If you were writing it today [1957] would you show him that way?" Shaw replied: "I wouldn't change it much. This is the breed that killed 20,000,000 people, and the people they killed are still dead." Brando: "But the world can't spend its life looking over its shoulder and nursing hatreds. There would be no progress that way. No nation is all good. There are Nazis and men of good will in every country. If we continue to say that all Germans were bad, we would add to the Nazis' argument that all Jews were bad."[55] The irrationality of Brando's argument here is surely matched by the travesty of his portrayal of the Nazi Christian.

In the film Christian's acceptance of Hitler is presented at first as a naive attitude, motivated by justifiable social bitterness and an honest hope for change. Later, as a soldier, he is admirably resourceful, using his military skill to triumph with as little bloodshed as possible. The superhero image is reinforced through Christian's interactions with women. He is tough and contemptible toward the flashy, seductive wife of his commander but gentle and considerate in developing a relationship with a sweet French girl who hated the Germans until she meets Christian. In general, Christian's positive personality emerges most conspicuously through the constant juxtaposition with his commander, Hardenburg (Maximilian Schell), who displays unlimited arrogance, kills unarmed prisoners, and supervises the torturing of suspects in the Gestapo offices.

In the novel, Christian does start out as a fairly innocent person. But he is corrupted into a monster as the typical product of the Nazi system. Initially holding Hardenburg, the commanding Nazi officer, in contempt for his unwavering and sadistic conduct, Christian gradually adopts more and more of Hardenburg's mannerisms and becomes at the end virtually a carbon copy of his sadistic and despicable commander. He identifies suspects for the Gestapo, listens to them being tortured, asks to be permitted to watch the executions, and, his appetite thus stimulated, he enjoys "a large breakfast, with eggs and sausage and real cream."[56] In the film, by contrast, Brando expresses revulsion when he realizes that prisoners are being tortured, and he requests that his commander transfer him. Another remarkable example of the character's revision involves his romance with the French girl. Brando meets her through his friend, Brandt. In the film, Brandt attempts to convince Brando to live with him and the girls and stay out of the war. However, Brando chooses to abandon the quartet because his patriotic allegiance overcomes any considerations of personal convenience, although he shows understanding toward Brandt's decision and sympathy for his predicament. In the novel, on the other hand, Christian does not even consider desertion; instead, he turns his girlfriend, Brandt, and his friend's wife over to the SS in full knowledge that this will result in Brandt's execution.

Finally, one of the film's unpardonable ironies is that it is Brando's expression—the German soldier's—which conveys the first reaction of shock to the concentration camp horrors. Brando looks unbelieving when the commander complains that, after the war, everybody in the government would deny any knowledge of the plan to exterminate twelve million people. Brando leaves the room with an expression of complete horror on his face, while the commander continues trying to edify him with talk about German honor and duty to the fatherland. In short, instead of the embodiment of a demonic character with the ironic name "Christian," the film projects a benign German soldier in World War II, a basically good, albeit temporarily misled, Christian.

In general, Shaw's novel gains force precisely as a result of such reversals, thematic and narrative, when the reader's expectations, conditioned by traditional conceptions and conventions of plot developments, are shattered and overwhelmed by manifestations of Nazi evil. But the film reverses completely these significant turns of plot, and thus, despite its ostensibly liberal concerns, it is indeed a reactionary piece. Notice also that the film's optimistic conclusion has resounding religious connotations. On the symbolic level, Noah survived the deluge and returns to "Hope" and a fresh start under the "Greens." The new beginning had been enabled through the sacrifice of "Christian."

The disregard for moral realities of history established in such films as *The Desert Fox* and *The Young Lions* eventually escalated to the point at which Judith Crist, in the mid-sixties, wrote sarcastically: "Screenwriter, with a revolutionary glint in his eye was telling me the other day he's going all-the-way original; he's writing a World War II movie with bad Nazis."[57] In the same spirit, Art Buchwald wrote that Hollywood was on its way to featuring Pat Boone as a U-boat commander who refuses to fire on a passenger ship, declaring, "I'd rather risk getting sunk than torpedo a ship with civilians aboard. Hitler would want it that way." Or Hollywood producing *Stalag Hilton* with Henry Fonda as the camp commandant and Doris Day as his wife rolling bandages for the Jewish prisoners in the hospital, and when SS sergeant Glenn Ford rushes in with the announcement that the prisoners are escaping, Fonda replies, "Don't talk to me. I'm in on the July '44 plot to kill Hitler," and Ford says, "Aren't we all ?"[58]

Remarkably, not until 1959, in filming *The Diary of Anne Frank*, did Hollywood address itself directly to the Nazis' genocidal treatment of the Jews in Europe. This is even more surprising because the movie was made in the last year of a decade which, according to Gorden Gow in *Hollywood in the Fifties*, was marked by "a tendency to reconsider the social structures and personality traits," and "delving into areas of sociology which Hollywood had touched upon only with caution in the financial heyday."[59] Not that commercial considerations were not paramount in the case of *Anne Frank*. The film followed the enormous success of the Broadway play by Goodrich and Hackett, which, in turn, was inspired by the popularity of the translated diary published in America in the early fifties.

Anne Frank has become a popular symbol of victimization under the Nazis. But notwithstanding the wonderful virtues of Anne and the moving story of her family, the transformation of her case into a symbol has compromised some of the more demanding aspects of the concentration camp universe. Anne's story, in its popular dramatic form, focuses exclusively on the period of hiding, excludes the depiction of her persecutors, and by ending with the arrival of the Nazi police (who are not seen), avoids the horror of her actual fate.

Lawrence Langer dismisses the importance of the original diary, contending that Anne's diary, "cherished since its appearance as a celebration of human courage in the face of impending disaster, is, in actuality, a conservative and even old-fashioned book which appeals to nostalgia and does not pretend to concern itself with the uniqueness of the reality transforming life outside the attic walls that insulated her vision."[60] Alvin Rosenfeld agrees that "to limit one's understanding of the Holocaust to such a book as Anne Frank's diary is to grasp only the most preliminary outline of the coming war against the Jew."[61] The diary is also characterized by several conventional narrative formulas: domestic frictions under tight, stressful conditions, the expression of a self-reflexive aspiring young writer, a youthful adventuristic approach to the family's predicament, and also a vivid, adolescent romance between Anne and Peter. However, Rosenfeld makes two important points. First he observes that the diary "is not without its more realistic and even fatalistic side, and its premonitions of a bad end, recorded more than once after the young girl peeked through her curtain of fancy onto the dark streets beyond, came to be borne out in a brutal way."[62] In addition, Rosenfeld claims, the story contained in the diary is inseparable from knowledge of her ultimate end, and he advises the reading of Ernst Schnabel's *Anne Frank: A Profile in Courage*, a detailed biography from her birth until her death, "which 'completes' the work [the diary] by supplying the details of the young girl's ending in Auschwitz and Bergen-Belsen."[63]

The Diary of Anne Frank is essentially a cinematic version of the popular Broadway play, which ignored the important points raised by Rosenfeld. The cast was made up primarily of the actors who had played the same roles in the stage production on Broadway for years, and the leading role of Anne was played by Millie Perkins, a former model whom director George Stevens had selected after allegedly screen-testing more than 10,000 applicants.[64]

Using film's realistic resources, Stevens aimed at achieving perfect verisimilitude to the authentic reality, and he shot the film in a studio replica of the original attic. The exterior scenes were made in Amsterdam, showing the actual exterior of the Franks' building and its surroundings. To convey a historical context beyond the "chamber drama," Stevens showed glimpses of marching German troops, grim processions of deported Jews, nocturnal air raids re-created by sound and image, and a dream sequence depicting a concentration camp. A special artistic achievement of the film was its black-and-white Cinemascope photography, which, by means of expressive lighting and elaborate camera movement, kept the action moving within the narrow, cluttered space.

The soundtrack was also a rich means of transcending the limitations of space. The radio, with its wartime reports and typical programs from the BBC and Nazi Germany, vivified the period of World War II and cued us into the general historical development. The immediate threat to the Franks was conveyed by sounds of soldiers marching in the streets, occasionally shooting at those violating the curfew. The noisy sirens and air-raid bombardments supplied audiovisual spectacles of terrifying danger. Seagulls chirping outside signified unattainable freedom, the repeated sounds of church bells form an ironic reminder of the enormous immorality of the crime against the Jews, and whistling trains foreshadowed inevitable doom.

However, much of the credit for the film's popular success is due to the authors of the screenplay, Frances Goodrich and Albert Hackett, who transformed the raw material of the diary into a fairly gripping story. The plot of *The Diary of Anne Frank* is based on the structure of classical drama, with prologue, epilogue, and five acts, designed to express the narrative movement of a tragic action. The film begins with postwar pictures of the only survivor of the family, Otto Frank, visiting the old hiding place, his appearance expressing the bitterness and pain of a father who has lost his entire family. In the attic, he discovers the papers of Anne's diary and as he leafs through them, Anne's voice emerges describing the first moments in the secret annex.

The first act introduces the main characters and focuses on their predicament. For the victims of the Holocaust, the road to death goes through a complete reversal of ordinary living. The Franks are forced to maintain a schedule which is the opposite of a normal lifestyle, being deadly quiet during the day and beginning to live during the night. The ethical aspect of the Nazi-inflicted disorder and of the reversal of norms of law and morality is demonstrated in a scene when a thief enters the building at night, terrifying the innocent people. Normally, of course, the discovery of a thief leads to the criminal's punishment. Here, however, the criminal might have inadvertently discovered honest citizens and brought about their doom by reporting their presence to the Gestapo for a reward.

The second act illustrates the full scale of the threat against the Jewish victims. Dussell joins the Franks and the Van Daans and informs them of the persecution against the Jews, of the arrests, disappearances, deportations, and rumors about exterminations in Mauthausen concentration camp. During one night, Anne hears screams and observes soldiers shooting civilians in the street. She dreams that her good friend Liz is in a concentration camp. This dream sequence visualizes crowds of women swaying during a massive roll call, their faces expressing hunger, exhaustion, and despair. The images were based on a sequence from Jakubowska's *The Last Stop*, and the sound, a symphony of *Sieg Heil*, is from *Triumph of the Will*.

The climactic third act features an actual clash with the antagonistic forces. It begins with a Hannukah party in a rare episode of bright celebration and harmonious happiness. Anne gives everybody a gift, and this gesture, along with the holiday mood, overcomes the tensions between the eight people. The modest revelry is interrupted when a burglar breaks into the building. He is scared away by Peter's cat, but German soldiers enter to investigate, and the Jews fear that the cat will give away their presence. Of this scene, the *Time* critic wrote: "In a scene more tension-packed than anything Alfred Hitchcock ever devised, two Germans search the factory by night after a burglar has broken in . . . as they prowl, Stevens' camera flashes to a shot of the family cat perched on a drainboard, its nose prodding a small funnel toward the edge; its rear legs scuffing against a plate. The fugitives— and the audience—can do nothing but watch the animal in paralyzed silence."[65] This breathtaking scene is also a focal point in the narrative. It conveys the extreme danger that the fugitives were facing, and it suggests their tragic end by highlighting the crushing power of their oppressors.

The next section of the film revolves mostly around the love affair between Anne and Peter. Generally in tragic drama the function of the fourth act is to create pathos and irony.[66] After the crucial crisis in the middle of the drama, the protagonists' doom is sealed and efforts to struggle against the inevitable end are both ironic (because of their futility) and pathetic (for we feel more empathy toward the losing hero). This is exactly the effect of the unfolding romance, whose help-lessness is poignantly ironic and whose innocence is wistfully pathetic. Similar feelings of pathos and irony are stimulated in the celebration of the beginning of 1944 when the fugitives believe that this is going to be their last year, and even more so when they rejoice over the news of the Normandy invasion, assured that their rescue is very near.

The impression of an imminent Allied victory underscores the unhappy end-ing. Here again, the authors of the play created a highly suspenseful climax. It is Sunday and the phone rings endlessly; the fugitives debate whether it is a trap or a genuine warning from their protectors. Otto Frank decides against answering the phone, as the others sit motionlessly in a state of nearly unendurable tension. Finally the police break in and the refugees await them with calm resignation. The scene dissolves to the film's final image, a reiteration of the opening picture of sky with clouds and birds.

The authors of the dramatic version of Anne Frank's *Diary* created an attractive drama whose narrative structure and action imitate the form of classical five-act tragedies: exposition of the predicament, manifestations of the central conflict, the major clash and crucial crisis, scenes of pathos and irony, and the final catastrophe. But can the Holocaust be used as an inspirational source for tragic vision?

Tragic heroes suffer because of a fatal flaw, an error or a sin, the *hamartia*, which triggers the disastrous process against them. The *hamartia* does not render the tragic hero a mere sinner, for it is always the result of an essentially humane flaw, or a universal human shortcoming; in committing a crucial and understandable error, the tragic hero assumes responsibility for his end and becomes a vital agent of the tragic action. But the Jews as individuals and as a people did absolutely nothing to provoke Hitler's wrath. The innocence of the victims and the enormity of their suffering not only exclude the possibility of a tragic punishment but also undermine any possible theories of retribution, and therefore pose insurmountable theological problems with regard to Providence and the concept of theodicy. It is indeed the reality of an absolute evil which manifested itself during the Nazi era. This stark reality is a scandal for a metaphysical conception that holds earthly evil and its examples as imperfections rather than as the product of an essential active force. Indeed, the tragic predicament is based on the protagonist's tragic choice between two fundamentally right forces. Thus, the metaphysical significance of the tragic conflict transcends issues of morality that can be theoretically resolved on an ethical level of comprehension and judgment. The forces in Hitler's time, however unsophisticated this may appear, conform to the melodramatic pattern of forces threatening innocent victims.

Finally, tragic heroes always exhibit a human grandeur vis-à-vis overwhelming antagonistic forces; their struggle is a demonstration of admirable human will, and the process of their fall is eclipsed by a gradual gaining of profound self-knowledge and spiritual triumph. Historically, the Jews behaved as other human beings would or could under the same circumstances, displaying the full range of possibilities from collaboration through submission to heroic resistance.[67] More significantly, however, it must be stressed that the victims had few chances to demonstrate nobility of spirit because of the duplicitous and vicious nature of the assault against them. Distinguishing between the classical dramas about man's fate and the Holocaust drama as the story of man's doom, Langer makes the following observation:

> The tradition of fate encourages identification: we may not achieve the stature of an Oedipus or a Phaedra, but their problems of identity, of passion, of moral courage, or retribution, are human—are ours. The tradition of doom—a fate, one might say, imposed on man by other men against his will, without his agency—forbids identification: for who can share the last gasp of the victim of annihilation, whose innocence so totally dissevers him from his end? . . . The drama of fate reminds us that Man, should he so choose, can die for something; the drama of doom, the history of the Holocaust, reveals that whether they chose or not, men died for nothing.[68]

The American authors of *The Diary of Anne Frank* preferred the action of the spiritually triumphant, classical drama over the actual crushing experience of the Holocaust. *The Diary of Anne Frank* downplays the place of evil by showing the threat to the Jews in very general terms without dramatizing the evil schemes of the Nazis and by ignoring their satanic ideology and their relentless motivation to destroy and to kill. Moreover, the film version succumbed to Hollywood's perennial optimism and did away with the agonizing effect of the tragic recognition either on the part of the characters themselves or on the part of the viewers who would watch the unfolding catastrophe. Indeed, the hopeful notes of the finale of *The Diary of Anne Frank* constitute a monumental dissonance with our knowledge of the victims' doom. After the Fascist police break in, Otto Frank's concluding words are: "for two years we've lived in fear; from now on we'll live in hope." The filmmakers visualize the strain of hope by showing the benign look of nature, with birds and clouds against the backdrop of the big sky, which is also symbolic of the metaphysical promise of heaven. The travesty of that final image comes across in full force when we remember that rather than clouds in the sky, what the victims of the Nazis found, or rather what they were transformed into, was the smoke of the crematorium.[69]

But *The Diary of Anne Frank* is not only an inadequate tragedy in terms of the reality it pretends to represent, it also subverts the true tragic overtones of the original text. The professional authors chose to use some of the most naive lines of the fourteen-year old girl, ignoring the more penetrating and insightful observations of a sensitive writer responding to her atrocious predicament. The film's motto is Anne's statement: "In spite of everything, I still believe that people are really good at heart." Just as the belief in human goodness remains unshaken, so is the faith in universal order, for the Anne of the film declares: "We are too little to understand the great patterns." The real Anne knew better. On May 3, 1944, about three months before her capture, Anne wrote: "There's in people simply an urge to destroy, an urge to kill, to murder and rage, and until all mankind, without exception, undergoes a great change, wars will be waged. . . . "[70]

The cinematic addition of "the great patterns," is more nonsense. The Nazis planned to liquidate all the Jews, and the genocide was deeply rooted in the everlasting incidence of antisemitism. Anne knew very well that she was persecuted because she was Jewish, and she offered this remarkable insight: "Who knows, it might even be our religion from which the world and all peoples learn good, and for that reason, and that reason only, do we have to suffer now."[71] One finds this thought in Nietzsche's works and in George Steiner's writings, which suggests that Anne's wise insights were indeed more mature, disillusioned, and specific than the adolescent's clichés one finds in the screen version.

When the commercial version of Anne Frank's diary enjoyed a tremendous success in America—the play had a long run on Broadway, winning the Critics Circle Award, the Tony Award, and the Pulitzer Prize; the film was received enthusiastically by the critics—there was a single voice conducting a quixotic campaign against it. The voice was that of Meyer Levin, who was bitter because his own version of the diary was never allowed to be produced. Meyer Levin had been a correspondent for the Overseas News Agency during the last month of World War II, and he was one of the first Americans to see Terezin, Dachau, and Buchenwald. His personal encounter with the Holocaust led him to revise his prior indifferent feelings toward his Jewish origins. He became a Zionist and after the war made a film in Israel, My Father's House, on the plight of a boy survivor who searches for his parents until he discovers that they perished in the Holocaust. The boy overcomes the tragic loss, thanks to the youthful and loving community in the Holy Land, and is psychologically and physically rehabilitated. This rather crude and amateurish work was for Levin "a symbolic story of the Jewish fate."[72] In 1947 Levin made another film, The Illegals, on the underground movement of surviving Jews from eastern Europe to the land of Israel. Levin, who made a successful career with his books in America, settled in Israel in the late fifties.

Levin read Anne's diary in French and was instantly aroused by its honesty and absorbing power. He contacted Otto Frank about publishing it in English and learned that prestigious publishing houses had rejected it because they believed "the subject too heartrending; the public would resist, the book would not sell."[73] Levin helped Otto Frank find a British publisher and later introduced him to literary circles in New York. They agreed that Levin would write the dramatic version of the diary. However, Levin was eventually removed from the stage production with Otto Frank's consent, allegedly for failing to produce a "stageworthy" play. For this he sued the producers and dramatists of The Diary, claiming that his own dramatization, after being read and rejected, was, after all, the basis for the popular and successful version. Literary critics concluded that indeed Levin had a strong case, and the court vindicated his claim of "plagiarism and appropriation of ideas," awarding him half the royalties the Hacketts were getting.[74]

For Meyer Levin, however, it was only a "moral victory." (The legal complications which followed caused him to renounce the promised royalties—about $50,000.) Levin's lasting obsession—his autobiographical account of the case is entitled The Obsession—stemmed from the fact that the world was left with the Broadway play and the film version while any other play production based on the original diary was suppressed. Even an amateur performance of Levin's play, staged by a group of soldiers of the Israeli army, was terminated by the long arm of the *Diary's* copyright holders. Numerous appeals from literary personalities, community leaders, and a massive petition from the rabbinate failed to persuade the *Diary* owners to grant permission for noncommercial groups to perform Levin's version.[75]

Levin maintained that he was victimized by a cultural "doctrinaire censorship of the Stalinist variety," for offering something too Jewish. Although in the commercial version the Jewish identity of the Franks is never concealed, and they are even shown celebrating Jewish holidays, what is completely missing is any attempt to present the Franks' predicament as essentially Jewish, within the context of the history of Jewish experience. Anne's published *Diary* demonstrates the concern of the young characters with their Jewish identity. Her sister, Margot, has a minimal role in the commercial drama, and Levin suspected that it was because she was a Zionist who planned to go to Israel after the war. By contrast to Margot's assertion of Jewish nationalism, Peter is the classical example of Jewish self-hatred, wishing to conduct postwar life without any reference to his Jewishness.

Jewish self-hatred is a phenomenon whereby Jews who fail to assimilate or who are singled out because of their ethnic or religious identity react with resentment to what they perceive to be the main reason for their troubles: Judaism. It is also demonstrated by people whose eagerness to assimilate and succeed in Gentile society impels them to express antagonistic remarks on Jewish matters or to adopt positions opposing the interests of the Jews. This self-hatred complex appears in many forms, and in the relatively open society of America it is often seen (as demonstrated by some of those who handled the *Diary* production) in the deliberate suppression of any forthright attempt to examine the Holocaust for what it was, an assault against the Jews. Meyer Levin maintained that the Jewish producers, writers like Lillian Hellman, and even Otto Frank pressed for a universalized presentation out of anxieties about a work that may seem too Jewish. The worst blatant example had to do with the character of Anne. The "American" Anne states: "We are not the only people that've had to suffer. There've always been people that've had to . . . sometimes one race . . . sometimes another." But the real victim of the Nazi genocide felt the Jews had to suffer because it is "our religion from which the world and all peoples learn good." Elsewhere Anne wrote: "Who has made us Jews different from all other people? Who has allowed us to suffer so terribly up till now? It is God who has made us as we are, but it will be God, too, who will raise us up again. If we bear all this suffering and if there are still Jews left, when it is over, then Jews, instead of being doomed, will be held up as an example."[76]

An even more extreme example of Jewish self-hatred is demonstrated in Sidney Lumet's *The Pawnbroker* (1965), which deals with the survivor's tortured life. This film is actually a sort of social drama, embedded with and reflecting the prevailing issues of the sixties in American society, concerning civil rights and the relationships between different ethnic and minority groups in American society. Directed by the Jewish Lumet in the East Coast, and featuring Rod Steiger in an outstanding performance in the role of the survivor, *The Pawnbroker* was based on a book by an American Jewish novelist, Edward Wallant.

Protagonist Sol Nazerman is a Holocaust survivor who owns a pawnshop in Harlem, and makes a nice living by serving as a front for a local mobster. Twenty-five years after the Holocaust he is still haunted by the period during which he was forced to witness the execution of his brother, the brutalization of his wife, and the death of his two children. In addition, New York City, especially the poor quarter of Harlem with its rampant street violence, continually reminds him of his experiences from the war years.

Sol Nazerman is highly respected in his neighborhood for his wisdom and stature. But he has built a wall around himself, blocking any emotional involvement with others. The pleas of the needy, the verbal assaults of the antisemites, the flattery of his admiring assistant, and the pleasantries of a local social worker who tries to befriend him—none of these gestures leaves any trace on him. His mechanical sexual intercourse with the wife of his dead brother has the look of an act of necrophilia, just to complete his image as a living dead.

The dramatic change in Sol's life occurs when a desperate black prostitute tries to seduce him, fearing that her boss will punish her for not giving him enough money. The present situation evokes Sol's memories of his wife being sexually abused by the Germans. When Sol learns that the prostitute's pimp is none other than the mobster with whom he has done business all those years, he is shaken, and for the first time in his postwar life he tries to take an active stand against injustice. Sol's feeble attempts to confront the mobster are crushed by the criminal's thugs. Fearfully he roams the rainy streets of New York throughout the night, and early in the morning he ends up visiting the sympathetic and helpful social worker.

Meanwhile his Puerto Rican assistant, Ortiz, agrees to collaborate with local hoodlums in a robbery of Nazerman's shop on the condition that there will be no shooting. But during the holdup, the old Jew, unaffected by the threatening guns, refuses to give up the demanded money. In the shooting that follows, Ortiz jumps in front of Sol and is killed, saving his boss's life. Struck by remorse and guilt, Nazerman is compelled to feel physical pain. Piercing his palm on a receipt spike, he leaves his shop with his hand bleeding, as people outside crowd around Ortiz. Sol kneels beside his dying apprentice and grimaces with silent cries.

The Pawnbroker has the look of a serious drama and was almost universally acclaimed as a penetrating exposition of the survivor's life. The concentration camp sequences are quite effective, for they deal with such extreme moments as the deadly overcrowding inside the deportation trains, the hunting of prisoners with bloodthirsty dogs, and the brutalization of women by Nazi soldiers. There are also some dubious fantasies, as for example when the filmmakers present the Nazi guards pulling rings from the hands of dead victims stretched over the barbed wires. But the sequences of the past are usually powerfully realistic, and the subliminal technique of very brief shots, indicating the process of the protagonist's flashy recollections, also contributes to the strong effect on the viewer.

In addition, stark photography of present-day Harlem is the setting against which serious social ills and contemporary prejudices are vigorously examined. But

the successful formal unity is ultimately the product of a specific ideological program. For the bogus analogy between the horrors of the Holocaust and living
conditions in Spanish Harlem is the main premise of this film as well as its main
fallacy. Andrew Sarris captured the crux of *The Pawnbroker*: "the idea behind the
production seemed to be that by combining the Jewish Problem with the Negro
Problem the picture would be twice as profound because the audience would be
twice depressed."[77] Indeed, despite Sidney Lumet's statement that "there certainly
was no attempt to show Harlem as a modern concentration camp,"[78] his film
projects exactly that notion. The contemporary locale is shown through pictures
of heaps of shoes and ragged clothes whose iconography is part of the Holocaust
footage and they function here to present an urban ghetto. Further, while in the
original novel Sol's recollections of the past are in dream sequences, the film shows
how scenes and images from the present trigger his hallucinations of the past. Thus,
through paralleling visual images and quick crosscutting, Lumet establishes the
disturbing comparison between urban street violence and Nazi brutality, or between
the prostitute's anxiety to please her pimp and the rape and sexual abuse of a Jewish
woman in a German concentration camp.

The film adds further insult and offence in its portrayal of the Jews vis-à-vis
the blacks and the Puerto Ricans. Harlem's poor tenements and their miserable
inhabitants are juxtaposed with Nazerman's family, his sister and her children, who
live in a nice suburban house. In contrast with the confinement of the urban
ghetto, the Jewish youngsters are planning a trip to Europe completely mindless
of the meaning of its past for their parents. The comfortable and leisurely lifestyle
of Nazerman's family is made possible by the money that Sol brings, which, as it
turns out, is actually the underworld's profits, earned at the expense of the black
ghetto residents. This money also sustains Sol's mistress and sister-in-law and her
elderly father, both survivors of the Holocaust. The sister-in-law is an unattractive
character, self-pitying, unappealing, and greedy. The father is a grotesque old man,
suspicious and querulous.

By contrast, the young Puerto Rican apprentice, his old mother, and his black
prostitute girlfriend represent the sympathetic exploited characters. They are all
full of vitality and domestic or passionate love. Ortiz is a handsome, industrious
young man who wishes to elevate himself from the swamp life of the black ghetto
through hard work and education. He is the opposite of the hollow Nazerman,
who emotionlessly takes people's dreams in exchange for dollars. Ortiz is nevertheless impressed by Sol's financial success and is fascinated by his Jehovah-like
sternness and rectitude. He tries to find out about the pawnbroker's background
and character. Sol responds with a bitter speech, explaining how a history of
persecutions and suffering accounts for Jewish business success. Thus the anguish
of Jewish history is used insidiously to strengthen one of the most negative stereotypes of Jews as heartless money-makers.

The book on which the film was based was written by Edward Wallant, a
young Jewish-American writer who died at the age of thirty-six.[79] Dorothy Bilik,
in her excellent study of Wallant's book, found in Sol's bitter speech "Wallant's
unease with Jewish materials, ancient and modern," adding that "Survivor guilt,

so often expressed by fictional characters, is here supported by the author."[80] Elsewhere, she remarks, Wallant's portrayal of some of the Jewish characters "descends to the level of anti-Semitic caricature."[81] The Jews in Lumet's film are also contrasted with the Gentile, conscientious social worker, Mrs. Birchfield; they are mindless hedonists, unscrupulously enjoying the comfort achieved by tainted money. The enormous tragedy of the Holocaust functions merely to add pathos to this negative portrayal: "They are unsympathetic, but you've got to understand because . . . the Holocaust and all that. . . ." This, in a nutshell, is the film's offensive observation.

But the offensiveness of this film does not end there, for The Pawnbroker goes on to offer the Jews redemption, as usual, through the exemplary Christian. Ortiz is the sacrificial martyr whose death saves Nazerman's life. In addition, heavy religious symbolism comes into play. Ortiz's first name is Jesus. Moments before the fatal robbery he had gone to the church and stared at Christ's figure, symbolically completing the identity between them. Through an act of ultimate sacrifice, Jesus saves Sol's soul—which leads us to the equally unsubtle meaning of the Jew's name. Consistent with the film's apology for the bogus negative stereotypes of the Jews, Nazerman, because of his traumatic experience at the hands of the Nazis, almost understandably behaves like one of his former tormentors: his name suggests that he is a kind of Nazi-made man. But at the end of the film, he is redeemed and is thus qualified to be looked at as the man of Nazareth. Piercing his hand on the spike is obviously an act of crucifixion, and he is literally Christianized through love, grace, and suffering. No wonder, then, that a Christian book entitled Theology through Film views the pawnbroker's role as "one of the finest cinematic experiences of transcendence," and declares, "The Pawnbroker is as central a contribution to a behavioral theology as could be hoped for."[82]

The film production Sophie's Choice (1982, director Alan Pakula) was also about the survivor's predicament in America, although in this work the Jew is not offered redemption; rather, he seems to be the chief obstacle to redemption. As in The Pawnbroker, Jewish-Gentile relationships present the Jew as a perpetrator of disaster, but with an additional offense: in this "Holocaust drama," Sophie, the victimized Gentile, is also the survivor, a former inmate of Auschwitz who lost her husband and two children during the war. The American foil is Nathan, an erratic, brilliant, and ultimately destructive Jew from New York.

Sophie's Choice was based on William Styron's best-selling novel.[83] In first-person narration (both in the film and in the novel), Stingo, a young aspiring Gentile writer who comes to New York from the South in the late forties, relates the process of his literary maturity, which is crystallized through his friendship with the two major characters, Sophie and Nathan, and his subsequent realization of the Nazi horrors. In reviewing the film, Andrew Sarris correctly observed that "William Styron's 200,000 word meditation on guilt and shame in the aftermath of the Holocaust is a more copious novel than most, which is to say that if writer-director Alan J. Pakula had really wanted to be faithful to the novel, he would have had to stop the narrative in mid-stream for a feature-length documentary on the Nazi death camps."[84] On the other hand, *New York Times* critic Janet Maslin contends that the film "follows the lengthy novel closely enough to capture it with amazing comprehensiveness in a little more than two-and-a-half hours. In fact, the novel is reflected so accurately that both its strengths and its weaknesses remain intact."[85] What Maslin has in mind here is the fictional narrative, exclusive of Styron's lengthy philosophical discussions in the novel. However, as is nearly always the case in transitions from books to film, the core of the cinematic signification lies in the narrative, with its characters and dramatic action.

Pakula's film focuses on the entangled relationships between the flamboyant lovers, Sophie and Nathan, and between the lovers and Stingo, who is more reserved and gentle but at the same time a perceptive and admiring listener. One part of the story revolves around Sophie's life before arriving in New York. For Stingo (and the audience) the unimaginable atrocities of Auschwitz create a dark, mysterious source of interest in her, and the lies she tells about her past provoke additional curiosity, tensions, and suspense. The plot contrives two sensational twists. First we discover that the sympathetic Sophie, who often speaks favorably of her late father and whose complex attitude toward men appears to be explained by her early relationship with him, was actually the daughter of a notorious antisemite who proposed in his writings the liquidation of all Jews even before the outbreak of the war. The second plot twist, which gives the film its title, is that in Auschwitz Sophie had been forced to choose which one of her two children would be immediately taken to the gas chamber.

All the extreme moments in Sophie's past are designed to portray her as a highly pathetic victim of the Nazi horrors. In New York, referred to by Styron's narrator as "the kingdom of the Jews," she finds neither shelter nor comfort, because her lover, Nathan, is her new tormentor. Their stormy relationship vacillates between moments of bliss and depression, but Nathan is an essentially destructive agent who fiercely beats her in moments of mad jealousy. His demonic character embodies many of the stereotypical notions of the successful Jew in American society. He is a musician, a scientist, a connoisseur of the arts and literature, and seems to have unlimited sources of money. Nathan is haunted by a Jewish sense of guilt for being so detached from the Holocaust experience. He displays a puzzling erratic behavior; however, in this case, the narrative surprise is disappointing for we find out that Nathan is simply unstable, insane, and addicted to hard drugs. Nathan views Sophie as both an antagonistic Gentile and an especially desirable object of conquest and possession. His complex attitude prompts several outbursts of unfounded jealousy that constitute focal points in the development of the trio's relationship; each crisis leads to closer contact between Stingo and Sophie, until they flee together from Nathan and New York. This time, though, Sophie's betrayal is both real and fatal; she returns to her Jewish lover and dies in a seemingly joint suicide pact. It is not clear whether Sophie's suicide was voluntary, but given the demonic control that Nathan exercised over her, he is certainly the clear cause of her death.

If we examine the core of the narrative of *Sophie's Choice*, it looks like this: a Catholic Polish girl, after suffering terribly in Auschwitz, arrives in the "promised land" but is trapped in the "Kingdom of the Jews," where she falls prey to the demonic Jew, whose initial help develops into manipulation and torment. Sophie's choice to stay with Nathan is the climax of her miserable life and leads to her death.

The perverse drama of Sophie and Nathan is presented as the inspirational source for the would-be writer Stingo. *Sophie's Choice* is a *Bildungsroman* or a *Kunstlerroman* on Stingo's process of maturity as a young man and as an artist. The young man's sexual obsessions make up the other major strain of the work. The virginal gentleman from the South is struck by the libertine norms in the "Kingdom of the Jews," but the "goddess of his unending fantasies" is Sophie, the mature, beautiful, and, above all, mutilated woman whose history of suffering and exploitation renders her all the more sexually desirable. One of Sophie's functions in the narrative is delivering Stingo from his timid virginity and teaching him, with "boundless lust," all the possibilities of lovemaking. After that Sophie's character is dispensable, and she indeed disappears on the following morning to her death in New York.

In the original book, Styron takes issue with two potential objections to his story. He explains that by choosing a non-Jew as the victim of Nazism he does not imply any diminution of the enormity of the crime against the Jews. After all, there were many others who perished in Auschwitz, and so Styron's choice is legitimate. Nevertheless, he does deal with Jews, and the manner of that treatment, in terms of both narrative functions and portrayal of character, is quite negative, and since the Holocaust constitutes the background of his story, it is quite unpardonable. However, it is important to note that this offensive treatment of Jews probably has nothing to do with antisemitic prejudices against Jews, but is rather a narrative strategy, designed to downplay the victimization of the Jews in order to drive home the universalization of the Holocaust.

Styron's other main issue involves the task of approaching historical events as the basis for fiction and artistic expression. He criticizes the call for silence made by Elie Wiesel, who has claimed that "Auschwitz negates any form of literature, as it defies all systems, all doctrines," and disagrees with George Steiner who maintains that it is best "not to add the trivia of literary, sociological debate to the unspeakable."[86] Styron's disagreement with the advocation for silence is nevertheless banal. Of course we must not be silent, that is, ignore, forget, or displace the incidence of the Holocaust; and literature, as a means of description, communication, and personal or cultural self-examination is an important tool of expression. Both Wiesel and Steiner are aware of it, as their books on the subject would testify. Styron misunderstood "the deep anguish and immense frustration of the writer who confronts a subject that belittles and threatens to overwhelm the resources of his language."[87]

There is a curious tendency of many authors to emphasize the limits of the literary discourse vis-à-vis the Holocaust and then try their own novels on the subject. Several years before the publication of *King of the Jews* (1979), Leslie Epstein wrote that "almost any honest eyewitness testimony of the Holocaust is more moving and more successful at creating a sense of what it must have been like in the ghettos and the camps than almost any fictional account of the same events."[88] George Steiner wrote *The Portage to San Cristobal of A. H.* In both cases the authors produced controversial pieces, charged with exploiting the Holocaust for either dubious moralization or incongruous entertainment.

The problem of silence is not merely rhetorical: it refers to the core of the concentration camp universe, to moments of human experience, personal tragedies, and massive horrors that are beyond the power of the narrative, that are undramatizable, so that they cannot become the substance of an "Auschwitz novel." In *Sophie's Choice*, Sophie's dilemma in Auschwitz is the "stunt" of the work, a sure tear-jerking scene aiming at the viewer's choice "To Cry or Not To Cry."[89] But what are we to make of this moment in terms of appreciating the artistic conception of the fictional character's state of mind and its meaning? Is Sophie's choice the product of literary ingenuity? Or, is it a daring treatment of recorded extraordinary human experience? Further, can it have any significance with regard to morality, human psychology, or any other realm of metaphysical reflection? Can it tell us anything on the complexities of human choice, even those made under extreme conditions? Then we ought to remember that in the context of the dramatic narrative this moment of choice must bear some significance on the character's subsequent career and personality. But is there any possibility to build up a character on the basis of such atrocity? And in daring to present this episode as a critical dramatic moment (so much so that it gives the work its title), what sort of intellectual catharsis does the author expect to elicit from the viewers? Before I point out the special conditions in the camps (and I would mention here that there was truly a case of a mother who had to make such a choice in regard to her three children!),[90] I challenge the reader to try to identify with this person in this extraordinary moment. The sheer horror of this atrocity entails a paralyzing shock, and a black hole at any attempt to pass judgment on such a choice.

In the death camps, inmates were usually denied any choice because of the ruthless mechanism of repression and destruction. If there was choice, it was so horrific that the reflective mind would literally have been paralyzed by it. For example, since mothers with young children were immediately sent to the gas chambers, the most excruciating incidents involved a mother abandoning her child during the selection, or another killing her newborn infant lest she be liquidated with him. We have such stories from eyewitnesses, who relate them with horror but also with understanding, the tellers' understanding actually conveying the impossibility of comprehending the effects of extreme terror on the mothers' behavior. Sophie's choice, like the two authentic situations mentioned above, is one of those unique moments in the life of an inmate which no one has the right to judge, or try to understand, or even dramatize. Such scenes are beyond the limits of artistic re-creation and authorial adventurism. The failure to realize that resulted in the obscenity of *Sophie's Choice*—as a novel and a film. The treatment of her choice is a crude intrusion into the deepest and most private recesses of an inmate's misery, and its depiction rules out any significant thought or lesson for the rest of us, the outsiders of "the other planet."

The American films that deal with the subject of the Holocaust are few but notable. Such movies as *The Mortal Storm*, *The Young Lions*, *The Diary of Anne Frank*, and *The Pawnbroker* were major productions, featuring superstars in leading roles, and they were distributed with a great deal of publicity, resulting in much critical attention and considerable popular success. Since all of these works were in a way mass media events, their treatments of the subject were inevitably affected by the popular setting. Notice also that all the films discussed in this chapter were based on best sellers or successful plays. The main reason for this is probably a fear to deal with sensitive issues in an original manner; it is less risky to draw upon material which had proven successful and appealing in literature or drama. In addition, these movies were often designed to turn a profit by converting a popular literary or dramatic text to the more popular mass medium of cinema. To the original popular material, Hollywood's formula added further rigidity through entertainment conventions and trivialization. Stark realities of extreme horrors, piercing pain, and unendurable dark realizations bereft of hope and of life are accommodated to popular taste. The unsettling historical trauma is usually transformed into conventional unhappy melodramas based on a stock of recognizable actions that the audience can easily relate to, concluding with traditional optimistic notes on the triumph of humanity and justice.

In spite of Hollywood's inherent incapacity when it comes to dealing with a subject of the magnitude of the Holocaust, the popular media can be instrumental in enlightening ignorant people about the course and nature of the Nazi evil. A dramatic demonstration of the formidable power of Hollywood's universal appeal was provided by the enormous impact of NBC's television drama *Holocaust*. This eight-hour teledrama series, written by Gerald Green, was faithful to the narrative conventions of Hollywood's "formula." Its story is too contrived (almost everything important in the history of the Third Reich and the persecution of the Jews from 1933 to 1945 happens to the members of two families), and there is even a happy ending (the young sympathetic hero makes it to Israel). At no point does *Holocaust* convey the impression of any searing pain or unendurable anguish or represent the actual experiences of starvation, suffocation in sealed boxcars, or other specific incidents of Nazi atrocities. Instead, the characters respond to stock narrative situations, such as forced separation between lovers, the death of a close friend or a family member, social corruption, and familiar forms of political oppression. The aesthetic shortcomings of *Holocaust* were pointed out by *Time* writer Lance Morrow: "One senses something wrong with the television effort when one realizes that two or three black-and-white concentration camp still photographs [displayed in the context of the narrative by a fictional SS officer]—the stacked, starved bodies—are more powerful and heartbreaking than two or three hours of dramatization." Morrow follows it by stating that the "last 15 minutes of Vittorio de Sica's *The Garden of the Finzi-Continis*, in which Italian Jews are rounded up to be taken to the camps, is more wrenching than all the hours of the *Holocaust*."[91]

Morrow's judgments are sound for any person with a sense of good taste, some basic knowledge about the events of World War II, and minimal sensitivity to the enormous suffering of the victims and the overwhelming evil of the victimizers. In America, the distance from the actual historical experience undoubtedly had some impact on the capacity of Hollywood filmmakers and their audiences at home to grasp and express the incredible atrocities; consequently, the treatment of the horrors on the screen has always been evasive or pussyfooting. But the popularization of the historical material into a sort of soap opera for prime-time American television is liable to diminish the horrors of the actual atrocities and to present a bland drama that fails to provoke a sustained aesthetic reaction corresponding to the extremity of the authentic human sufferings. Reacting to the scandal triggered by the NBC teledrama, screenwriter Paddy Chayefsky stated simply and correctly: "Trivialization is television." I don't think much can be added to this argument, except that the moral outrage aroused by the inevitable trivialization is countered by the recognition of the enlightening force of a popular media that can inform the ignorant about the basic tenets of the Nazi evil and about the massive victimization of the Jews. These seemingly irreconcilable considerations apply also to the Hollywood film, which basically shares the same aesthetic norms of television. Ultimately, popular versions of the Holocaust should be evaluated in terms of their faithfulness to the historical truth, the general concerns or ideological thrust, and their impact on an oblivious and otherwise mindless audience. Gerald Green's *Holocaust* appears to me to be a positive contribution to the consciousness of the Holocaust one generation after Auschwitz. In Germany the program destroyed a taboo and compelled new widespread interest in the subject and a reassessment of attitudes toward the national past. As one critic put it: "Germany has been enriched by a new American word 'Holocaust,' which simultaneously covers the Jewish genocide, the tv movie and its personalized tragedy, and the emotional and political reactions it promoted."[92]

Hollywood films do not merely trivialize history, but project images and attitudes that distort it and violate its incontrovertible moral lessons. When Hollywood treats tragic themes, it usually does so with the eighteenth-century conventions of the bourgeois tragedy, that is, with a special drive to press a fairly neat moral lesson. The action may be serious or even awful, but the moral codes that underlie decline or prosperity are always clear, and they are, moreover, appealing and acceptable to the large audience. The result is that the works are loaded with ideological overtones that conform to prevailing social attitudes and convey a comforting, rather than a challenging, message. The relationship between the popular cinema and ideology is usually summarized by concepts of imposition and reflection; the first means that a certain value system is perpetrated and reinforced by each product of the film industry, and the second implies that popular art always reflects sociocultural trends, attitudes, fears, or desires, but it expresses them unconsciously or indirectly, like dreams which are disguises for hidden wishes or fears.[93] However, popular cinema is distinguished by the presence of ideological overtones which are usually part of the subtext, and they attest to prevalent social attitudes toward specific topics.

The social ideology advocated by the American film denies the singularity of the Jewish catastrophe. The strategy of generalization either takes the form of eliminating all references to the Jewish identity of the Nazi victims, presenting them rather as vague "non-Aryans," or else it has Jewish victims, like Anne Frank, declare that all kinds of people suffer, as if this were the lesson of the Holocaust. Hollywood, partly as a result of its continuous search for the most common denominator of its audience, evidently did not wish to emphasize the tragedy of the Jews, lest it be perceived as a specific Jewish tragedy.

Most of the films discussed in this chapter were crude attempts to universalize the Holocaust. *The Mortal Storm* defied reason and normal expectations when it persistently avoided specifying the Jewish identity of the Nazis' victims whom the film was presenting. *The Young Lions* marks the absurdist reversal of the moral stature of victims and victimizers, the Nazis and those who fought against them in World War II. *The Pawnbroker* establishes bogus analogues between the Holocaust and contemporary social ills. The universalization of the Holocaust is based on the idea that the Nazis' atrocities and the manifestations of bestiality and inhumanity in World War II demonstrate man's vilest instincts and crimes against humanity. The universalist approach led also to a failure to appreciate the true nature of Nazi antisemitism. The American films chose to treat the persecution of the Jews as a form of intolerance rooted in social prejudices; in the process they ignored the importance of anitsemitism for Hitler and his henchmen, the murderous—indeed genocidal—thrust of Nazi antisemitism, its roots in the history of the Jews in Christian Europe, and thousands of years of Christian antisemitism. But the main problem with this approach is that it forgets that the inhuman crimes enacted during the Nazi era were not crimes against humanity—a catching phrase, but actually a meaningless one—rather, if anything, they were the crimes of humanity against the Jews.

Lawrence Langer observed that "the American imagination seems reluctant to take the non-Kierkegaardian leap into unfaith."[94] Langer was rightfully appalled by the tendency in American film and theater—the statement above was made in reference to *The Diary of Anne Frank*—to treat the subject of the Holocaust by glossing over its unsettling horrors, preferring instead to drive home positive, optimistic messages on Providence, the nobility of the human spirit, and belief in progress toward a better future. It is not so much the inherent naiveté, or simplicity, of these ideas that provokes the critical outrage, but rather the incongruous usage of the Holocaust experience to foster such views. But the fact of the matter is that the American film does not simply display a "reluctance of the imagination" to confront the universe of atrocities. What we actually have in most American Holocaust films is a deliberate refusal to leap into unfaith, an attitude rooted in the embracing of solid faith, namely that of Christianity, which dominates the cinematic treatment of the Holocaust. Indeed, the striking aspect of the observation of the Christian content of those films is its persistence. Films made in different decades, using different modes of production, with different cultural codes, and, more specifically, reflecting entirely different attitudes toward the theme of the war and Jews in American society—a propaganda movie from the early forties, an antiwar film of the late fifties, a social drama of the sixties—all share in common the fostering of Christian ideology on the back of the Jews and their tragedy.

The manifestation of Christian attitudes and Christian symbolism varies from film to film. We have a Jewish character behaving like a Christian, an implicit conversion of the Jew to the dominant religion; a Jew appearing as a Jew but advocating Christian ideas; a Jew being presented through the prism of Christian stereotypes of Jews; and a presentation of the greatest tragedy of the Jews being neatly resolved in Christian terms. Sometimes the imposition of Christian symbols would be contradictory. In *The Pawnbroker*, for example, Nazerman is both a "Nazi man" and "the man of Nazareth"; the two concepts are evidently irreconcilable, and when pressed together, along with the martyr-assistant Jesus and the special relationships between the two characters, the heavy religious symbolism becomes frustrating rather than suggestive, confusing more than illuminating. *The Young Lions* also involved some "competition" regarding the Christ-like figure between the Jewish character and the German soldier, Christian. The origin of this film's double meaning can be traced, in part, to the production itself. Marlon Brando suggested to the director, Edward Dmytryk, that in his final scene instead of just falling down the hill and dying face-down in a puddle of water he would land on a roll of barbed wire and one of the strands encircle and cut into his forehead like Christ's crown of thorns. According to Montgomery Clift's biographer, Robert LaGuardia, Dmytryk seriously considered the idea until Clift expressed his objections, threatening to leave the production if Brando got his wish. LaGuardia noted that "according to the endless published accounts, the story presumably is symbolic of the rivalry between Monty and Brando for top-dog status as Christ figures."[95]

This lack of any clear and specific consistency indicates, I believe, that the extensive use of Christian themes is not part of an indoctrination campaign or a conspiracy to vilify the Jews. Aside from the contribution of sociopolitical factors—whose nature, motives, and extent are subjects beyond the scope of this study—the extensive usage of Christian ideas and symbolism is also the failure of the artistic imagination. This failure comes in the form of the uncritical adoption and, at times, sheer exploitation of the suggestive communicative power of Christian motifs and symbols, whose imposition on the Holocaust distorts the crucially authentic details of the historical experience and projects ideological strains which betray the memory of the victims.

American films have failed on both accounts, of representation and presentation. These two terms constitute categories of aesthetic approaches, but they are also charged with moral implications: the first, representation, in the sense of creating a truthful account of the Holocaust horrors, has the responsibility of registering the Nazi reality without any popularistic compromises or evasions; the second, presentation, in the sense of identifying and paying tribute to the Nazis' Jewish victims and their unique predicament—unique in terms of their particular situation during World War II in the context of the complacent western civilization, the unprecedented crime of genocide, and the Jewish history of persecutions in the Christian world—is bound by the moral call to avoid sociopolitical distortions or deceptions.

Unlike the personal drives of west and east European filmmakers, who deal with the Holocaust in order to explore and express their own national traumas

(many continental Holocaust movies are indeed based on autobiographical experiences of the film directors or their screenwriters), the American interest in the
subject is motivated by other considerations which are not necessarily rooted in a
genuine concern with the disturbing truth of the historical tragedy. Unlike the
Czech films, whose abstraction of the historical persecution was aimed at exploring
metaphysical premises about the human condition, Hollywood's universalization is
rooted in specific social concerns that seek to avoid burdening a basically indifferent
public with the unbearable facts of the Nazi genocide of the Jews. It consciously
avoids indicating that that genocide, rooted in Christian antisemitism, grew out
of the heart of western civilization, was initiated by the "Allied" Germans, and
was carried out while the entire Christian and western world stood by, unable and
unwilling to stop the process of destruction. "The Jew is a living reproach," declared
Steiner,[96] and Hollywood, in order to diffuse this ethical burden, or to avoid
confronting or offending the public, or even to try and appease the audience when
the subject is as disturbing as the Holocaust, distorts the identity of the victims—
far worse, presents them as little better than the victimizers or bystanders. And it
provides the banal, comforting message that everybody is guilty, and everybody
suffers, but redemption is still possible, or else that "people are still good at heart,"
a significant statement not because of its meaning but because of its purpose,
namely, to disburden the conscience from the implications of unsettling events of
the magnitude of the Holocaust.

AN INTERLUDE

Chaplin's *The Great Dictator*

Charles Chaplin's *The Great Dictator* (1940) was the period's boldest cinematic attack on the German leader as well as the first film in the west which showed a Jewish protagonist against the background of the Nazi world. The uncanny resemblance between Chaplin and Hitler—many had referred to the Austrian-born dictator as "the little tramp" even before Chaplin created his movie—made the project quite expected. Here is Chaplin's account of the development of the germinal idea.

> Alexander Korda in 1937 had suggested I should do a Hitler story based on mistaken identity, Hitler having the same moustache as the tramp: I could play both characters, he said. I did not think too much about the idea then, but now [1938] it was topical, and I was desperate to get working again. Then it suddenly struck me! Of course! As Hitler I could harangue the crowds in jargon and talk all I wanted to. And as the tramp I could remain more or less silent. A Hitler story was an opportunity for burlesque and pantomime. So with this enthusiasm I went hurrying back to Hollywood and set to work writing a script. The story took two years to develop.[1]

The production itself began in September 1939 and continued until March 1940. The film was released in October of that year. During the making of *The Great Dictator* Chaplin received threatening letters and was attacked verbally by groups unhappy with the film's anti-Nazi theme. American officials also warned Chaplin that an anti-Hitler picture would inevitably be banned.[2] Thus, because of the resemblance between Hitler and Chaplin, "the blow was waiting to be struck," but it took a great deal of courage on Chaplin's part to strike it.

In *The Great Dictator*, Chaplin portrays both a little Jewish barber and the barber's physical double, the dictator of Tomania, Adenoid Hynkel. In a mixture of farce and satire, Chaplin mocks the Nazi racist ideology and Hitler's megalomania, while, at the same time, showing the suffering of the Jewish community under the Nazi regime.

Chaplin sets up a comic tone to the film even before the story begins. But he also uses Brechtian alienation effects, which frame the narrative and the ensuing comedy in the context of the serious situation of World War II and the persecutions of the Jews. Thus the film starts with an epigraph that "any resemblance between Hynkel the dictator and the Jewish barber is purely coincidental." The joke, of course, is that Chaplin plays both. The statement also introduces one of the main themes, namely, the exposition of the absurdity of Nazi racism, which is ridiculed through the basic irony of the story: the great dictator looks so exactly like the small Jew that at the end of the movie the closest colleagues and ardent admirers of the former cannot distinguish between the two. The comic tone of the opening statement also inverts its literal meaning—the racist "excuse" when, as it happens so often, "superior" Aryans look like "inferior" Semites and vice versa. Finally, the epigraph is a parody of the common practice of Hollywood films to emphasize their fictionality and possibly avoid libel suits. Here, on the other hand, the implied irony suggests that we had better treat his film more seriously, rather than dismiss it as fiction, and thereby draw the right lessons for concrete actions.

The story itself is also introduced with humor. A second epigraph reads: "This is a story of a period between two World Wars—an interim in which insanity cut loose. Liberty took a nose dive, and humanity was kicked around somewhat." Funny but sadly true. Telling the truth with laughter and a touch of pathos is Chaplin's underlying approach in *The Great Dictator*. Chaplin indeed had a paramount concern with a pressing reality and its distasteful facts in a time when most of the world preferred to ignore them. Acknowledging the escapist temptation of a fundamentally entertaining film comedy, he believed that his comic talent could be used to convey the urgency of current political realities, and he sought to entertain his audience without obscuring the message of his work.

The first episode in the movie is set amidst the notorious trench battles of World War I. Here Chaplin creates a war comedy reminiscent of his *Shoulder Arms* (1918). He focuses on familiar Chaplinesque elements of the little fellow caught up in a threatening environment yet managing through fool's luck to survive. Another element characteristic of Chaplin's comedy is the mechanized character of the threatening forces. One of Chaplin's favorite concepts is that machines created by man for his convenience and improvement can menace, dehumanize, or enslave us. The first gag involves Charlie's attempts to check the fuse of a huge shell he has just fired and which failed to explode. The huge, eggy shell keeps rotating ominously and making strange noises, literally following and matching the actions of the terrified little soldier, before blowing up.

In the Fascist systems which Chaplin has set out to condemn, human mechanization or regimentation is all pervasive. Charlie, the soldier, is eventually saved exactly because of his inability to be regimented like all the others. He loses his unit in the fog and confusion of the battlefield, and when Schultz, a wounded aviator, needs him to fly an aircraft and deliver important dispatches he quickly seizes this opportunity to get away from the battlefield. Schultz is the opposite of Charlie. He is motivated by strong patriotic feelings and a sense of military duty. The comic mood from Aristophanes to Chaplin sees these ideals as a threat to life-enhancing impulses. Schultz is actually a version of the classical *miles gloriosus*, used by Chaplin as a caricature of the German attraction for the image of romantic warriors. The chivalric character is presented in a grotesque fashion—as his plane is nosediving to destruction Schultz launches into a poetic evocation of Spring in Tomania, of gentle sweet Hilda and the flowers in her garden, stating that Hilda "could never bear to cut the daffodils—it is like taking life to cut them." This little parody of a chivalric love poem reveals two major themes characteristic of the reality of World War II. First is the artistic or poetic pretensions of many Nazis while engaged in committing atrocities, and second is the sentimental concern with pets and flowers juxtaposed with the enormous insensitivity to the sufferings and deaths of millions of human beings.

The transition from the end of the First World War to the Nazi era is accomplished by a montage sequence of newspaper headlines: "Peace," "Dempsey beats Willard," "Lindbergh flies the Atlantic," "Depression," "Riots in Tomania," "Hynkel party takes power." The second and the third items in this list demand a special explanation. Lindbergh had his own small role in the critical events of the time. A heroic figure in the United States for his successful crossing of the Atlantic, Charles Lindbergh became a supporter of Nazi Germany and was actively calling for better relations with Germany, helping thereby to becloud American awareness of the Nazi evil. The boxing headline about Dempsey and Willard is intended to evoke another boxing match which had become one of the most curious episodes associated with the Nazi state during the thirties. The boxing match between the "Aryan" German Max Schmeling and the black American Joe Louis was for many a great deal more than a sporting event, a symbolic struggle between the races, and a platform to foster general ideologies. For the Germans, it was a test to demonstrate the ultimate superiority of the Aryan man; for most others, a Louis victory would have been seen as proof of the fallibility of the racist theory. Schmeling was a member of Nazi high society and Louis was a folk hero in the United States. Like the Dempsey-Willard fights, they split the two matches. Schmeling won the first, but in the second he was humiliated by a knockout in the first round.

In the central portion, the film focuses on the Jews in the ghetto and the escalation of persecutions planned by the dictator and his top aides. The narrative action is minimal. Hynkel decides to invade Osterlich, which requires a loan from Epstein. To appease Epstein, a Jew, the persecution against "his people" ceases temporarily. Hynkel finds out that Epstein refuses to deal with "a medieval maniac." Ominously cracking nuts, Hynkel declares that he will "deal" with his (Epstein's) people.

The dictator himself is first introduced in his most characteristic behavior—delivering a fanatical speech to the multitudes of his faceless followers. Chaplin accomplishes a "marvelous mimicry of the Hitler delirium, particularly the pursed-lip rendering of the German gutturals—'mit der ach hic,' etc., ending in a coughing spell."[3] The content of the hateful speech comes through by using German-English double-talk. But one of the most curious aspects of this scene has to do with the English translation of Hitler's words. Chaplin was painfully aware of the dubious role the media were playing in terms of portraying the true nature of Hitler and Nazism. The exchange on the soundtrack between the words of the Phooey (i.e., the Fuehrer) and the English interpretation is a nice illustration for the Nazi art of deception as well as the wishful rendering of Hitler in the west. Hynkel yells: "Democration shtunkt!" Translator: "Democracy smells." "Liberated shtunkt!"— "Liberty is odious." "Frei sprachen shtunkt!"—"Free speech is objectionable." Then the dictator bursts into a wild, incomprehensible tirade forcing the microphones to wilt as he roars. No euphemism can deliver the content of this passage. The translator, maintaining the necessary sense of factual tone and decorum, simply remarks: "The Phooey has just referred to the Jewish people."

Hynkel is surrounded by Herring and Garbitsch, modeled after Goering and Goebbels. The top aides represent two essential but different aspects of the great dictator. The plump, bumbling Herring has the shape of a Falstaff and the mind of an idiot. He embodies all the buffoonish elements in the dictator's character. Garbitsch, on the other hand, is tall, slim, and cunning. Always dressed in black or grey and speaking in a soft, sneaky voice, he is the devil engineering all the evil schemes. He is also the driving force behind the persecution of the Jews, remarking at the end of the Phooey's speech that the tirade against the Jews was too restrained and that violence against the Jews can boost the people's morale. Significantly, the implied competition between Herring and Garbitsch results in the triumph of the dark, humorless enemy of humanity.

Hynkel's first speech ends with a beat of burlesque. Herring, bowing to a lady, butts the dictator down the stairs. The Phooey's fury is expressed in stripping the medals off Herring's chest and giving him a poke which indents his paunch. But the wild comic gag, like other slapstick moments in *The Great Dictator*, never obscures the realistic background. The pictures of the admiring adherents which immediately follow are based on authentic photographs from *Triumph of the Will*, including the greeting by a little flower girl and the dictator's posing with a baby. In Chaplin's version, the baby, to be sure, fails to show proper respect, wetting the disgusted dictator.

Meanwhile, the Jewish barber returns to the ghetto after escaping the hospital where he had been kept since the end of World War I suffering from amnesia. The encounter between the little man, who is ignorant of the Nazi takeover, and the Storm Troopers, who represent the new reality, is the source of many jokes. When two Storm Troopers paint "Jew" on his shop window, the barber goes out to wash it off. After one of the Troopers begins to kick him around, the barber appeals to the other uniformed bully to arrest the aggressor. The Jew is about to be lynched by the Storm Troopers when Schultz, now high officer in the Phooey's Reich, recognizes and greets him with the words "You saved my life, strange . . . and I always thought of you as an Aryan." The barber replies, "I'm vegetarian." At this point, the quality of the barber's ignorance is ambiguous. On the one hand, his amnesia guarantees a special moral stature of supreme innocence. But it also contains a certain amount of criticism. Amnesia, Chaplin seems to suggest, is the Jewish malaise which is responsible for the forgetfulness of history of persecutions and hence the unpreparedness for coping with newly erupting dangers of antisemitism.

Even though Chaplin was fully aware that the first victims of Nazi antisemitism were the socially progressive and integrated Jews of Germany, he features a traditional Jewish community living in a ghetto. The purpose of this portrayal was to underscore the benign quality of traditional Jewish life, especially vis-à-vis the evil of the new social forces, and also, perhaps more important, to stress the communal tragedy of the Jewish predicament. The physical weakness of the Jews is contrasted with the bullying Storm Troopers. The Jewish characters are mostly middle-aged people and are physically unimpressive, speaking with an accent, and clinging to one another. The range of responses to the new reality is expressed by the following exchange. "Good morning," Mr. Mann, the respectable leader of the small community greets the scurrying and ever-fatalistic old Jaeckel. "What's good about it?" grumbles Jaeckel, and Mann replies, "Conditions could be woise." The two typify atavistic modes of behavior Jews had acquired in the ups and downs of their history. Mann represents the accommodative, optimistic, reasonable man who believes in good reason, reconciliation, and fair play even in the most dangerous situation. On the other hand, we find the ever-panicked Jaeckel, with his characteristic bitter pessimism.

The most pathetic figure in the film is Hannah, an orphan who lost her father in the war, presumably fighting on the German side. Aside from her pathetic background, she is the only young person in the ghetto and the only one there wishing for and trying an active resistance against the oppressive forces. When the barber fights back she helps him by knocking the Troopers with a frying pan. This cooperation inevitably develops into a touching romance. Hannah's romantic role and her striking beauty, charming spontaneity, and healthy moral instincts make her the only character in the whole movie who is not comically grotesque, and therefore the character with whom we most identify. Chaplin declared that for him, Hannah "typifies the whole Jewish race, their strength, their resentment against senseless persecution, their hope for a better future."[4] But one must concede that although played by Paulette Goddard, a Jewish actress and Chaplin's third wife, it is impossible to detect a specific Jewish trace in the character of Hannah. She rather perfectly conforms to the prototype of a pathetic female figure in a sentimental melodrama.

Likewise, the Jewish barber as played by Chaplin is yet another version of the old tramp figure. His lowly social stature, oversize clothing, hat and walking cane, and the entire stock of comic gags which revolve around him come from the storehouse of the classical Chaplin comedy. His struggles against the Storm Troopers are little more than reiterations of the old Charlie vs. the cops from the Mack Sennett Keystone comedies. But in *The Great Dictator* the character of Charlie the little tramp, set against the background of the Jewish ghetto and its inhabitants, serves to convey the moral strain of the work through constant contrasts with the political monster. The barber speaks very little, whereas the dictator is a compulsive talker, specializing in inflammatory tirades. The barber is absentminded—excited by the presence of Hannah in the barber's chair, he unwittingly starts to give her a shave! The dictator is ridiculous exactly because of the opposite traits; all of his moves are calculated to the second, including brief posings of two seconds with his private artists. Interestingly, Hitler was indeed hyperkinetic, a biographical fact exploited by Chaplin for comic effects.

The contrast between the dictator and the barber is total, excepting, of course, for the physical appearance. At times Chaplin uses an outstanding acting talent to convey the differences, as, for example, when the two characters are seen in similar amorous situations. In Hannah's presence, the barber displays tenderness and touching embarrassment; the dictator considers his secretary as sexual prey, grimacing and growling like a beast about to attack its victim. One little detail of the mise-en-scène shows the great concern with which Chaplin approaches the systematic juxtaposition. Chaplin's shop as well as other houses in the ghetto are full of small utility objects used for the ongoing life there. By contrast, the monumental palace, with its huge walls, is strikingly empty. Even the closet behind Hynkel's desk has only mirrors to reflect the image of the self-admiring dictator. The mirrors in the barber's shop are, of course, intended, more practically, for the use of customers, or for people other than the barber. Hynkel, we learn, has turned the magnificent palace library into his private barber's shop.

Ultimately, the contrast between the dictator and the barber is that of inhumanity versus humanity. Inhumanity in its simplest form is illustrated by the way Hynkel utilizes human beings as functional objects. A flunky sticks out his tongue so that Hynkel can seal an envelope—an unambiguous image of dehumanization. Hynkel's total disregard of human life is illustrated in the following examples. Herring presents a new invention of a "perfect" bulletproof suit. Hynkel tests it by shooting the devoted inventor, who falls flat dead. Hynkel dryly remarks, "far from perfect." Herring then brings another inventor, who is wearing a contraption, salutes the dictator, and jumps out of the window to demonstrate the power of a new parachute. As this man falls dead Hynkel complains: "Herring, why do you waste my time like this?"

On the other hand, the barber's humanity is based on the unique quality of the old tramp character. According to Gerald Mast, "Charlie's tramp character [was] plucky, human, sensitive, warm, alternately generous and tough, down and out in society's eyes."[5] In essence Charlie has always celebrated human endurance in the face of threats and pressures, along with the demonstration of shrewd and healthy survival instincts which never violate the basic moral codes but rather contribute to and justify our sense of justice. Chaplin correctly felt that the leader of the German nation in his time was the complete antithesis for everything that he, the little tramp, ever stood for. Indeed, the dichotomy between the little tramp and the great dictator goes beyond this particular film. For instance, Hynkel's posing with the baby recalls the famous picture of Charlie in *The Kid*, when at the end of the film he embraces his adopted child. The latter is one of the greatest filmic expressions of pathos and human affection; Hynkel's gesture is unambiguously arranged for the camera and the dictator can barely conceal his disgust with the incontinent baby.

While Chaplin's pathos always stirs a universal cord, Hynkel is obsessed with megalomania, illustrated in his dance with a balloon designed like a globe. The accompanying music is, as might be expected, Wagner's, the slow Prelude to act I of *Lohengrin*. After scrutinizing the object of his desire, Hynkel embraces the globe balloon like a dear little toy. He spins it, tosses it up, kicks it, and butts it with his head and his rear. The slow movements and the silence of the dance itself, plus the character's complete absorption in this game, are hypnotic. The dream or hypnosis abruptly ends when Hynkel leaps to grasp the balloon and bursts it. Breaking into tears like a child who has ruined his toy, the dictator sobs on the desk.

Immediately after the hypnotic ballet, the barber shaves an elderly customer to the strains of Brahms's Hungarian Dance No. 5. In perfect harmony with the lively rhythmic music, Chaplin displays a tour de force of physical performance, of quickness and precision, rinsing and wiping his hands, stropping and testing the razor, lathering the face, shaving, wiping the face and the razor, removing the sheet, and putting the customer's hat on his head. Although engaged in practicing his profession—at the end the barber holds out his hand for the fee to the last beat of sound—the pattern of recurrent movements, perfectly synchronized with the rhythmic music, renders this sequence a purely artistic ballet performance. The differences between the two ballets are succinctly defined by Gerald Mast: "The barber's human work contrasts with the dictator's inhuman dreams of glory, just as snappy movement and music contrasts with the ethereal slowness of Hynkel's dream ballet—percussion and pizzicato rather than obbligata, razor rather that lighter-than-air balloon."[6]

But the effect of these differences goes beyond the fictional story of the barber and Hynkel. The two consecutive ballet sequences present an essential dialectic inherent in the nature of art. On the one hand, Wagner's heavy, sophisticated, highbrow music, which has a special elitist and nationalistic appeal. It was especially significant to the Nazis, who saw Wagner's art and dedication to racist mythology as the expressions of a proto-Nazi. Hitler himself took a personal interest in the annual festival devoted to Wagner's music in Bayreuth, which Richard Grunberger observed "ranked supreme in the Führer's affections." A festival handbook from 1938 included the following statement:

> Wagner's work teaches us hardness in the figure of Lohengrin . . . through Hans Sachs, it teaches us . . . to honor all things German. . . . In *The Ring of the Nibelungen* it brings to our consciousness with unexampled clarity the terrible seriousness of the racial problem . . . in *Parsifal* it shows us that the only religion Germans can embrace is that of struggle towards a life made divine.[7]

Regardless of the nationalistic interpretations, the Germans found in Wagner a lot of "heavy stuff," metaphysical pretensions and ambitious superprofundity, the opposite of Charlie's art, whose humor never failed to warm the heart because of his simple yet forceful grasp of human sensitivity and basic humane ethics. The piece by Brahms fits into this vision of humble and benevolent humanism. It is originally a folk dance, vivacious, exciting, and fundamentally life-enhancing. The Hungarian dance is the true expression of the folk, rather than Wagner's ponderous sounds with their pompous intention to express the "Volk."

Wagner's art notwithstanding, the German composer was also a notorious antisemite, and many Nazi leaders followed his example, trying to accommodate their love of art and music with their hatred of humanity. They respected high culture and, perhaps because in their subconscious they were troubled by their barbarism, sought in it an affirmation for their goals. Wagner, to be sure, was one of their major inspiring forces. Hitler once said: "Whoever wants to understand National Socialist Germany must know Wagner."[8] Chaplin caricatures the Nazi subversion of art by showing in Tomania the famous statues of the Venus de Milo and Rodin's *The Thinker*, each with an arm raised in a Nazi salute as Hynkel's car passes by them. Also not to be forgotten, the ex-corporal himself was once an aspiring artist. Chaplin simply shows the incomprehensible coexistence of art and atrocities by following the Storm Troopers' assault on the ghetto and the burning of the barber's shop (a dramatization of Kristallnacht) with an image of little flames on two candlesticks, providing the light for Hynkel, who plays a brief tune on the piano. The adjacent shots indicate the simultaneity of both events and throw light on another horrific, yet essential, characteristic of the great dictator and of Nazism in general.

Less abstract than the issue of high culture, and a much more pressing issue in the late thirties, was the universal cowardice which accommodated and compromised with Hitler's imperialist ambitions. One specific scene exemplifies this attitude. After Schultz quarrels with Hynkel he finds shelter in the ghetto. He schemes for the assassination of the dictator and wants one of the ghetto Jews to undertake this deed. Five men meet conspiratorially for this purpose. They sit at a table and are informed that the assassin will be the one who finds a coin in his cake. It turns out, however, that Hannah has put a coin in each cake, but when each participant (other than the community leader) discovers his coin he immediately passes it to his neighbor's plate. Although all these characters are ghetto Jews, Chaplin points to a universal phenomenon of cowardice and duplicity. In particular, the central business in this scene reflects the way European countries and the rest of the world avoided confronting the Nazi menace by passing responsibility to one another, hoping to be individually spared by Hitler.

The film's next part features the hilarious episode involving the two dictators, Hynkel and Napaloni. The two little men frantically compete with one another in various ways to demonstrate their power and "grandeur." Chaplin's comedy is an incredible mockery of the two European leaders, and Hynkel in particular is the subject of constant humiliation. In the palace barber shop, they raise their chairs higher and higher until Hynkel hits the ceiling and crashes down. This reduction of political figures and world affairs to purely comical gags of wild physical humor culminates in the pure farce of the food-flinging battle at a buffet table prepared for a treaty-signing ceremony.

In spite of these farcical scenes, Chaplin retains the connection with reality by drawing on some of the well-known episodes associated with Mussolini and Hitler. Hynkel's panic at Napaloni's presence is rooted in the respect the Nazi Fuehrer had for the Fascist leader, which led, among other things, to the adoption of the Fascist hail as the standard Nazi salute. The comic business with the erratic trains at the beginning of their meeting recalls one of Mussolini's achievements in Italy, having the trains come on time. Mussolini's notorious disregard for his wife is reflected in a scene in which Mme. Napaloni is ignored by her husband, gets lost in the train station, and is pushed in the face by policemen as she tries to identify herself. Later the plump and ugly Mme. Napaloni is neglected at a big ball in Hynkel's palace. Garbitsch urges Hynkel to invite her to dance, which propels a nice comic sequence with the big woman leading and Hynkel being carried, raised, and moved like a weightless wax doll.

In the last part of the film the mood changes drastically. The invasion of Osterlich is presented without a glimpse of humor. Tanks appear out of haystacks to trample fields and houses, and the newspaper headlines announce "Ghettoes are raided," "Property confiscated." Hannah, who fled to Osterlich with her adopted family, is brutally knocked down as Storm Troopers take possession of their farm. The invasion of Osterlich is, of course, the invasion of Austria, which was far from being an act of war. The only onslaught of the campaign was directed against Jews. Chaplin shows us a scene resembling the notorious news pictures of the Jews of Vienna being forced to rub and wash the streets. Then, one young Jew tries to resist the humiliation and vandalization of the Jewish shops and is immediately shot—the only depiction of death in the whole film.

In the final sequence, the roads of the barber and the dictator finally cross, after the barber and Schultz escape from a concentration camp near the Osterlich border. The expected occurrence of mistaken identity is finally realized. Prison guards arrest Hynkel, who is dressed in Tyrolean costume and has been seated in a small boat, duck hunting. Meanwhile, the barber is taken for Hynkel, and with Schultz by his side, he leads the invasion of Osterlich. Invited to make a speech to millions of victorious soldiers, the barber is terrified; but Schultz pushes him forward. "You must speak, it's our only hope." The word "hope" rings with the sentimental musical theme associated with Hannah. Then the barber rises and goes to the microphone.

We expect to see the character of the barber at the podium, and indeed most critics refer to that final speech as delivered by the Jewish barber. But the little man near the microphone is not the Jewish barber, nor is he, of course, the dictator. The surprise is subtle, for Chaplin changed his character's appearance between two shots in the middle of the scene. At the end, then, it is Chaplin himself, with white hair and somber expression, addressing the world with the absolute seriousness of a man expressing his most important credo. Chaplin steps out of the role to give a direct appeal to the audience. The only persona before us is that of Chaplin, the author of the little tramp, who grew old and disillusioned and is visibly agonized by the contemporary eruption of evil in the world: his expression possesses the extraordinary burden of having foreseen a forthcoming catastrophe.

Chaplin's speech is simple and moving. After an initial hesitation, apologizing, "I'm sorry, but I don't want to be an emperor," the simple and modest Everyman passionately urges human brotherhood, freedom, and happiness. The simplicity of these notions led some critics, like Gerald Mast, to consider the speech a "poetic failure of the words to add up to the grand concepts they attempt to express . . . Marxism sweetened with American idealistic cliches."[9] Nevertheless, given the politics of the time, Chaplin does express a few daring notions. He declares: "I should like to help everyone—if possible—Jew, Gentile, black man, white," at a time when the very mentioning of "Jew" in the cinema was almost a taboo. Remarkably, he blends references from Christian sources to divert any parochial interpretation. "In the seventeenth chapter of St. Luke it is written: 'The Kingdom of God is within man.' " Finally, Chaplin's conclusion is unambiguously militant. Acknowledging the real threats to the noble humanism he envisions, he declares: "Now let us fight to fulfill that promise! Let us fight to free the world. . . . Let us fight for a world of reason. . . . Soldiers! In the name of democracy, let us unite!"

The film concludes with pictures of Hannah listening to Chaplin's voice coming from the sky. "Look up, Hannah, look up!" calls Chaplin, ending his speech on the hopeful note of a lighter and brighter future. Hannah, the character with whom we most identify, is seen in a final close-up, against the clouds, with her hair blowing in the wind, and smiling hopefully through her tears. Her final word is "Listen!" as she responds to Charlie's speech. Chaplin's final scene shows Hannah, the symbolic representative of the oppressed Jews, listening to the voice of hope. Chaplin has rounded his "comedy of oppression and fanaticism" with a vision of hope in one of history's darkest hours. But the excessive sentimentality of this finale, with its heavily romantic music and unconvincing change to a hopeful tone, creates a syrupy optimism, which forms "a severe stylistic disruption in the form— from human comedy and political burlesque to humanistic hearts and flowers."[10]

The last quote was originally made by Gerald Mast to criticize Chaplin's final speech and his passionate plea for the return of decency and humanity. When the film was released, many shared the same view, and the adverse criticism aggravated Chaplin, who declared: "They had their laughs and it was fun, now I wanted them to listen. I did this picture for the return of decency and kindness."[11] Shortly after the film's release, Chaplin was upset and bitter. In an interview with the *New York Times* he said: "I had a story to tell and something I wanted very much to say. I said it. . . . The picture is two hours and three minutes in length. If two hours and three minutes of it is comedy, may I not be excused for ending my comedy on a note that reflects honestly and realistically, the world in which we live, and may I not be excused in pleading for a better world?"[12]

Interestingly, the "final speech" was a common device in Hollywood War propaganda movies. Alfred Hitchcock ended his 1940 anti-Nazi film *Foreign Correspondent* (released before *The Great Dictator*) with a broadcast to the U.S. citizens: "The lights are going out in Europe, ring yourself around with steel, America." The climax of Edward Dmytryk's *Hitler's Children* (1943) is a scene in which the young hero delivers a speech on the radio, denouncing Nazi ideals and expressing the hope for the triumph of freedom and democracy. However, in these movies, the rhetorical propaganda was always an integral part of the story (the hero's attempts to make it to the radio is a central narrative line), or it was provided after the narrative's closure. Chaplin's speech is an extraordinary case, not only because it is "a severe stylistic disruption," but moreover, it defies the expected closure of his story. In other words, Chaplin's fantastic comedy has no ending, for the author chose to ignore the fictional demands in favor of direct address to real matters of the pressing hour.

Chaplin's movie was the most daring, unequivocal, and comprehensive anti-Nazi movie of its time. Viewers today, however, would probably be less upset by the final speech than by what precedes it. In other words, the biggest problem with *The Great Dictator* arises from its very essence, the comic treatment of Hitler and the Nazi phenomenon. On its satiric level, Chaplin's film reduces the seriousness of the historical situation, it transforms the human to the mechanical, it ridicules the absurd, and it often merely entertains. But given the enormity of the Nazi crimes—the worst crimes were still to come—few would dispute that Hitler and the Holocaust cannot be subject matter for laughs and fun.

Chaplin has had good reasons to regret some moments in *The Great Dictator*. That the Holocaust surpassed the limits of human imagination is nowhere more evident than in some of Chaplin's jokes. We ought to remember that much of the film's humor serves to demonstrate the absolute insanity of the Nazis, their maniacal evil ad absurdum. Thus when Chaplin has Garbitsch surprising even Hynkel himself with the statistics of five or ten thousand people arrested daily, Chaplin intended those numbers to represent a gross, unrealistic, absurd exaggeration. One or two years later, the number were much higher in reality, and they applied to daily murders. But the most unfortunate jokes are the references to gas. The 1940 audience undoubtedly laughed, and present-day viewers probably chill, when Herring breathlessly announces to Hynkel the discovery of a "marvelous gas" which "will kill everybody!" Another "joke" which would have been innocent before the Final Solution but appears monstrously incongruous after is Charlie's teasing question to the guard in the concentration camp—if he can go to the smoking room!

The comic style also misses several fundamental aspects of the political realities Chaplin set out to denounce. The depiction of Nazi Germany is the most unrealistic element in *The Great Dictator*. Tomania appears as if taken from Swift's imagination. The name evokes Germania, deliberately containing the word "mania" to convey the prevalent madness, and it also means Ptomania—ptomaine is a poisonous organic matter. Tomania is a fairyland created in the image of the dictator's perverse mind, full of huge banners with the national symbol of the double cross, two X's, one above the other. The cult and worship of the dictator are total: Hynkel's portrait is visible everywhere, and as his car passes the streets and the gardens, even the classical statues bow and salute him. Amidst this madness, the Jewish community occupies a little island of simple and ordinary life, but even this island has a stylized Brechtian introduction—the word "Ghetto" defines the locale on a little sign, painted in old Gothic letters, surrounded by quaint flowers. Although this unrealistic approach can be justified for the sake of allegorical signification, there are moments which are offensively erroneous. The concentration camp, for example, is a spacious place whose inhabitants are ordered to goose-step all day long and are allowed to joke with their guards. Likewise, the depiction of the Storm Troopers as a bunch of street bullies in uniform obliterates the true menace of the SA and ignores completely the extraordinary terror of the SS. Chaplin also displays a poor understanding of the anti-Jewish policies of Nazi Germany. He reads them in terms of the classical socioeconomic antisemitism—Jews are arbitrarily chosen as the scapegoats for social ills and the regime's economic failures. Concentrating the Nazi assaults on the ghetto, Chaplin appears to conceive of the Nazi perse-cutions as nothing more than a pogrom of specific function and limited duration.

But without doubt, Chaplin's chief concern, as the film's title indicates, is the character of Adolf Hitler. Humor is Chaplin's weapon against Hitler's ideo-logies, especially his racism and megalomania. In both cases, Chaplin focuses on the absurdity of these programs. Racism is ridiculed through the film's basic irony, namely, the exact resemblance between Hynkel and the barber. At one point, the dark Garbitsch seductively advises the black-haired dictator to eliminate all the brunettes:

HYNKEL: "We shall never have peace till we have a pure Aryan race. How wonderful—
Tomania, a nation of blue-eyed blondes."
GARBITSCH: "Why not a blonde Europe—a blonde Asia—a blonde America?"
HYNKEL: "A blonde world!"
GARBITSCH: "And a brunette Dictator!"
HYNKEL: "Dictator of the world!"

The most important political goal of *The Great Dictator* was the shattering of the image of Hitler, who in 1939–40 was still venerated by many. Regardless of Hitler's political views, the fact that he was the popular leader of the German nation made many people, even in the antifascist countries, doubt whether he could really be so monstrous. Indeed, to this day, there is not a single film com-parable to *The Great Dictator* in terms of its absolute assault on a living political figure. Chaplin's laughter was aimed at undermining the automatic respectability assigned to heads of state. By vilifying Hitler with humor, Chaplin wished, in his own way, to nullify the Hitler phenomenon.

Chaplin's presentation of Hitler conforms to that historiosophic view which tends to belittle the actual impact of the individual Adolf Hitler on the course of history. According to this view, Hitler was essentially a nonentity, an ex-corporal obsessed with mad ideas of megalomania and racism who happened to appear on the historical stage at a moment when the masses supported these ideas, and a highly efficient bureaucracy lent itself to serve blindly the mad dictator. However, whether Hitler was a "great man" or a special product of historical circumstances, the Austrian-born Fuehrer had an unambiguous comic side to his personality. Consider, for instance, the following exchange between Hitler and Prince Philip of Hesse, on March 11, 1938, at 10:25 P.M., in the critical point of the Austria crisis when the German emissary called the Chancellery from Rome to inform Hitler that Mussolini gave up to the German demands.

> P: I have just come back from the Palazzo Venezia. The Duce accepted the whole thing in a very friendly manner. He sends you his regards. . . . Schuschnigg gave him the news . . . Mussolini said that Austria would be immaterial to him.
>
> Hitler was beside himself with relief and joy.
>
> H: Then, please tell Mussolini I will never forget him for this!
> P: Yes, sir.
> H: Never, never, never, no matter what happens! I am ready to make a quite different agreement with him.
> P: Yes, sir. I told him that too.
> H: As soon as the Austrian affair has been settled I shall be ready to go with him through thick and thin—through anything!
> P: Yes, my Fuehrer.
> H: Listen! I shall make any agreement. I am no longer in fear of the terrible position which would have existed militarily in case we had gotten into a conflict. You may tell him that I do thank him from the bottom of my heart. Never, never shall I forget it.
> P: Yes, my Fuehrer.
> H: I shall never forget him for this, no matter what happens. If he should ever need any help or be in any danger, he can be convinced that I shall stick to him whatever may happen, even if the whole world gangs up on him.
> P: Yes, my Fuehrer.[13]

Aside from the ironies implied in this display of gratitude in return for a great crime, and the assurance of support and loyalty coming from the greatest political villains of all time, there is a great deal of buffoonery in Hitler's emotional outburst. Chaplin, of course, could not be familiar with such specific details, but he had the keen eye to observe this side in the Fuehrer character and then the guts to render him on the screen and make the idolized leader of the German nation a mere laughingstock.

Chaplin's comic strategy in dealing with the figure of Hitler is twofold: he parodies actual incidents and characteristics, exaggerating to the point of a complete grotesque picture, and he also draws from the traditional stock of comic gags to create a perfect buffoon. The universal appraisal of *The Great Dictator* is as a brilliant political satire. Gerald Mast calls it "a political cartoon—very funny, very successful at reducing serious questions to silliness."[14] And for Andrew Sarris, "Chaplin's satiric assault on Adolf Hitler, alias Adenoid Hynkel, had already lost most of its context, if none of its conviction, with the outbreak of WWII."[15]

Although, prima facie, *The Great Dictator* is a satire of a sort, there is another, more profound level of comic attitudes which reveals Chaplin's conception of Hynkel. Rather than a mere worthless buffoon whose stupidities we enjoy because of the resentment we feel toward the real ominous figure of Hitler, Chaplin shows Hynkel as a character with demonic dimensions. The hyperkinetic nonentity—he fails in everything he tries to do and literally cannot conceive or accomplish any-thing by himself—is the perpetually active nothing which is the philosophical formula for, or one of the definitions of, the devil. Throughout this film, Chaplin plants numerous references, somehow ignored by all critics, to present Hitler as Satan on earth, whose schemes spring from the root of evil and who threatens to perform an apocalyptic disaster.

The comic form signifying a temporary triumph of the devil is the carnival. The carnival began as a religious festivity in the late Middle Ages, a noisy and riotous revelry in the season immediately preceding Lent. Its unique feature had been the appointment of a distinctly lowly figure from the community as the master of the celebrations. In the context of the pious and hierarchical medieval world, the carnival signified a reversal of universal order: the momentary sovereignty of the devil and an opportunity for the community to revel in satanic temptations. In *The Great Dictator* the emphasis on food, culminating with the hilarious buffet dinner for Hynkel and Napaloni, is a carnivalistic element. Interestingly, the open-ing sequence prepares the ground for the carnivalistic interpretation. We have to remember that in the first battle scenes we don't know whether Charlie plays the barber or the future dictator. After all, Hitler was indeed a mere corporal in the German army during World War I. The deliberate ambiguity is rather important because what the two characters share in common is an innate identical physical appearance and a similar social point of departure. However, in the beginning the little moustached soldier is defined as being the last in the line. The orders go from one commander to the second in rank, and Charlie is the last one, with nobody behind. In time, his replica is going to turn the world topsy-turvy. This development is foreshadowed in the famous sequence where, due to a mechanical problem, the plane in which Schulz and Charlie are escaping turns around and they see and experience the world upside down.

In addition, there are numerous supporting elements which underscore the satanic character of the great dictator. For example, when Schultz betrays Hynkel by refusing to go along with his mad policies, Hynkel cries, "Why have you forsaken me?" Through the reversing humor, the use of Jesus' words establishes the dictator as an anti-Christ figure. The dictator's name implies another hint of his satanic stature. *Hinken* in German means to limp, and this particular disfiguration associates Hynkel with another famous devil, the wooden-legged Mephistopheles from Goethe's *Faust*. And Hinzel or Hinzelmann is also the name of a German demon.

Chaplin, then, did not merely ridicule Hitler but also suggested a satanic figure threatening to create universal havoc. But still, can we derive fun and be stirred to laugh from the comic presentation of Hitler? Hitler's "achievements" were too real and too awesome even for the subtle tragicomic attitudes of the "absolute comic."[16] And yet, decent people watch *The Great Dictator* and usually enjoy it, even when they are aware of the enormity of the Holocaust. The solution to this apparent paradox is that Chaplin's film is successful to the extent that it deals with the general phenomena of megalomania, racism, social prejudices, and totalitari-anism. We develop moral identification with the comic vilification of the character who stands for all these immoral issues. But the Holocaust was too awesome, too concrete and too painful to be measured or even comprehended in the general terms of megalomania, prejudices, and totalitarianism. Its enormity and singularity defy the comic. Charles Chaplin, one of the greatest comedians of all time, fully acknowledged this: "Had I known of the actual horrors of the German concentration camps," declared Chaplin, "I could not have made fun of the homicidal insanity of the Nazis."[17]

Transport from Paradise. The Transport.

Transport from Paradise. The "Paradise."

The Fifth Horseman Is Fear. Dr. Braun in the çonfiscation center.

Diamonds of the Night. Hunger and terror of the young fugitives in the hostile Sudeten regions.

Diamonds of the Night. A flashforward surrealistic image of the extreme emotions of hope and fear.

The Shop on Main Street. Tono's family, his wife (on the right), her sister, and Markus: the complacent collaborators and bystanders.

The Shop on Main Street. Tono and Mrs. Lautmann (Ida Kaminska): his genuine human concern and her horror at the face of crumbling humanity.

The Garden of the Finzi-Continis. The beginning: Mikol (Dominique Sanda) and Alberto (Helmut Berger) hugging in the center; the distance between the characters reflects the social divisions of the Jewish community.

The Garden of the Finzi-Continis. The end: everybody united in the old school building, sharing the fate of the Jews during the Holocaust.

The Damned. The beginning of glamorous opulence and apparent family harmony. Sitting around the table from right to left: Elisabeth (Charoltte Rampling), Martin (Helmut Berger), Friedrich Bruckman (Dirk Bogarde), Sophia (Ingrid Thulin), Konstantin (Rene Kolldehoff), Guenter (Renand Verlay), Aschenbach (Helmut Griem), and Baron Joachim von Essenbeck (Albrecht Shoenals).

The Damned. The end: Hitler's last days in the bunker with Eva Braun inspired this grotesque wedding ceremony which marks Martin's rise to power.

The Damned. A dramatization of The Night of the Long Knives of orgy and destruction serves as a central metaphor for the Nazi rule of orgy and destruction.

Night and Fog. The irony of Goethe's oak in Buchenwald. The tree was destroyed by the Allies' bombardment at the end of the war.

Distant Journey. The band provides music for the funeral march of the marchers.

CHAPTER V

Modernist and Post-Modernist Comprehensions of the Nazi Terror and Inhumanity

To the post-Auschwitz mind, the greatest challenge of the Nazis' attempted genocide of the Jews is, perhaps, neither representation nor presentation but that of comprehension. The Holocaust appears to be incomprehensible because it demonstrates the existence of states and events composed of fundamentally contradictory elements. Dictionaries define contradictions in terms of linguistic statements or logical forms. To contradict usually means "to assert the contrary or opposite of; deny directly and categorically, to speak or declare against." The terrifying aspect of the Holocaust was the actualization of contradictions. It presents a disorienting reality on which the mind always stumbles, a horrific existence that haunts our belief in humanity and culture. The basic notions and precepts of understanding forms relating to human nature, historical developments, the value of social norms, God's very existence—in each of their various alternative intellectual positions they suffered a severe blow in the universe that created Auschwitz.

Germany, the nation of Kant, Beethoven, Goethe, Brahms, Thomas Mann, became the nation of Goebbels, Himmler, and Hitler. The fine democratic system of the Weimar Republic gave birth to Hitler's totalitarianism (there was no "seizure of power"; Hitler became the tyrant of Germany following elections and legal political maneuverings). Masses of people who had been raised on the tenets of humanist education adhered to Hitler's satanic theories. Goebbels, a Ph.D. in the liberal arts, underwent a "spiritual rebirth" after reading *Mein Kampf.* Hitler was an aspiring artist. Goethe's oak in Buchenwald. Music in Auschwitz. . . . Advances in twentieth-century technology became the tools of massive destruction. Scientific research produced Zyklon B, the gas used to exterminate

millions of people. The elaborate bureaucracy of annihilation was ordered to perform "productively." Human psychology revealed unprecedented reversals: a
mother killing her baby out of courage and mercy; a Nazi killing a child to obtain
the child's apple; children being thrown alive into ovens. "Why?" asked the judge
in the post-war trial. "Why? To save bullets," answered the Nazi. An Auschwitz
doctor wrote in his diary: "Bicycle trip. Wonderful weather . . . present at 11
executions, three women begged for their lives, fresh samples taken from lower
spleen and pancreas." After the war this doctor declared: "The purpose of this
work was purely scientific," explaining that human flesh was used "because the
guards ate the beef and horse meat received for use in our bacteriological research."[1]
If science, technology, art, liberal education, democracy, and cultural tradition
were all diverted to the service of the devil, where was God? If there is Providence,
why was God silent when his "chosen people" were being liquidated? And why
did his deputy on earth, the Pope, remain silent despite direct appeals for interference and assistance?[2] Perhaps this silence is related to the oldest contradiction
of all, the terrible cultural malaise of antisemitism, or, as Anne Frank put it, that
"the people who brought good to the world" have been perpetually persecuted by
most of their fellow human beings.

In our final chapter, we shall see how a few remarkable films, created by
cinema *auteurs*, have attempted to meet the challenge of giving penetrating and
thoughtful visions to the searing contradictions of World War II. Compared with
Chaplin's movie, these works manage to go a step further, or deeper, in their
conceptual approach to the Final Solution. *The Great Dictator* displays the shortcoming of the artistic imagination to cope with the special nature of Hitlerism, in
spite of the film's outstanding triumph as the first unqualified attack against the
ostensible evils of Nazism. (Actually, Chaplin's failure and triumph are closely
interrelated. For in order to secure the success of his anti-Nazi film in sociopolitical
terms—that is, maximum exposition of the Nazi monster to most audiences, and
an uncompromising conceptual vilification of the Hitler phenomenon—Chaplin
used the weapon of humor and the arsenal of comic gags and motifs which had
brought him unmatched fame and popularity.) After the war, without the political
urgency that fueled Chaplin's commitment, and in a climate that allowed—and
at times even encouraged—serious cinematic art works, we find new attempts to
reflect on the profound crises encompassed by the Holocaust experience. First,
some brief general remarks on the cultural, socioeconomic, and historical background of these works.

In the late fifties cinema entered a new phase of its development into the
modernist stage. The works of Ingmar Bergman (*The Seventh Seal*, 1957), Federico
Fellini (*La Dolce Vita*, 1959), the French New Wave (Jean-Luc Godard's *Breathless*,
1959), and Alain Resnais's (*Hiroshima Mon Amour*, 1959) heralded an entirely
new approach to the language of cinema, to the range of subject matters and
sensibilities expressed in the medium, and to a new mode of film production. By
the latter I am referring to a new kind of authorship in cinema: the creation of
films that are designed to exhibit the distinct personal visions of their directors,
who choose cinema as the medium to express their artistic and philosophical at-

titudes. In his book *Cinema Eye, Cinema Ear: Some Key Filmmakers of the Sixties*, John Russel Taylor cites a statement made by French critic Alexander Astruc "as the manifesto of the new cinema."

> I call this new age of cinema that of the Caméra stylo. This image has a very precise sense. It means that the cinema will break away little by little from the tyranny of the visual, of the image for its own sake, of the immediate anecdote, of the concrete, to become a means of writing as supple and as subtle as that of written language. No area must be barred to it. The most austere meditation, attitudes to all human works, psychology, metaphysics, ideas, passions are very precisely its province. Indeed, these ideas and visions of the world are such that today the cinema is capable of giving them full realization.[3]

Most artists who tried to realize Astruc's manifesto have worked in western Europe, especially in Italy and France, which, along with Hollywood, have been the main centers of film production in the west. Individualistic filmmakers had the opportunity to develop in France and Italy because these countries were free from the rigid political impositions of Communist bloc countries or the equally tyrannical demands of Hollywood to secure financial profits. Therefore, they did not have to succumb to popular taste and convictions or to previously proven successful formulas, but rather were able to pursue their personal style and vision.

For nearly two decades after the war and its immediate aftermath, the west Europeans were reluctant to treat openly their war experiences. Indulgence in recovery, and perhaps a sense of shame about the past, were key reasons for the apparent suppression of the subject. Whereas in eastern Europe the socialist regimes fostered the lessons of World War II as a heroic struggle against western fascism, in the west the foregrounding of the subject was carried out mostly by the rise of a young generation who treated the war with much curiosity and little traumatic complexity.

In regard to the Holocaust, the people of western Europe were spared the atrocities of mass killings by *Einsatzgruppen* and death camps for millions of people. They witnessed the persecutions up to the point when the Jews were deported to the east. However, the impact of massive victimization of the Jewish communities on the mentality and cultural makeup of western Europe was enormous. The Jews of western Europe were, by and large, assimilated and highly integrated within Gentile society. They participated in its politics and sometimes attained high political positions; they were active in social trends at all levels of the social fabric, made significant contributions to the national culture, and in most cases developed benign friendly and deep relationships with their neighbors. The uprooting of the Jewish community was, therefore, an act of literal and brutal amputation, which, excepting the antisemites, most sensitive people found painful. Moreover, when the tragedy happened, the local population by and large remained passive bystanders, doing little or nothing to help their Jewish compatriots. For most honest people the fear of the Nazi terror paralyzed action but not the sense of guilt or shame. Finally, the most reflective attitudes show awareness of the fact that Nazism was born in the culture of western Europe. Hence, they regard its momentary triumph and monumental disasters, exemplified above all by the onslaught against the Jews, as crucial testimony to the failure of western culture either to prevent Nazism from happening or to stop it when it became destructive.

The films that express such attitudes are the products of artists with distinct modernist sensibilities and consciousness, employing forms and themes derived from the major trends of twentieth-century literature. Each film in this category focuses on a different kind of participant in the historical drama, the Jews, the bystanders, and the Nazis. But more important, each of them displays a distinct approach to its subject in terms of narrative strategy, mise-en-scène conception, and the thematic concerns that the narrative entails. We shall study the films in order to define and explain these approaches and analyze their applicability to the subject of the Holocaust.

Mythical Patterns and Apocalyptic Visions

In 1969, Luchino Visconti created The Damned, a sort of "Elizabethan drama" on one Krupp-like industrialist family whose career reflects the story of the Third Reich. Hailed by many critics as one of cinema's masterpieces, The Damned embodies Visconti's attempts to explore seriously the roots, cultural makeup, and social fabric of the Nazi state. In addition to its somber content, the film's formal approach is highly complex, employing stark realism, heavy symbolism, expressive visualization, and mythological figurations.

The Italian filmmaker Luchino Visconti, who had begun his career with social dramas heralding the style of neorealism, later distinguished himself as one of the most stylistic directors in the world. Visconti usually drew his themes and stories from the works of such great literary masters as Thomas Mann and Albert Camus, and incorporated elements from classical mythology. Visconti prepared the script for The Damned after a thorough study of the historical material, augmented by his own personal impressions of Nazi Germany formed during a visit there in the mid-thirties.[4] The story outline was finished in November 1967, and the ambitious production was financed by Italian, Swiss, American, and British companies. The international nature of the project is best reflected in the cast, made up of well-known actors from seven European countries. Each of the leading actors gave a remarkable performance as an associate of the central family and as a representative figure for German society, portraying realistic character and behavior while simultaneously projecting mythical dimensions.

The head of the family is Baron Joachim von Essenbeck, played by Albrecht Shoenals. An old, dignified man, he plans to retire as chairman of the family's industrial empire, a move that sparks a bloody struggle for control and leads to his murder. Shoenals projects "a distinguished-looking old man with something of the pathos of an ancient bloodhound about to be put away for its own good."[5] The tragic fatigue—associated with the Baron's old age, his dying class, and the past disasters of his family and country—is poignantly conveyed when we see him staring at the picture of his only son, who was killed in World War I. The baron also represents the figure of Hindenburg, the respected old president of the Weimar Republic who, out of feebleness and shortsightedness, was instrumental in giving power to Hitler. The aging aristocrat in Visconti's movie is the first victim of the Nazi schemes, an apt demonstration of the expiring process of his class and the beginning of the new order of an unrestrained, murderous political system.

Ingrid Thulin from Sweden plays the role of Baroness Sophia von Essenbeck, the widow of Joachim's son. The aristocratic lady is deeply involved in bloody intrigues designed to promote her lover, Friedrich Bruckman, to the ruling position, but at the end they both fall prey to SS schemes. Monica Stirling remarked that Thulin's "mixture of abnormal strength with equally abnormal fragility made her an ideal choice for Sophie—who is in many respects a perfect illustration of Goethe's dictum that, in Germany, romanticism sought to be classified as a notifiable disease."[6] Sophie's changing visual appearance signifies the full cycle of her character's development and its broader implications in the context of Nazi Germany. She first appears seductive and smiling, her whole face filling the screen, which is lit in red and black to convey her demonic dimension. At the end, moments before her ceremonial suicide, Sophie's deathly white face, with its blood-red lipstick, black-rimmed eyes, and yellowish teeth, displays the grotesque horror of her metamorphosis and the total damnation of her kind.

Friederich Bruckman was played by the Dutch-born British actor Dirk Bogarde. Bruckman is not part of the aristocracy, but as a skillful manager and Sophie's lover he seeks to control the Essenbeck family. Presented in the script as the film's protagonist,[7] Bruckman represents the lust for power, bound by no moral inhibitions. At the same time Bruckman's relatively low status is a constant source of his inferiority complex and lack of confidence. The true force behind him is Aschenbach (another reference to Thomas Mann, as this is the name of the hero of *Death in Venice*), the Baron's nephew and the family's member of the SS. Helmut Griem portrays the SS prototype—flashy, impeccable, intriguing, and highly civilized. Aschenbach regards *Mein Kampf* as somewhat common and quotes Nietzsche with dubious cynicism. He also possesses considerable understanding of the weaknesses of human nature and the characters around him, which allows him to manipulate them at will. He is the chief perpetrator in the drama, orchestrating intrigues and murders to achieve the final triumph of his organization.

The bullying Konstantin von Essenbeck (Rene Kolldehoff) is the opposite of Aschenbach as the gross and rumbustious SA officer. Although von Essenback's historical model is the notorious Ernst Roehm, Rene Kolldehoff projects a charm bestowed by energy and self-indulgence so as to give an impression of good nature. Even his depraved homosexuality appears pardonable vis-à-vis his manipulation and ultimate victimization by the snaky Aschenbach.

The younger generation in the drama is also composed of a gallery of representative characters. Herbert Thalmann (played by the Italian Umberto Orsini) has the name of the leader of the German Communists who was murdered by the Nazis. In the film Thalmann is the liberal leftist who is framed as a murderer by Aschenbach's plotting. He is forced to give himself up to save his two children after his wife (played by the British actress Charlotte Rampling), a member of the

Essenbeck family, dies in a concentration camp. Gunther (played by Renand Verlay from France) is Konstantin's son, who begins as a sensitive young musician but after his father's death he is lured by Aschenbach to join the ranks of the SS.

And finally we come to Martin, who is undoubtedly the central figure in *The Damned*. The grandson of Baron Joachim and the future heir to the family steelworks, Martin grew up spoiled, neurotic, and a drug addict. His mindless attitudes toward politics and the family's business give the others the opportunity to struggle for control of the Essenbeck fortune. Martin himself indulges in perverse sexual pleasure. He is a transvestite and a molester of little girls, and he finally rapes his mother. Despite his decadence and perversities, Martin, with the aid of the SS, ends up as the Essenbeck in control. The role of Martin was played by Austrian-born Helmut Berger in his first major performance. Stirling noted; "Guided by Visconti, who saw Martin as the complex result of 'a profound dis-education,' Berger gave the vicious little crown prince a touch of soon-to-be-lost vulnerability, as well as tyrannically willful petulance."[8]

The Damned begins with a family dinner at the Essenbeck's castle. The preparation and the family gathering recall Thomas Mann's novel *Buddenbrooks*, subtitled *The Decadence of a Family*. Beneath the magnificent setup and the perfect manners of the family members, there are stormy undercurrents: wild passions, external political turmoil, and the unrelenting struggle within the family hierarchy would soon shatter the apparent harmony. The dinner is in honor of Baron Joachim's birthday. The entertainment which follows dinner begins with young Gunther's cello performance of Bach and ends with Martin's transvestite show impersonating Marlene Dietrich. Martin's performance is interrupted by the news of the Reichstag burning. At the end of the evening Baron Joachim is murdered by Bruckman, and Herbert Thalmann is forced to flee because Aschenbach is about to arrest him for the murder.

Afterwards, Bruckman is appointed president of the board of directors of the steelworks, to the unconcealed dismay of Konstantin. Realizing Aschenbach's intrigues and maneuvering, Konstantin tries to pave his own way to power by blackmailing Martin. While living in a town apartment where he regularly met his mistress, Martin had seduced a Jewish child living in the neighboring apartment. The child committed suicide, and her death is exploited by Konstantin against Martin.

Sophie seeks to protect her son against Konstantin and appeals to Aschenbach. The removal of Konstantin is part of one of the most stunning sequences in the film. Visconti dramatized the "Night of the Long Knives," Hitler's ordered massacre of SA men and their leader Ernst Roehm, on June 30, 1934. The first scene exhibits the rowdy joviality of the vacating Storm Troopers and their depraved orgy at night. When the revelers are asleep, the natural setting of the beautiful countryside is lulling, romantic, and even wistful. The arrival of the SS is observed from a great distance. Gradually the first sounds are identified as motorboats. The steady approach of the SS vehicles' cold lights is particularly expressive against the background of the shadowy figures, dressed in black, whose ominous darkness is visible in the dim light of dawn. The anticipation of death and damnation is actualized with an orgy of destruction, a ruthless manhunt, and systematic cold-blooded murdering of the young SA members in bedrooms, hallways, and bathrooms. Konstantin is the last to die, shot by Bruckman at the instigation of Aschenbach.

The bloody spectacle is the climax at the center of the plot. The rest of the film shows Martin's rise to power as the completion of a demonic cycle, with numerous ironic parallels to the action in the first half of the film. Beginning with another dinner scene around the same dinner table of the film's impressive opening scene, the empty seats constitute an eloquent testimony to the family's casualties. The ongoing process of deterioration is further emphasized by the open hostility which has replaced the former refined politeness. Martin, encouraged by Aschenbach, undermines Bruckman's authority and plans his eventual overthrow. Sophie attempts to help her lover against her son, but she fatally underestimates Martin's wild passions. The bedroom encounter between the mother and son ends in incest as the drugged Martin rapes his mother.

The final act features a grotesque marriage ceremony between Bruckman and Sophie, which, like the Baron's birthday, is doomed to lead to their death. Unlike the unexpected shock of the first death, this scene shows a macabre ritual of execution. Martin, dressed in a Nazi uniform, is the master of ceremonies. The house is full of Nazi flags; soldiers and whores engage in an orgiastic, depraved party which is the complete reversal of the "cultural entertainment" for the old Baron in the beginning. Sophie and Bruckman are forced to poison themselves, and as they lie dead Martin clicks his heels and salutes like a good Nazi. Martin has degenerated to the position of the new great dictator, embodying the full triumph of the Nazi Third Reich. Ironically, this scene was inspired by the bizarre marriage of Eva Braun and Hitler in the Berlin bunker during the last ten days of Hitler's rule, followed by their common suicide. For Visconti this event is not simply a finale to the darkest drama in human history. By displacing it to the beginning of the Nazi reign he presents this macabre act as symptomatic of the entire period and characteristic of its horrific nature.

Visconti focused on the years 1933–1934, for he intended to explore the roots of Nazism. While preparing the script he thoroughly studied the historical material and had declared that William Shirer's The Rise and Fall of the Third Reich was "La nostra Bibbia"—"our Bible."[9] The shocking incident involving the suicide of a young Jewish girl was probably based on the real story of a six-year-old Jewish girl who after being harassed by her schoolmates returned home and hanged herself. When The Damned was released, distributors insisted on cutting a shot of the girl hanging from a rafter, presumably to avoid an unbearable visual horror.[10]

The Essenbecks, all critics hasten to claim, were modeled after the Krupp family. Visconti maintained that he had in mind other prominent industrialists who supported Hitler, "not merely the four-star Krupp, but also the Kirdorfs (coal), Thyssens (steel), Voeglers (steel), Schnitzlers (I. G. Farben chemical cartel), Rostergs and Diehns (Potash), Schroeders (Bankers)."[11] The Marxist Italian director ignored the role of the low-income masses in the rise of National Socialism. However, his work is not a vehicle to a Marxist reading of history. Rather, it appears that Visconti's focus on a representative wealthy family was a harsh reckoning with his own personal background, treating the fundamental flaws of the dying European aristocracy. Ultimately the concerns of *The Damned* are more of character than of social forces, existentialist and not political, mythically oriented rather than materialist.

The mythological trend in the Holocaust discourse is expressed by works employing apocalyptic visions, mythical characters, and the presentation of mythic forces which symbolically operate in the specific historical setting. The underlying thesis of such creations is that the universe of atrocities became the stage for the outburst of dark irrational forces which had previously been artistically conceptualized in both the Greco-Roman mythology and the Judeo-Christian tradition of narrative and visionary writings. Two central aspects of the historical experience lend themselves to mythological approach: the extreme evil of the Nazis, often interpreted as satanic or demonic, and the magnitude of suffering and destruction of the victims, which appears almost literally apocalyptic. Sidra Ezrahi elaborates on that point:

> The images, of course, are at hand; the Jews were branded on their arms with numbers which easily recall the decree of the "second beast" in the book of Revelation: "He compelled everyone—small and great, rich and poor, slave and citizen—to be branded on the right hand or on the forehead." (Rev. 13:16). Certainly the abundance of death and even the manner of death (in a "huge furnace" [Rev. 9:2]) have their analogue in the massive death which precedes redemption in the New Testament version of the Apocalypse. And the religious imagination had already built the bridge between the visionary events and the historical victims by identifying the Jews with the hosts commandeered by the Antichrist, who are destined to battle the army of Christ in the final Armageddon.[12]

The Damned is dominated by mythical overtones. The European title *Gotterdammerung* (in the published Italian script *La Caduta degli Dei*) emphasizes the universal mythical concern rather than a psychological, realistically concrete approach to characters. The film abounds with numerous references to mythic elements. The title, the recurring fire imagery, and the dramatic amber and red lighting suggest an infernal dimension to the story. Martin and his mother Sophie act out the classical Oedipus complex, while Frederick is like Faust to Aschenbach's Mephistopheles. The plot, acting style, makeup, and music evoke the world of Wagnerian opera. Kinder and Houston add:

> Visconti stresses the universality of his theme about the corruption of power by creating a strong mythic level. Struggles move inward and outward, forming concentric circles that comprise an orderly vision of Chaos (as in Dante's *Inferno*). The pervasive tension between chaos and order gives the film a cosmic scope.[13]

Visconti's method in incorporating the mythical material is designed to reverse the inherent meaning of the original form. Serious Holocaust writing tends to employ traditional literary forms but usually turns them upside down. Thus instead of showing a movement toward a positive, life-affirming climax, they concentrate on the process of expiration and annihilation. In *The Damned* Visconti follows rituals of renewal—like the Baron's birthday, the final wedding, the SA spring holiday—with bloody murders. The film begins and ends with images of fire from the steelwork factory, signifying the movement from industry to destruction. The entire action follows a cyclical pattern whose landmarks are spectacles of death enclosed within the man-created hell and the fires of damnation.

Visconti's film is distinguished by its rich and often stunning visual style. The dominant colors are red and black; there is almost no green, the color of natural growth and renewal. The prominence of black contributes to the atmosphere of doom and destruction as well as the dark nature of the unfolding drama. Red is employed in the most expressive manner. The film begins with the orange flames and sparks of the steelwork furnace, signifying the might of the Essenbecks and foreshadowing the outburst of wild forces. The SA orgy is lit in red, to suggest the uncontrolled exercise of lust and perverse passion. Then, in the bloodshed which follows, the red conveys the bloody essence of the Nazi period. The deadly disfiguration of Sophie in the final episode is defined by the black dress, white face, and blood-red lipstick—the national colors of Nazi Germany. The dim red lighting in the final sequence signifies the ultimate twilight as the Nazi party is taking over with the gigantic red flags covering the entire room. The film ends with a dissolve from Martin's face to pictures of the factory's furnace, this time the red is unambiguously the fire of hell.

As most critics agree, "the Von Essenbeck family becomes a microcosm of the entire German society, and Martin plays the role of Hitler."[14] There is no problem in the representative stature of the old baron, Konstantin, Herbert Thalmann, Aschenbach, and even Gunther. But Martin presents the most intriguing and most problematic character, especially for his allegorical portrayal of the great dictator. The conception of Martin's character, particularly the emphasis on his sexual perversions and his representative stature, has irritated some critics. Richard Schickel charged:

One emerges from *The Damned* with the strong impression that the yeast causing the rise of the Third Reich was exotic depravity—transvestism, child molestation, incest. No one denies that the pre-war German power elite was, to put it mildly, an unhealthy organism. But to imply a cause-effect relationship between sexual perversion and political perversion is both historically inaccurate and socially irresponsible. For it has an odd, insulating effect on us, making us feel that totalitarianism is a rare bloom, one that can flower only in very special soil.[15]

The answer to Schickel's complaint is that Visconti does not offer a "cause-effect relationship between sexual perversion and political perversion," but rather allegorical relationships. In Visconti's mythological approach the ancient Eros/Thanatos figuration becomes the underlying mythos for *The Damned*, a key to Visconti's reading, and not rendering, of the Nazi phenomenon.

The connection between Nazism and sexual deviance was first treated in cinema by Roberto Rossellini. In *Rome Open City* (1945), the Nazi commander of the Italian capital and his female assistant are both sexually perverse. It is remarkable that Rossellini's presentation of the German headquarters, a micropicture for Nazi culture in general, is strikingly similar to Visconti's vision—both directors used an attractive baroque setting projecting an image of a highly civilized environment, but in essence the appearance is artificial, covering up a decadent existence. In *Germany Year Zero* (1946), Rossellini again features a schoolmaster who has been dismissed from his job because of his unrepentant Nazi views, and who in his current unsavory lifestyle indulges in the seduction of young children.

The combination of Nazism and sexual perversity has become a popular motif in film and literature. This motif is usually used to highlight both physical decadence and moral degeneracy, emphasizing the inherent linkage between the two. It was Sigmund Freud, through his study of the Eros/Thanatos complex, who established a direct linkage between sex and violence. Freud gained a universal reputation with his instinct theory on the primacy of Eros as the source of human behavior and psychological complexes. Eros represents the life-enhancing forces, egoistic and self-preservative impulses, and sexual desires. Under the shocking influences of the massive carnage in World War I, Freud modified his views, claiming a dualistic theory of instincts by positing Thanatos, a death instinct which works against the life instincts of Eros. Thanatos refers to an innate tendency to self-punishment in the individual, and in more general terms, to all those forces that deny life and disrupt civilized existence.[16]

Interesting conclusions emerge from Freud's work which can apply to theorizing about the Nazi phenomenon. First, if Nazism means essentially destruction and the ultimate assault on civilized existence, then it demonstrates the triumph of Thanatos and the defeat of Eros with its healthy life instincts. But the Nazi barbarism grew and developed in the heart of civilized Europe, and, notwithstanding some German attempts to show it as the invasion of external forces, it was born in the German-speaking parts of the continent. This means that Nazism implies the existence of an inherent destructive inclination, or a profound disturbance of the organism; in this context the organism is the German society or even western culture in general. According to Freud, sexual perversities (such as sadomasochism) are the most conspicuous examples of the dynamic interaction between the positive Eros and the negative Thanatos. Moreover, the existence of excessive sexuality, in any of its forms, indicates the uncensored operation of primal instincts. In *Civilization and Its Discontents* (1930), Freud argued that cultural progress is preconditioned on the taming of the primal impulses, and that social and civilized stability necessitated the restraint of instinctual strivings. These ideas are the underlying premises of such social thinkers and philosophers as Wilhelm Reich, Herbert Marcuse, and, more recently, Michel Foucault, who explore the relationships between political trends and sexual drives.

Hitler's obsession with the threat of Jewish sexual corruption, and the pornographic Nazi magazine *Der Sturmer*, published by one of the most prominent and most obnoxious Nazis, Julius Streicher, indicate that sexuality was a major element in the dynamics of the Third Reich. In Freud's terms, the Nazi obsession with sexuality demonstrates the retreat from life guided by cultural values to instinctual behavior. Remarkably, but not surprisingly, the fanatic Nazi claims for racial biological elitism led to the persecution of homosexuals while many Nazis were themselves homosexuals. The most notorious examples involve Ernst Roehm, leader of the SA, and the relatively high incidence of homosexuality throughout the SS.[17]

In *The Damned* Martin and Aschenbach represent the essence of Nazism. Aschenbach is the epitomy of the smooth, yet extremely sinister cultural refinement, whereas Martin embodies the truly dark forces, the primal demonic drives which ultimately made use of the Aschenbachs to draw the world into an orgy of destruction. What Visconti projects then in *The Damned* is the collapse of cultural appearance and civilized existence—a point clearly illustrated by the mise-en-scène as we compare the Essenbeck's palace at the beginning and the end—resulting from the assault of dark instincts, mythical in their dimension, sexually perverse in their nature, and satanic in their effects.

To sum up, Visconti features the apocalyptic and the demonic through visual evocations of inferno, further suggested by the film's title, the Mephistophelean character of Aschenbach, whose black costume and extraordinary cunning is also reminiscent of the devilish snake from the Bible, the employment and then inversion of mythological rituals of growth and renewal, and finally the invocation of the Eros/Thanatos forces. At the same time, Visconti's concern is ultimately with a very concrete reality, and his work is often classified as a demonstration of fine realism.[18] Consequently, *The Damned* displays an unresolved tension between the mythical dimension and its level of psychological realism. The uneasy marriage between strong realistic referentiality and highly suggestive mythologization is brought into sharp focus in the case of the dramatic agents, who need to play both mythical roles and psychologically complex characters. Some critics found this combination confusing and unbridgeable. John Simon wrote a raged critique: "*The Damned*, included in the ten-best pantheon of both Vincent Canby and Judith Crist, is meant to be tragic and terrifying, but it emerges as the ludicrous flailings of puny puppets in inscrutable wooden frenzies."[19] But Visconti's main goal was to project the extraordinary nature of the era as truthfully as possible. On the other hand he mythologized this reality out of certain metaphysical convictions, but also because relatively unstylized, believable realism might have "the effect of humanizing the incomprehensible terror, of making it comprehensible, and therefore diminishing it."[20]

The apparent stylization of the concentration camp universe creates an interesting problem regarding the representation's cathartic effect. There is always the danger that the indulgence in the tragedies and horrors is designed to elicit aesthetic effects at the expense of moral sensitivities to issues of humanity and inhumanity. We shall elaborate on this point through a comparison between Visconti's *The Damned* and Chaplin's *The Great Dictator*, for these two films deal with the subject of evil, whose artistic conceptualization always risks confusing moral perceptions with aesthetic gratifications. George Steiner makes an interesting observation about the delicate relations between aesthetics and morality, or the potential danger of dealing with the Holocaust in artistic terms.

Not only is the relevant material vast and intractable; it exercises a subtle, corrupting fascination. Bending too fixedly over hideousness, one feels queerly drawn. In some strange way the horror flatters attention, it gives to one's own limited means a spurious resonance. . . . I am not sure whether anyone, however scrupulous, who spends time and imaginative resources on these dark places can, or, indeed, ought to leave them personally intact. Yet the dark places are at the center. Pass them by and there can be no serious discussion of the human potential.[21]

Visconti's *The Damned* attempts to expose the dynamic of the German society which culminated with the triumph of Nazism. As noted before, each of the characters represents a distinct and general political attitude. In Chaplin's work, the focus is on the single man at the top of the social pyramid. Chaplin ignores the implications of general social developments and their contribution to the Nazi phenomenon, considering the multitudes of Hitler's supporters as victims of tyranny. For Chaplin, the collapse of moral decency in the Nazi state is rooted in the Fascist dictatorship and its regimentation, which turned the people into mindless functioning machines.[22] Chaplin's approach concentrates the evil in one individual and in a way might give some credence to the Nazis' claim that they were "just" obeying orders.

Visconti's views of human nature are much more complex. His examination of Nazism involves a problematic treatment of fundamental and profound human instincts. For Chaplin, the case is much simpler. In one of Hynkel's feverish speeches, Chaplin shows the dictator pausing for a glass of water. Mast observed that after cooling his overheated throat, "he also splashes some water down his trousers; his genitals are as overheated as his tonsils. With this gesture Chaplin implies that the Nazi mania has as much to do with the sex organs as with words, and more to do with either than with ideas."[23] This view is obviously untenable to the post-Freudian mind. Visconti's is the disillusioned, modernist world which cannot ignore, actually because of the Holocaust's impact, an inherent complicity of human nature—notwithstanding its basic physical needs—and human ideas with man-inflicted disasters.

Chaplin, on the other hand, denies the existence of an active evil in the human realm by presenting Hitler as a satanic figure, the Devil on earth. Visconti's mythological attitudes are more equivocal because of the ambiguity of the mythical reference in *The Damned*. The use of mythology is intended to enrich our understanding of the central characters. By drawing our attention to literary archetypes and placing the film's characters within the context of the entire western heritage Visconti emphasizes the enormity of Nazism. At the same time, the complementary realism illustrates the literal incarnation of what was formerly conceived of as only imaginary evil. Chaplin, then, created a topsy-turvy world, a crazy Tomania in the image of the devilish dictator. Visconti's inferno is concrete—the factory's flames are real, and they produced the machine guns which in the hands of the *Einsatzgruppen* killed nearly two million Jews. Having the advantage of hindsight, Visconti did not have to imagine hell, he simply showed it, or, more accurately, showed its roots and beginning, and alluded to or visually suggested its infernal implications.

To sum up, while Chaplin's reading of Nazism is given in terms of the treatment of general issues of Fascism, dictatorship, imperialism, and regimentation, Visconti displays a greater awareness of the unique character of the Nazi era. Thus, when asked why he chose to deal with Nazism rather than with Fascism, Visconti made an intriguing statement:

> Because of the difference between tragedy and comedy. Of course Fascism was a tragedy in many many cases. . . . But as a perfect archetype of a given historical situation that leads to certain types of criminality, Nazism seems to me more exemplary—because it was a tragedy that, like a hideous bloodstain, seeped over the whole world. . . . Nazism seems to me to reveal more on a historic reversal of values.[24]

Chaplin has in a way defined the limits of the comic approach to Nazism through the presentation of Herring and Garbitsch as the archetypal Nazi characters. One projects physical power and a weak mind, treating his victims with brutality, but is "punished" by being ridiculed as a mindless bully—the comic attitude thus fulfills the audience's revengeful resentment toward the bad Nazi. The other one is flashy and impeccable, controlling his victims through intrigues and shrewdness. This Nazi cunning is combined with manifested, often self-conscious and self-satisfied immorality which projects a particularly detestable character. Garbitcsh, then, is the precursor of Aschenbach, and Martin is a dramatic offspring of Herring.

However, the most important differences between *The Damned* and *The Great Dictator* that postulate them as exemplary modes of attitudes toward the Nazi reality lie in their aesthetic approaches to their subject. The vast aesthetic difference between *The Damned* and *The Great Dictator* is visible in practically every image. Chaplin's mise-en-scène is in the style of classical Hollywood studio realism, subordinated, in this specific work, to its allegorical significations. The precise reproductions of authentic photographs are intended to achieve the effect of political cartoons, reminding the audience of a true reality but inverting its literal meaning with the weapon of humor. In *The Damned*, the mise-en-scène is an essential part of the fictional story and its multiple ideas. Thus, the book-burning scene in *The Damned* is a powerful dramatic re-creation of the original event, and it exerts profound effects on the fictional character Guenther. The destruction and burning of the barber's shop in *The Great Dictator* is primarily a reminder of the Kristallnacht, intended to elicit the feeling of general pathos without any specific dramatic implication (it can be viewed as an indication of Charlie's return to the role of the homeless wanderer). Hynkel's palace represents the vanity and pomposity of the great dictator. Its huge dimensions and the funny baroque decorations underscore the empty space in which Hynkel operates. The few objects in the room prove to be props for comic gags, ridiculing Hynkel's disorientation. Interior shots of the Essenbeck's palace have an entirely different effect. The external style is in truly good taste, and not exaggerated or grotesque. Through deep focus shots and elaborate camera movement Visconti shows how the vastness of the big rooms reflects deep psychological voids. The different characters, each with a distinct dramatic personality, are scattered in the large space, the physical distance between them reflects the emotional distance despite the familial relationships. The multiple meanings of *The Damned*'s mise-en-scène and its various effects on the dramatic characters make it an important source of symbolism. On the other hand, Chaplin's use of the mise-en-scène to further emphasize his single-minded approach to Hynkel makes the visual images allegorical rather than symbolic.

At the same time, the complexity and ambiguity of *The Damned* are potentially dangerous in terms of the moral impact of the work. In Chaplin's work, the moral codes are unambiguous, and his condemnation of Hitlerism is manifested in every aspect of the film's style, narrative, characterization, and mise-en-scène. By combining the pathetic story of Hannah with wild, cinematic political cartoon, Chaplin made direct appeal to the basic emotional and intellectual faculties of the viewers, determining the desired moral attitudes. On the other hand, the complexity and sophistication of Visconti's film result in a rich work of art, designed to exorcise Fascist malice and decadence through catharsis. But the cathartic reaction is never predictable, simply because it is based on the strategies of absorption and rejection. It is possible that the second stage of rejection, or purgation, will not materialize. In that case the cathartic approach achieves exactly the opposite effect in regard to the desired reaction of the beholder toward the represented subject matter. Susan Sontag relates a curious incident which exemplifies this observation. "The left-wing organizers of a current exhibition of Nazi painting and sculpture (the first since the war) in Frankfurt have found, to their dismay, the attendance excessively large and hardly as serious-minded as they had hoped. Even when flanked by didactic admonitions from Brecht and by concentration-camp photographs, what Nazi art reminds these crowds of is—other art of the 1930's, notably Art Deco."[25] Similarly, the attempt to re-create the Nazi reality on the screen could end up more appealing than appalling; or, the aesthetic pleasure derived from effective realism and the achievements of verisimilitude can be associated with the appeal of the reproduced reality.

Visconti's somber, highbrow drama enjoyed a surprising popular success. Unfortunately *The Damned* has contributed to a distinct kind of fascination with the Nazi era, a new cultural trend which sees in Nazism a source for cheap romantic indulgences and aesthetic attractions. Visconti's work, undoubtedly inadvertently, has inspired numerous works which exalt in the perception of a period with uncensored behavior, and yet a period characterized by a special attention toward aesthetics and quasi-ritual ceremonies. In particular, reflections on the Nazi era serve to release the human impulse to play with the dark spheres of human nature. Nazism is a model for the realization of the terrifying effects of these dark forces—instinctual forces, which are often conceptualized in mythological terms—but, at the same time, the Nazi concern with formal aesthetics helps to define a distance of playfulness in reflections on the era. In other words, this approach to Nazism offers sensual, or instinctual, stimulations, and then their gratification through the medium of artistic verisimiltude, which also ensures a comfortable distance from the real terror of Nazism because of the inherent playfulness of the discourse of art.

The most conspicuous demonstration of this trend can be found in a branch of pornography, including x-rated movies and dime novels, which makes extensive use of World War II settings and Nazi paraphernalia to play upon the pornographic imagination. The examples range from highbrow works like Lina Wertmuller's *Seven Beauties* and Liliana Cavani's *The Night Porter* to the cheap sexploitations of the porno industry. These works feature the interaction of Eros and Thanatos, sex and violence, uncensored gratification and brutal oppression, which in the historical case of Nazism were also particularly demonstrated in a special concern with biological reproduction coupled with the creation of factories of death. The vices of these works, in the context of our discussion, lie in their distortion of the real nature of the Holocaust. They spread false notions on the historical experience— for example, suppression of sex rather than excessive resort to it was characteristic of Nazism—and they neutralize the moral sensitivities by focusing on the aesthetic or on other forms of dubious gratification. Thus the evasion of moral indignation in favor of indulgence with aesthetics, sensual stimulation, or all kinds of supposedly amoral speculations, such as the nature of instinctual behavior, has become one of the serious pitfalls of many works about Nazism and a strategy of reprehensible falsification of the true meaning of the Holocaust.[26]

The Fall of Mr. K.

The enormity of the Jewish tragedy was the result of horrors and atrocities perpetrated by the Nazis and their collaborators. The most atrocious aspects of the war against the Jews were the victims' unimaginable sufferings and the victimizers' unbelievable evil. However, the central universal experience during this critical period was the undisturbed continuation of commonplace existence shared by the millions of those not directly involved with the genocide of the Jews. George Steiner feels that one of the most disturbing contradictions that has emerged from the Holocaust reality is what he calls "the time relation," by which he means the incomprehensible contemporariness of Auschwitz with the general pace of human culture, the temporal and also the spatial affinity of "the other planet" to the ongoing progress of ordinary life. Writes Steiner:

Precisely at the same hour in which Mehring or Langner [victims of the camps] were being done to death, the overwhelming plurality of human beings, two miles away on the Polish farms, five thousand miles away in New York were sleeping or eating or going to a film or making love or worrying about the dentist. This is where my imagination balks. The two orders of simultaneous experience are so different, so irreconcilable to any common norm of human values, their coexistence is so hideous a paradox—*Treblinka is both because some men have built it and almost all other men let it be* [emphasis mine]. . . . it becomes exceedingly difficult to grasp the continuity between normal existence and the hour at which hell starts, on the city square when the Germans begin the deportations, or in the office of the Judenrat or wherever, an hour marking men, women, children off from any precedent of life, from any voice "outside," in that other time of sleep and food and humane speech.[27]

Of all the peoples of Europe, the French presented the most dramatic example of living under the Nazi occupation with an astonishing degree of complacency.

Initially, France along with Great Britain gallantly declared war against Germany following the Nazi invasion of Poland. But the French army never seriously engaged the Wehrmacht on its western front, passing eight months of inaction in the so-called phony war. When the Germans invaded France from the north on May 17, 1940, they crushed the French army in five weeks, entering Paris on June 13. The French acceptance of the humiliating defeat by a historical foe was extraordinary, considering the cultivation of a proud consciousness as the last grand empire in Europe and their self-esteem as leaders of western civilization and progress. More-over, most French citizens during the war did not allow the new conditions to disturb their petty concerns with personal security and comfort. Paris maintained its status as the center of entertainment, and most Frenchmen in the countryside and the big cities ignored underground calls for active resistance. In southern France the Vichy government was formed under humiliating terms. The Germans gave the French the illusion of sovereignty over one part of their land by installing a pro-fascist regime that cooperated with the Nazis. One of the interviewees in *The Sorrow and the Pity* summarized the French experience during the war.

France collaborated. It is the only European country which collaborated. The others signed armistices, capitulated. This is the only country in Europe which had a gov-ernment which adopted laws which on a socialist level went even further than the Nuremberg laws, since the French racialist criteria were even more strict than the Germans. France was covered with concentration camps: Lurs, Avgeles, Rivesaites, Drancy.

Mr. *Klein* (1976) is a film on both the French duplicity and what Steiner defined as the terrifying "time relation." The movie is a French production, written by an Italian, Franco Solinas (*Kapo, The Battle of Algiers*), and directed by an American-born British director, Joseph Losey, who had previously distinguished himself with several films based on Harold Pinter's screenplays (*The Servant*, 1963, *The Accident*, 1967, *The Go-Between*, 1971). The artistic cooperation demonstrates the socialist concerns of Franco Solinas and a Pinter-like action of "a thinking man's thriller," or "a metaphorical mystery melodrama," about a wartime successful art dealer, Robert Klein (Alain Delon), whose life becomes fatefully entangled with that of a Jewish Klein who is persecuted by the new racial policies.

The germinal idea of Mr. *Klein* can be traced to *The Sorrow and the Pity*. One of the characters in Ophuls's documentary was a Monsieur Klein, a merchant who during the war years was concerned that his name could be mistaken as Jewish and therefore published advertisements assuring his clientele that he was both 100 percent Aryan and 100 percent French.[28]

The obsession with racial segregation is the basis for the opening sequence in Mr. *Klein*. Under the Nuremberg laws and the Nazi racial regulations, to avoid persecution a Gentile had to produce baptismal certificates showing that all four grandparents were Christian. Those who could not obtain these proofs had to attend physiognomy clinics where doctors measured their noses and cheekbones to determine their affiliation with the Jewish race. This practice inspired the ghastly introduction to the Holocaust universe depicted in this film.

A face fills the screen, shot in extreme closeup. We see eyes, a nose, mouth: not enough, for the moment, to decide age or sex. The eyes are wide open perhaps in wonder, perhaps in horror. Now we see the fingers of a second person palpating the flesh of this face, neither gently nor roughly, folding back the upper lip to examine the teeth; turning the head to inspect the lobe of an ear. The camera draws back, and it is seen that the face is that of a middle-aged woman, naked. The fingers are those of a white-coated man who seems to be a doctor. This man now speaks, dictating notes to a secretary: lower lip fleshy . . . prognathous jaw typical of non-European races . . . could well belong to the Semitic race . . . case doubtful.[29]

This powerful scene accomplishes several things. It makes visual the monumental obscenity involved in citizens' readiness to lend themselves to this humiliating process and physicians' commitment to providing this "service." The doctor's inhuman attitude toward his subject—he treats her like a laboratory specimen—and the woman's vulnerable nakedness and pitiable expression project a sharp sense of a victim-victimizer relationship. What we actually see is not only an illustration for the initial stage in the persecution process, the identification of the victims, but actually a selection episode with the man in white evoking the satanic character of doctor Mengele, who determined the lives and deaths of thousands after brief "clinical" observations and with a slight nod of his head.

Though the central character in *Mr. Klein* is not Jewish, the film deals with the issue of antisemitism as an essential component of the war reality. Losey is not interested in the overt and coarse forms of antisemitism. He chooses to focus on the mainstream of French society, whose members would publicly deny the existence of prejudices and yet deep inside professed anti-Jewish attitudes.

A delicate and yet penetrating exposition of embedded anti-Jewish sentiments is shown in the Strassburg sequence. Klein travels to visit his father and obtain the Christian birth certificate of his ancestors to prove that he is not Jewish. The conversation between the father and son is a long play of innuendos as the protagonist tries to explain his problem. Avoiding mentioning the word "Jew," Klein assures his father, "it's the law," "just a formality." The father, evidently understanding the situation, simply refuses to come to grips with it. The conversation culminates in the following exchange:

FATHER KLEIN: Well, why do they ask you for all these certificates?
KLEIN: Because it's the law. . . . And besides . . . (Pause; he leans on the back of the armchair, realizing that he can no longer hide the truth) . . . because there is . . . (he sits down in front of his father) another Robert Klein, and it seems that he's Jewish.
. . . .
FATHER KLEIN: Jewish? (Klein approves with a slight nod of his head). Impossible! . . . That's impossible! Or then, this might be the Dutch branch.[30]

Although Pere Klein's antisemitism is comparatively mild, its most disturbing aspect is that it is not self-conscious and it can be maintained without realizing the actual consequences of these attitudes. His son shares the same dangerous insensitivities. When his unsophisticated mistress flees an antisemitic show with disgust, Klein is astounded. He is a man of good humor, and later on when even he himself is deeply entangled in the Jewish persecution, he still enjoys the anti-semitic cartoons in the newspapers. (Losey demonstrates good taste when he avoids satisfying voyeuristic impulses by not showing the obscene cartoons.)

In general, in Klein's circles Jews are virtually nonexistent. The only real contacts he makes with Jews are when he buys their artistic pieces during the war, taking full advantage of their predicament to make ruthless deals. Though not realizing it, Klein actually professes the stage of expropriation and confiscation in the Nazi assault against the Jews. Conveniently, he never notices the signs pro-hibiting Jews from the restaurants and other public places which he freely enters. When he is eventually forced to begin to see things from the victims' point of view, he bursts out in a revealing statement:

> KLEIN: My identity papers have been confiscated, and my car. . . . My paintings were taken away. I'm forbidden to sell or to buy. No more bars, no more buses, no more restaurants, no more movies . . . nothing anymore. Everything is forbidden! According to them, I can't go anywhere anymore, not even to the public restrooms! And all that because my grandmother's certificate has not arrived![31]

Mr. Klein highlights the identification stage of the genocide process. The prologue in the clinic shows one form of identification. The perpetrators' shrewd tactics and efficiency are manifested when Klein learns from the editor of the local Jewish journal that issuing and distributing the paper had been encouraged by the police, who later went on to seize the subscribers list. The process of identification is also illustrated in the image of a huge office where people work on endless files, presumably identifying and sorting out their Jewish victims. This Kafkaesque image is part of a series of brief scenes that interrupt the ordinary flow of the narrative, until we find out at the end that they depict the preparations for a massive roundup of Paris Jews. The two most recurrent pictures include a group of dark figures in massive black coats, symmetrically arranged on both sides of a huge table, sitting in some kind of an administrative office, while the background wall in the center shows the map of Paris. The other image is that of black cars, seen going out on their missions from the central headquarters like black rats, agents of death em-barking to spread a plague. The demonic vision is combined with the stark visu-alization of the modern means (i.e., cars) and the bureaucratic efficiency employed in the service of satanic schemes.

The film's narrative builds up to *la grande rufle*, the notorious day when the French police rounded up thousands of Jews in Paris. Unlike another French movie, *Black Thursday* (Michel Mitrani, 1974), which contrasts the bright daylight of a midsummer day and otherwise a beautiful setting of Paris (the film's original title is *The Gates of the Louvre*, and the magnificent façade of the famous museum is a recurrent image) with the ongoing horrible crime, Mr. Klein provides a grim vision, deliberately setting the event in gloomy winter weather, all in all showing a stark picture of a ghastly situation.

The stadium (Velodrome d'Hiver) in Paris, to which all the Jews are taken, is presented as a concentration camp despite its transitory function. Barbed wires, watchtowers, and guards in black uniforms with huge, intimidating dogs constitute an important part of the scenery. Losey choreographed multitudes of people in situations of extreme overcrowding, expressing confusion and despair amidst scenes of separation and loss, while the soundtrack carries the loud and monotonous roll-call announcements trying to impose order by sorting out the victims before sending them to their deaths. The final image of numerous cattle cars containing the deportees, endlessly crossing the screen, conveys some sense of the magnitude of the Six Million. Thus, after dealing with the themes of identification, concentration, and deportation, the film's climax is dominated by violent images to render in visual terms the inevitable extermination that the deportees were facing. Foster Hirsh described it:

> In the final sequence, the hints sprinkled throughout the film of approaching doom are dramatized with stunning impact. To depict the pogrom, in which the Jews are herded into a stadium and arranged in alphabetical groupings, Losey drains the image of color—the action is shot in a deadly, neutral gray. The frames become increasingly crowded, and Losey uses jerky hand-held cameras to give the sequence a sense of documentary immediacy. Visually, these gray, densely populated, movement filled scenes are set off from the rest of the film. Mr. Klein ends with a chilling descent into darkness, as the protagonist's eyes stare out at us from among the huddled, shadowy figures that surround and engulf him in the packed car.[32]

Although the representation of historical realities is more than a mere background in Mr. Klein, the film, as is indicated by the film's title, does focus on the career of one man. Moreover, according to the published script the presentation of the final roundup sequence against the backdrop of a gloomy winter climate was made in order to reflect the protagonist's condition and state of mind.[33] Indeed, the individual fate of one remarkable character is the main concern of the unfolding drama, the subject of narrative exposition and artistic exploration, and the key to the film's significance and meaning.

While the hero's name was evidently inspired by the incident related in Ophuls's The Sorrow and the Pity, "Klein" in German means small, and the title conveys the notion that Klein represents a common everyman. However, Delon's character is far from being mediocre or commonplace. Mr. Klein is a highly successful social being, leading a glamorous life in a luxurious apartment and surrounded by beautiful women and objets d'art. Quite expectedly, he is overconfident and self-centered, disrespecting others not out of callousness or bad manners but rather because of his consciously high self-esteem. He obviously enjoys his superiority and power. He eyes the Jew who is forced to sell him a painting with a shadow of a smile, appearing like a hunter cornering its trapped prey, deriving pleasure from the inevitable triumphs of his game. An even more sinister outlook of his character is suggested when he is compared to a vulture, for his flourishing business during the war is, after all, based on the remains—the treasures—of the doomed victims, who are as good as dead.

When Klein gets mistakenly entangled in the machinery of persecution his immediate response is to try to correct the mistake and forget about the whole affair. Thus, in addition to his egoism, arrogance, and mindless antisemitic dispositions, his subsequent efforts to prove his non-Jewishness exhibit a morally reprehensible response, showing his refusal to come to terms with the enormous crime being perpetrated against the Jews. He openly declares that he does not question the law—his only concern is to demonstrate that it does not apply to him. In compliance with the Nazi definition of a Jew, Klein tries to prove that his parents as well as all four grandparents were not Jewish. The basic irony of his search is that he finds out that there indeed is Jewish blood in his family. Moreover, since his maternal grandmother was probably Jewish, he seems to be classified as a Jew according to the Nuremberg laws, as well as according to traditional Jewish laws (in Judaism, the offspring of a Jewish mother is defined as a Jew).

The irony of Klein's predicament eventually assumes tragic dimensions. Klein's efforts to remove the threat against his life develop into a serious quest for self-identity involving an existentialist revision of his former ideals and lifestyle. Losey employs numerous mirror shots throughout the movie to indicate the evolving process of self-reflexivity. In the beginning the mirrors function simply to please the hero with his own image. Later on his somber reflections convey a new level of unyielding soul-searching. The protagonist's spiritual development, culminating with the final gaining of a new, elevated moral stature, is correlated by the gradual fall of his material world. Klein's accumulated losses involve his properties, mistresses, and his few dubious friends, but his obsession with his quest makes him indifferent to his physical predicament. What does the protagonist ultimately discover? The film suggests that the full circle of Klein's searches leads to a complete identification with the Jewish Klein he is after. The similarities between the two Kleins extend beyond their identical names and include also their affinity to the arts, their each having a young attractive mistress and an older married lover, and even such little details as each possessing a copy of Moby Dick.[34]

Although we never see the mysterious other Mr. Klein, the identity of the double is further complicated, for the narrative establishes a surrogate "Mr. Klein" as the person who sells Klein a Dutch painting in the beginning of the film. The similarities between them haunt Delon's character as he discovers that like this person whose family had come from Holland, he, too, has a Dutch-Jewish branch on the family tree. When he begins to realize his unjust conduct toward the Jewish victims, Klein develops a special attachment to the Dutch painting he bought from the Jew. When his apartment is emptied out under the rule of expropriation he frenziedly clings to that painting yelling that it's something personal and not merchandise. At the end, after missing a crucial chance to meet the other Klein, he returns to his bare apartment on his last night as a free person and spends the night staring at the painting. This moment illustrates the full change in Klein's personality. He abandons his cynicism, cool manners, and arrogance, and develops new sensitivity toward moral and aesthetic values. The man who considered paintings only in terms of their size and financial value begins to appreciate works of art for what they really are—sources of stimulating reflection and spiritual excitement.

In the final sequence, Klein ignores his lawyer's calls offering him the papers for release and chooses to follow the announcement of "Mr. Klein" in the roll call. In the stadium roll call it is unclear whether he is rushing to the cattle cars to seize and be with the other Klein, or whether he is frantically responding to the announcement of his name. However, he follows the Jewish deportees because his quest to find the other half of Mr. Klein, the metaphorical existence of his deep true self, became for him a matter of life and death. At the very end of the film, Klein is standing inside the cattle car. Immediately behind him is the Jew who sold him the painting. The soundtrack achieves closure by repeating the dialogue between them in the beginning of the film. Thus, the most crucial change in Klein's character is manifested as a growing sense of identification with the Jewish Klein, and the ultimate stage in Klein's development involves a complete identification with the Nazi victims, signaling both the absolute reversal of his career and the new dimension of his character.

Klein's victimization is also a due punishment for his uncritical acceptance of the persecution of the Jews. However, all that befalls Klein is the result of his own doings; like a classical tragic hero, Klein advances his own end and willingly accepts the ultimate conclusion. Mr. Klein assumes almost the tragic stature of Oedipus— the two dramatic characters set out to uncover the source of social and personal unrest, developing in the process a more profound quest for self-identity, only to find out that they themselves are the culprits; in the process they both attain a new level of self-knowledge. The internal action that involves the development of Klein's character reaches one climax when he gains a new understanding of the fundamental flaws in himself and his society and culture. The moment of recognition occurs when he states to his lawyer: "It's all over, I've begun to be fed up with France of today. In this country we are too civilized, too polite, too processed."[35]

Mr. Klein's life is presented as a story of fall and damnation, but as the last quote indicates, the failures of the representative protagonist have broader implications reaching out to the questioning of the entire fabric of a developed civilized society. Klein's business as an art dealer underscores his stature as representative of respectable social status and high culture, whereas his apparent worldly success suggests the profitability of art. The basic ironic attitude toward high culture is implied in showing the expert on the value of art pieces, who is also expected to demonstrate cultural refinement and moral sensitivity, ignoring the pressing reality around him, and when forced to deal with this reality, he chooses the wrong course of action.

The theme of disenchantment with culture is systematically treated in *Mr. Klein*. Setting the story in Paris helps to juxtapose the pretensions of civilized society with the horrors of the war. Major institutions of western culture are introduced as being decadent, bankrupt, impotent, or even as accomplices to the Nazi evil.

The chilly opening in the laboratory features the specter of scientific medical methods in the service of pseudoscientific racist ideology. This beginning—a sort of prologue, unrelated to the narrative itself—defines the film's major theme as well as setting up the mood of the whole work. The lab's glacial colors of foggy white and icy blue dominate the other scenes. Paris has never looked so grim and depressing. The "city of lights" was transformed by Losey into a dark, cold place of mostly narrow lanes in slum neighborhoods, and the urban centers and meeting places are always overcrowded, presenting a gloomy jungle of multitudes of anonymous people devoid of any genuine human rapport between them.

When Klein goes to a church to meet his lawyer friend, the visual splendor of the place and the highly stylistic ritual ceremony present a sharp ironic contrast with the turmoil in the outside world. The irresponsible obliviousness to harsh realities is especially illustrated when Klein's lawyer ignores the desperate look of urgency on Klein's face, silencing him so that he can concentrate on the communion ceremony of his son. Another irony involves the priest's act during the communion service, for the way he touches the waiting open mouths of the tense looking children is reminiscent of the doctor's dehumanized treatment of his patient in the clinic scene.

The castle, where Klein arrives to trace the other Mr. Klein, is another place of pompous cultural pretensions. Numerous paintings on the walls display respect for art and a well-preserved tradition. The landlords organize private chamber music concerts and demonstrate perfect social manners. But aristocratic refinement is merely a veil: there is not a glimpse of human warmth behind the frozen formalities of this decadent environment. The deceptive character of the castle is further reinforced when we find out that the aloof madam actually is having an affair with the mysterious Mr. Klein, who happens to be one of her husband's best friends.

Klein takes his mistress to a cabaret performance, a rather common form of entertainment in Paris during the war. They watch an antisemitic vaudeville act, reminiscent of the infamous Nazi film *Jew Suss*, which had been shown to packed houses in occupied Paris. The act features a sneaky Jew stealing the jewelry of a street singer. Losey chose the grotesque style for this scene to underscore the monstrous combination of entertainment and atrocities. The singer is a female impersonator, dressed and made up in dark expressionistic style, singing a piece from Mahler's *Kindertotenlieder*. Losey allows the hypnotic performance of Mahler's song to go for a while to register its macabre effect before the beginning of the Jew's act, focusing on the audience's reaction rather than on the show itself. The scene was nicely described by Foster Hirsch: "The lighting from below in this scene makes the faces look grotesque, reptilian: the rich, decadent audience, which carries to surreal dimensions the film's motif of indifference, laughs lasciviously at a burlesque of Jewish persecution. In a ghoulish premonition of the holocaust, this well fed audience screeches like a pack of vultures at the mock antics of the onstage racial comedy."[36]

Finally, *Mr. Klein* presents a mechanism of evil perpetrated by established social and cultural institutions. The accessories to the persecution include medical doctors, church goers, aristocrats, and theatrical entertainments, but, ultimately,

Klein is persecuted by the law and is rounded up, as indeed were the Jews of Paris on July 17, 1942, by the legitimate French police force.

While one archetypal model for Mr. Klein can be Oedipus, the real literary model for Losey and Solinas's film is the work of Franz Kafka. Mr. Klein is a Mr. K., and like Joseph K., his life is suddenly disturbed due to the intrusion of a mysterious force. Haunted by an unspecified charge against him, our hero is spurred to conduct a campaign to prove his innocence. The end of this campaign is a new knowledge, namely, the disenchantment with culture, that is somewhat sordid in its philosophical ambiguity but leads however to the protagonist's acceptance of his doomed fate.

A number of motifs, such as the narrative function of the dog, the emphasis on individual paintings and their cabalistic meanings, and the image of the two men carrying the victim between them to his end, further reveal the indebtedness of the film to Kafka's work. The castle sequence, where Klein arrives following an anonymous invitation only to realize that nobody there actually knows him, obviously evokes Kafka's *The Castle*. And Paris as an infernal, urban labyrinth resembles the Kafkaesque setting of *The Trial*. Finally, it is the law which persecutes Klein, and he consciously struggles with that fact. At first he wants to comply with it, but at the end, in his outburst to his lawyer expressing his disgust with France and its excessive civilized life, he declares, "we are too processed." (Kafka's book *The Trial* has the original title *Der Prozess*).

Many critics have noted the connection between Kafka's work and the concentration camp universe. Sidra Ezrahi wrote that "Kafka is the writer whose fiction so fully expressed the logic of modern technology, mechanized sadism, and bureaucratic depersonalization that Auschwitz appears almost as the realization of the fantastic world blueprint in *The Penal Colony*."[37] Gerson Shaked, the prominent Israeli literary critic, in his book on contemporary Hebrew literature discusses the influence of Kafka on modern Israeli writers, particularly on those like Aharon Appelfeld whose fiction revolves around the effects of the Holocaust experience. Shaked asserts: "The Holocaust was a second-to-none realization of the Kafkaesque terror (Angst), and the Jewish victims—a collective K., persecuted by an authority more arbitrary and cruel than anything Kafka depicted in his nightmares."[38]

Other critics as well have noted the indebtedness of Holocaust writers to Kafka. In this connection, Langer mentions such authors as Isaac Rosenfeld, Hermann Kasack, Ilse Aichinger, Primo Levi, and Jakov Lind. But one should also bear in mind the qualifiers used in establishing the analogies between Kafka and the Holocaust. Ezrahi says Auschwitz is "almost" like Kafka's "The Penal Colony" and Shaked admits that the Holocaust was "more" than Kafka's nightmares. Alvin Rosenfeld fully delineates the limits of the analogy.

Nevertheless, even in Kafka's case—as, say, in "In the Penal Colony" or "The Metamorphosis"—we are never led to abandon altogether our hold on a normative, stabilizing sense of things, on the saving power of the mundane. We may be released by his fiction into a universe of absurd and frightening proportions, but it is a highly composed universe, and while few would welcome a prolonged residence there, it is not a totally alien place. . . . "In the Penal Colony" is an uncanny prefiguration of Holocaust literature, a premonitory text. Nevertheless, in reading it we are still a step or two away from a direct knowledge of *history* as Holocaust, and no reader of the novella would confuse the infernal torture machine that is its elaborate centerpiece with the actual machinery of Auschwitz or Treblinka, just as no reader of "The Metamorphosis" would accept Gregor Samsa's transformation into a giant insect as a change that could ever actually overtake him. We accept these intricate literary devices as complex acts of initiation—a series of bridges that we must cross to enter the Kafkaesque world—and once we acknowledge them as such, we are usually content to let the stories take over and develop in their own terms. Since we do not read Kafka within predominantly realistic or naturalistic frameworks, credulity is not unduly strained by these inventions, which we recognize as the components of a profoundly disturbing but nevertheless fictional universe.[39]

The conclusion is then that despite the potential metaphorization of the Kafkaesque world it cannot be equated with the concentration camp universe. Rosenfeld, in effect, calls for unambiguous, indeed incomparable and quite literal depictions of the Holocaust reality to do justice to its singularity. And in *Mr. Klein*, Joseph Losey complements the metaphorical Kafkaesque references with stark pictures of the historical terror, inspired by specific moments of the actual events in France of 1942, and more general icons which have become associated with the concentrationary universe.

Mr. Klein is what is sometimes called an "arty" movie. Complex and sophisticated on the formal and thematic levels, it demands the viewer's full attention and concentration. Hirsh observed: "Losey's pacing is solemn, heavy. There isn't a single light moment in the film. Everything is carefully prearranged—objects, paintings, and tapestries are there for symbolic intent."[40] In addition to the depressing, somber mood, reinforced by the dominant dark and icy colors of the mise-en-scène, Delon's performance is very cool, matching with the narrative strategy to prevent excessive identification with the protagonist.

The film's use of thriller conventions proved to be especially problematic. While the intention is to use thriller narrative devices to make a statement on the concentration camp universe and the general human condition, the accumulation of ambiguities, most left unresolved at the film's end, might be too daunting for most audiences. Others, like the *Time* critic, felt the combination of a promising thriller and the Holocaust was totally inappropriate: "If this were simply a chase film, watching Alain Delon's weak face fall apart and his well-clothed body scuttle might be just passable fun. Since it is a film about Jews being shipped to death camps in cattle cars, it is a gross and nearly unbelievable lapse of taste and artistic intelligence."[41] Remarkably, the film was highly acclaimed in France where most critics related easily to its more profound aspects, such as the influence of Kafka and the serious metaphysical and psychological points treated by the story. In the United States, Pauline Kael's reaction was typical. The self-proclaimed populist reviewer condemned the film's "weighty emptiness," adding that "the atmosphere is heavily pregnant, with no delivery." She complains that "we're not meant to have any sympathy for Klein," and makes an incredible comparison between Losey's film and the vacuous *Gentleman's Agreement*—"The movie is a solemn, medicinal variant on *Gentleman's Agreement*."[42]

In general, artistic treatments of the Holocaust display an uneasy tension between conventional forms of expression and a traditional stock of thematic concerns on the one hand and the unique actuality of the specific event on the other. Mr. *Klein* is, in my opinion, a rare success, combining an effective presentation of the initial stages of the concentration camp universe and a stimulating discourse of the fundamental issues involved in that universe. The key concept, the underlying concern of the entire work, is the subject of identification. On one level it refers to the first stage of the genocide process. The film exposes the tragedies, horrors, contradictions, and absurdities involved in that attitude, namely the singling out of Jews on the basis of pseudoscientific theory and the deterministic factors of ancestors' background. Beyond the critique of, what used to be during the war, a commonly accepted practice of Jewish identification, the problem develops into the more profound issue of human identity. A serious reflection upon the notion of human identity leads to reassessment of social institutions and of the most important cultural and moral values. The failure of the bastions of western civilization to resist the Nazi evil leads to one specific conclusion, exemplified in the protagonist's dramatic change and his final action: the right way for bystanders in such a situation, if they wish to maintain human dignity and moral stature and to avoid self-deception, is to practice the ultimate act of identification: to identify completely with the victims.

Remembrance of Things Past

One narrative form highly common in Holocaust literature is the *Bildungsroman* or *Erziehungsroman*, the novel of development and education. Many survivors spent their youth under the oppression of Nazi Germany, and their memoirs relate stories to this crucial phase of their mental and physical development. However, given the nature of the deadly circumstances under which they made the transition from adolescence to maturity, their gains are as etheral as the smoke of their family members, friends, and fellow inmates in the camps. The positive note found in the traditional *Bildungsroman* or *Erziehungsroman* of newly acquired knowledge and belief in life's vocation is replaced by notes of anguished disorientation, serious spiritual crisis, and expiration. Two notable examples are Primo Levi's *Survival in Auschwitz* and Elie Wiesel's *Night*, which present, in Rosenfeld's words, "a kind of reverse *Erziehungsroman*, a narrative of miseducation or an unlearning and relearning of human possibilities."[43] Both works, each in its own way, touch on the most important aspects of the monumental cultural crisis embodied by the Holocaust. Levi, a secular, westernized scientist, comes across as a rationalist witnessing the complete collapse of orderly civilized society into an inferno governed by absolute irrationality. Wiesel had a religious, orthodox background and his account of Auschwitz describes "many of the same trials recorded by Primo Levi, but [he] sustained an additional one as well: the trial of a tormented and finally broken faith."[44]

Vittorio De Sica's *The Garden of the Finzi-Continis* (1970) was adapted from Giorgio Bassani's distinguished novel, a kind of *Bildungsroman* whose creation was motivated by Bassani's desire to pay tribute to the memories of the people he had known in his childhood in the northern Italian town of Ferrara.[45] The quasi-autobiographical book describes the personal experiences of Giorgio, a young student from a middle-class family who is trying to complete his doctoral degree in Italian literature shortly before and during the war.

The story focuses on Giorgio's relationships with the family of the Finzi-Continis, especially his frustrated love for their daughter, Micol. The Finzi-Continis represent a rare branch in European history, an old family of aristocratic, landholding Jews. This unique position as Jewish aristocrats in European society led them to be aloof and secluded in their mansion. The emergence of antisemitic restrictions imposed on them a new type of social isolation and caused their expulsion from the local country club. Consequently they invite some of their acquaintances to play tennis on their own land, a flattering invitation which draws one of the young guests to sarcastically remark that "we can thank our Fascists for the privilege." The film opens with the arrival of Giorgio and four other students who feel embarrassed in the opulent magnificence of the Finzi-Continis' estate. Their hosts try to put them at ease, being gracious and friendly. The Finzi-Contini parents stroll in the garden smiling politely to the newcomers; their children, the young hosts Micol and Alberto, attempt to develop genuine friendships through open and uninhibited behavior as if they were in the company of old pals.

Micol (Dominique Sanda) is an extremely attractive young girl who plans to write a dissertation on Emily Dickenson. She is free and animated but often given to moments of melancholy when, according to her, she "feels like an old aunt." In dealing with the new acquaintances from lower social classes, Micol appears imperious, provocative, and aloof, while her beauty and remoteness render her an unreachable object of erotic desire. Alberto's (Helmut Berger) remoteness is conversely ghostly—he is literally and figuratively lifeless, pale, languid, and morbidly sick. Giorgio (Lino Capolicchio) is possessed by images of Micol and Alberto from childhood in the synagogue and the local school, where communal and institutional activities brought them together but never bridged the fundamental gap between them. His lifelong attraction to the aristocratic couple now materializes, but his passionate love for Micol is met by chilly rejection. Micol initially befriends Giorgio with honest compassion and warmth, but she is unable to have a physical relationship with him. When Giorgio declares his love to her she answers, "But I don't love you. Lovers have a tendency to overwhelm one another. But the way we are alike as two drops of water, how could we ever overwhelm or tear each other to pieces? It would be like making love with a brother."

Micol's rejection of Giorgio as too brotherly to be a lover is not entirely honest. Her relationships with her brother Alberto abound with sexual overtones which suggest a form of repressed incest. They are like the brother and sister in Cocteau's *Les Enfants Terribles*, which Micol is seen reading. Her fascination with it is apparently translated into her attempt to act out Elizabeth's role from the novel. Micol's sinister side eludes Giorgio, whose gentleness, delicate manners, excessive considerations, and social insecurity make him "a truly noble fellow," but also one who "has the dullness of virtue."[46] Giorgio never suspects that their good friend, the hollow socialist Malnate, whom Micol once told that he was "too industrious, too Communist, and too hairy," would eventually become her lover. David Denby observed: "Despite his nobility, Giorgio the lover turns into Giorgio the Voyeur. In one of the screen's greatest images of sexual exclusion, he steals into the garden of the Finzi-Continis to spy on her and discovering her in the arms of Malnate, he suffers the extreme mortification of the unloved."[47]

The portrayal of complex and absorbing relationships between the main characters in the atmosphere of a sensuous youth-filled summer garden is a major achievement in *The Garden of the Finzi-Continis*. Bassani's novel is an impressionistic, Proustian *Bildungsroman*, mixing nostalgia with a tragic sense of lost past. Both De Sica and Bassani—each in his own way—created a poetic universe of the past, the heart of which is the family of the Finzi-Contini. Yet the film turns out to be a more forceful exposition of the period because it emphasized and elaborated on the historical context of the characters' experiences, thereby investing these characters with the searing pathos of the Holocaust casualties.

The Finzi-Continis are both unique and symbolically representative of the Jewish victims. Their seclusion is essentially willful, which allows them to preserve the rare elegance of their lives. Their lethargic passivity vis-à-vis the deteriorating political situation is the result of an aristocratic refusal to be tainted with rough struggles against harsh realities. They belong to a dying class and to a doomed race, for their elegance and high culture cannot withstand the erupting barbarism around them. Their decadence, inherent morbidity, and imminent doom are personified in Alberto's sickness, his gradual deterioration, and his perverse sexual inclinations to homosexuality and incest. After Alberto dies, his funeral signifies the end of the Finzi-Continis' world. A small procession of people dressed in black march slowly behind the hearse as an air-raid siren pierces the monumental silence; the Finzi-Continis, true to their style, ignore the ominous sound and quietly continue to follow the coffin.

The garden of the Finzi-Continis is the central poetic symbol; through its visualization De Sica shows the process of decline and destruction. In the beginning its beauty is shown in scenes of long summer afternoons when the twilight color is the only hint to the evolving tragic fall. The end of the *Finzi-Continis* takes place during the winter, and the full destruction is disclosed in the film's epilogue, which shows the neglected garden in an autumnal setting at twilight. Adding to the elegiac quality of the visuals is Manuel De Sica's hauntingly beautiful music— one of the most exquisite scores ever written for a motion picture. The visual approach was aptly described by Denby:

De Sica and cinematographer Ennio Guarnier have achieved a soft tone more appropriate to elegy. Their color photography is slightly grainy and intentionally overexposed, with an occasional softening of focus. It's a style that has its dangers, and they labor to avoid sentimentality or a merely static prettiness by keeping everything in motion, adapting the super-active manner of the sixties—with its zooms and rapid pans and fast cutting—into a smoothly meshed flow of constantly changing perspectives.[48]

In dealing with the historical material, De Sica employs an alternative style. One memorable scene in the film (which does not exist in the novel) involves Giorgio's trip to visit his brother, who had been sent by the family to study in France. Giorgio's journey provides ample opportunity to reveal glimpses of the stark political situation, illustrated through the presence of soldiers, the tension near the border, the waving flags of France and Italy, and a suspicious passport check. Giorgio meets his brother in the company of young students obsessed with current politics. One of them had been imprisoned in Dachau and carries a tattoo number on his arm. Giorgio is innocently curious about the tattoo, never having heard about Dachau. His ignorance ignites the former German prisoner, who delivers a succinct and angry speech about the function of a concentration camp in the Nazi state. The visual style throughout this sequence is drastically different from the rest of the film. Bright colors, sharp focus, and fast pace of cutting portray the existence of harsh realities devoid of any Proustian sentimentality.

This scene also highlights how De Sica's film differs substantially from the spirit and the content of the original novel in its emphasis on the historical context of the drama. The opening title introduces the movie with the following statement: "Ferrara Italy, 1938–1943. By 1938, the fascist government of the Il Duce, Benito Mussolini, was applying the so-called Racial Laws against Italian Jews." Bassani's novel ends in early September, 1939, after Giorgio's realization that Malnate is Micol's secret lover. In the film, this scene occurs in the middle of the plot, and the fate of the Finzi-Continis, described briefly in the novel's epilogue, occupies the entire second half, which is also devoted to showing the cruel eradication of the Jewish community of Ferrara. In addition, the film's treatment of specific historical incidents is more precise and concrete than the vague impressionistic memoirs in Bassani's novel. Toward the end of the book, Bassani describes Giorgio's relationship with Malnate. The two pals spent many evenings in literary discussions—the subject of politics was "dropped"—and mild erotic adventures. This chapter includes the following scene:

> One particular sultry evening in August we landed up at an open-air cinema, where I remember they were showing a German film with Christina Soderbaum. When we went in, the film had already started, and as soon as we sat down I started whispering ironical comments without paying attention to Malnate, who kept telling me to be careful, not to bausciare [to make a row], that in any case it just wasn't worth it. And he was quite right. A fellow in the row in front of ours, suddenly jumping to his feet against the milky background of the screen, threateningly told me to shut up. I retorted with an insult, and he shouted back: "Fora, boia d'un ebri" [Get out, you filthy Jew: Ferrarese dialect] and flung himself on me, grabbing my neck. It was lucky for me that Malnate, without a word, was ready to hurl my assailant back into his seat.[49]

In De Sica's film the references to the Holocaust are more concrete, for Giorgio and Malnate watch newsreels on the war and the Nazis. Hitler and Goebbels appear on the screen and Giorgio shouts: "The clown! Bunch of riff-raffs!" The image of Goerring and marching Nazi troopers prompts Giorgio's laughter and his remark "Stupid bastards." Giorgio's outburst irritates one thug who yells at him: "Get out, you dirty Jew!" A few local hoodlums threaten to beat Giorgio but Malnate helps Giorgio escape the theater. Immediately after this scene, De Sica shows how one of Giorgio's friends is chased by the local police. He is discovered in the movie theater and the menace of the approaching police is underscored by their silent and efficient conduct. The chase sequence is extremely powerful, for it illustrates a literal manhunt. The young Jew is innocent, yet a large police force is after him while his fearful face and heavy expirations clearly convey the stakes of this chase.

The film presents the worsening of the Jews' condition as a slow, gradual, but painfully palpable process. The beginning is marked by the expulsion of the Jews from the tennis club. Giorgio's academic ambitions suffer a critical setback when he is denied access to the public library for research. Terrorizing anonymous phone calls ruin the celebration of Passover, the constant ringing of the telephone literally drowning out the beautiful singing of traditional Jewish songs. Giorgio's father argues with his son: "So there aren't any more public schools for the Jews, no mixed marriages, no phone listings, no obituaries in the newspaper, public schools is more serious but still . . . we can still live, move about, own property, in effect, be a citizen."

The last remark reveals De Sica's unusual portrayal of the Jews. Giorgio's father is inclined to dismiss the seriousness of their predicament because he is a member of the Fascist party, believing that, after all, Mussolini is still better than Hitler. The Finzi-Continis are proud of their continuing contributions to government charities, but apart from inviting Giorgio to come and use their library— which, according to the father, has everything important but is "more selective" than the public library—they never use their stature and connections to help themselves or anybody else in the Jewish community. The Finzi-Continis present an almost scandalous refusal to understand and face the threatening situation. They shutter themselves from external reality in their private ghetto, preoccupied in Italian and western literature, avoid reading the daily newspapers, and spend the Passover night trying to read the future in a crystal ball.

De Sica also deals with the perennial divisiveness of the Jewish community, which is brought forth sharply by the angry words of Giorgio's bourgeois father, who opposes his son's associations with the aristocrats: "The Finzi-Continis are not for us. They're not our sort. They don't even seem Jewish." But nor does his son "seem Jewish," with his blue eyes, shy behavior, and sensitive character as the embodiment of "the dullness of virtue." Indeed, the Jews in *The Garden of the Finzi-Continis* contrast with the prevailing popular stereotypes of Jewish characters in cinema, but as typical assimilated Jews of a western society they are a great deal more truthful. They are not clannish or exotically different, not members of an arrogant middle class or poor tailors; they are not shrewd intellectuals or old sages— with or without magical power—not hysterical mothers or mindless fathers too busy to climb in the social ladder, and they don't all have dark eyes and black hair. Most important of all, their Jewish self-consciousness lacks the sickening complexes, so often found in cinema, which usually present either a stubborn adherence to Jewish tradition in defiance of or opposition to Gentile society, or a relentless ambition to assimilate to the point of self-negation. De Sica does not de-emphasize his characters' Jewish identity, nor does he account for their character and actions in terms of exclusively Jewish concerns and norms of behavior. The idiosyncracies of the Finzi-Continis and the mild flaws of Giorgio's family render these characters real and humane. Pauline Kael observed that unlike the Patimkins in *Goodbye, Columbus,* De Sica's characters present the opposite of the survivors.[50] Nevertheless, De Sica's success in arousing a great sympathy toward these characters is evidenced in the reaction to the Finzi-Continis' lethargic passivity: "We would like to reach up to the screen," wrote Denby, "and shake them by the shoulders, even though there's no reason to think it would do any good."[51]

The final phase of the movie, featuring the liquidation of the Jewish community of Ferrara, is handled with remarkable restraint and understatement. The earlier poetic rendering of the Finzi-Continis and their effete splendor was so emphatic that, as one reviewer observed, "when the unshaven, nondescript fascist agent carelessly smashes a chira vase while searching the house, a perceptible shudder went through the entire audience."[52] As true aristocrats, their behavior is dignified, even in moments of oppression. There is no yelling, bargaining, or pleading for mercy. When their names are read, they report with resignation that Alberto has died, and nobody suspects any possible trickery. Micol proudly corrects the announcer when he calls "Nicol," displaying pride in the foreign sound of her name with its possibly Jewish origin (the name is probably a version of the biblical name Michal). Then the entire family is taken to the local school—Micol and Giorgio's school, seen before in a few touching flashback pictures—where all the Jews have been sequestered. The Jews' composure and quiet obedience and the expensive black coats of the Finzi-Continis suggest the depressing silence of a funeral procession, or the uneasy quiet before a major catastrophe. In the hallway the family is ordered into two different classrooms. There is a limit to the number of Jews in each room, and the Finzi-Continis are forced to separate. Micol looks at her parents as they quietly turn the other way, and the pain of this moment of separation is infinitely subtler, but surprisingly also greater than any involved in a tearjerking melodrama like *Sophie's Choice.* The scene ends with Micol joining Giorgio's father. Giorgio apparently managed to escape. But all the other Jews of Ferrara are now united. There is no irony here but rather a painful pathos as all the Jews await their fate together—deportation to the death camps in the east— with calm despair and resignation. Lance Morrow summarized the power of this scene by noting that "The last 15 minutes of Vittorio de Sica's *The Garden of the Finzi-Continis,* in which Italian Jews are rounded up to be taken to the camps, are more wrenching than all the hours of [NBC teledrama] *Holocaust.*"[53]

De Sica's film concludes with an epilogue, a moving recitation of *Yizkor* (*In Memory*), a special Jewish prayer for the dead. The deep vibrating cantor's voice, using the names Auschwitz, Treblinka, Maidanek for the names of the dead, elicits a strong emotional response. The elegiac stance, based on nostalgia and distance, is replaced by palpable notes of grief for those newly dead. The camera shows the garden, whose current state of neglect and ruin is all the more devastating when we recall its former glory. The final picture is of the massive tomb of the Finzi-Continis, an ancient monument and a final silent memorial to the cruel annihilation of a special kind of people and culture.

The finale of *The Garden of the Finzi-Continis* expresses the dying mood found in authentic *Bildungsromans* of the Holocaust. Bassani created a story relating a series of poignant losses: Giorgio fails to get a degree, finds no love, and above all loses his father, his friends, and the admirable Finzi-Continis. De Sica added another essential dimension to the narrative by shifting the emphasis from the personal concerns of a semi-autobiographical hero obsessed with the process of his maturity, to the plight of the entire Jewish community and the process of its destruction. Giorgio, in fact, disappears completely in the last fifteen minutes of the film. There is no denouement to the story, no gratifying aftermath. The Jewish prayer at the end provides no moral statement or ideological conclusion. The underlying attitudes of *The Garden of the Finzi-Continis* emphasize the pain over the human loss. The potential psychological complexities of the main characters, the references to social divisions, and even the intriguing aristocracy of the Finzi-Continis are all overshadowed by the concern with the senseless and total liquidation of the Jewish community in Ferrara. Indeed, the narrative details and thematic allusions serve to enhance the vitality and humaneness of the innocent victims. De Sica committed himself to depicting the ordeals and trials of the Jews during the Fascist era, culminating with their uprooting and deportation. He wisely acknowledged that in the face of such tragedy, any intellectual ventures, ideological, psychological, or metaphysical, are secondary or even irrelevant. Hence, the unfinished story line and the powerfully emotional finale. Whereas the perpetrators and the bystanders compel serious reflections on issues of human nature and moral responsibility, the six million innocents defy philosophical probing because of their senseless and monumental victimization. The commemoration of the perished Jews should evolve the kind of respectful mood people have in funerals: somber recollection, compassionate tribute, and pain and anguish over the loss.

Conclusion

The three films discussed in this chapter, *The Garden of the Finzi-Continis*, *Mr. Klein*, and *The Damned*, deal with the fundamental implications of the Third Reich. De Sica presents an exquisite elegy for an admirable tradition and cultural refinement brutally liquidated; *Mr. Klein* is the story of a tragic fall, mingling, however, sharp, ironic expositions of the bankruptcy of cultural institutions in the face of Nazism; and Visconti suggests the existence of psychic disease in the cultural makeup that allowed the rise of Nazism.

The employment of Proustian attitudes, Kafkaesque angst, Marxist concerns, Freudian ideas, and mythical patterns demonstrates that *The Garden of the Finzi-Continis*, *Mr. Klein*, and *The Damned*, in style as well as in content, draw upon the artistic arsenal of modernist tradition.

The central theme in all of these films is what Lionel Trilling called the modernist disenchantment with culture. Trilling traces the roots of this idea to the writings of Nietzsche, Frazer's *The Golden Bow*, Conrad's *Heart of Darkness*, and Freud's *Civilization and Its Discontents*.[54] Irving Howe, in his introduction to *The Idea of the Modern* observes:

> In most modernist literature, one finds a bitter impatience with the whole apparatus of cognition and the limited assumption of rationality. The mind comes to be seen as an enemy of vital human powers. Culture becomes disenchanted with itself, sick over its endless refinements. There is a hunger to break past the bourgeois proprieties and self-containment of culture, toward a form of absolute personal speech, a literature deprived of ceremony and stripped to revelation.[55]

The crucial question, however, is how serious treatments of the Holocaust differ from earlier, post-World War I modernist works, or how these films represent the sensibilities of the post-modernist mind.

George Steiner, begins his essay "A Season in Hell" with the following questions: "How is one to address oneself, without a persistent feeling of fatuity, even of indecency, to the theme of ultimate inhumanity? Is there anything new to be said regarding the causes and forms of the breakdown of the European order in the 'Thirty Years' War' from 1915 to 1945?"[56] Notwithstanding the importance of these questions, Steiner's endeavor ignores the singularity of the Holocaust, the crucial differences between the two world wars, or the difference between modernism and post-modernism.

The first "Great War" shattered many of the notions about man's basic goodness and the promises of a rational western society. To be sure, disillusionment with Enlightenment ideals was expressed before by authors like Nietzsche, Dostoevsky, and Ibsen, but World War I gave the Enlightenment mood a final intellectual blow, with broader social effects (in its wane, Spengler wrote his influential *The Decline of the West*, and the Dadaists and the surrealists tried to demonstrate their defiant avant-garde postures in public spectacles). The unprecedented carnage of the First World War was essentially purposeless and meaningless. The political developments leading to its outburst were equally incidental and senseless, and the continuous killings between the deadlocked armies presented the battling forces as equally reprehensible or guilty. Numerous artists found themselves caught in the bloody battles (many of them perished during the war), and their moving reports, the cultural canon of poems, novels, essays, and paintings on the war horrors, are dominated by the sharp pain of inhuman massacres and atrocities and the despairing recognition of their senselessness.

The Nazi era manifested a different reality with different cultural implications. The carnage was not "senseless" since it was rationalized and motivated by strong ideological convictions, some of them nourished by the ideas of no other than Friedrich Nietzsche. It is impossible to lose the grip of categories of wrong and right, evil and good, throughout the career of the Third Reich. And the specific evil forces were not merely responsible for bloodsheds and massacres on a large scale, but they directly planned, calculated, and supervised a systematic process of extermination. The satanic logic of the concentration camp universe signals not simply the fall of reason before dangerous irrationality, but something else.

Still, the modernist heritage offers a rich body of symbolic references that can be used to depict the cultural crisis caused by the Nazi era. There is, however, a specific danger implied in uncritical adoption of modernist attitudes: the nihilistic irony and pessimistic visions of modernism might overwhelm compassion for the innocent victims and expressions of condemnation of the manifest evil. Moreover, the overwhelming objective facts (and in many cases, the personal searing experiences) cannot be effaced or evaded by the modernist journeys into realms of artistic fantasy such as expressionist allegorical nightmares, the fantastic visions of futurists, or the surrealists' dream world. (This is the pitfall that Czech films on the Holocaust successfully avoid.) Finally, according to many, the modernist nihilistic mood of post World War I was one cause for the rise of Nazism. Siegfried Kracauer's celebrated study of the German cinema in the twenties is entitled *From Caligari to Hitler*, trying to demonstrate how expressionistic German cinema reveals the fascination with trends and ideas that culminated in the election of Hitler.[57] Jacob Talmon contends that the conclusion that the Holocaust proves the absence of historical laws, moral lessons, and humanistic vocations, and rather the existence of irrationality, brutality, and meaningless atrocities, implies a submission to patterns of thought and norms of behavior characteristic of the Holocaust perpetrators.[58]

Whatever meaning the Holocaust has, its artistic treatment requires an indispensable allegiance to the basic historical facts. These facts concern the unequivocal identification of the victims as Jews, the perpetrators of the atrocities as Germans, and also members of local populations, who by and large assumed the role of indifferent bystanders. The facts also involve the main stages in the genocide process: racial laws, identification of Jews, concentration, deportation, and physical liquidation, and scores of recorded events, practices, and personal actions that reveal the incredible degree of inhumanity and the unprecedented scale of systematized horror. Holocaust art, then, is generally impelled to contain a crucial layer of truthful referentiality. Other artistic elements, in particular reflective insights and formal conceptualization, are liable to transcend the facts, but these must not overwhelm the artwork's basic respect for fact. The practical consequences of such attitudes are that Holocaust film tends to display an unresolved tension between verisimilitude and actuality of the historical references, and the stylistic imposition that can take any form such as melodramatic narration, existentialist mood, or mythical pattern. The universe of atrocities functions as a transcendental entity which few if any films, or for that matter, any other artwork, can penetrate and express without the intrusion of narrative conventions, ideological positions, or metaphysical preconceptions. But to dismiss the existing films as inappropriate and hence as worthless would be erroneous, for this attitude fails to acknowledge the limitations of the medium and of art in general.

Aristotle in his *Poetics* declared that history describes merely what has happened whereas poetry deals with what may happen. "Poetry, therefore, is a more philosophical and a higher thing than history: for poetry tends to express the universal, history the particular."[59]

The Holocaust poses a special challenge to the Aristotelian position. The singularity of the Holocaust reality, combined with the urge shared by many film-makers to relate excruciating and extreme experiences accurately, lead many to feel that faithfulness to the historical material is more important than poetic adventures. This approach recalls the modernist definition of realism as "a form of aesthetic experience which . . . lays claim to a binding relationship to the real itself, that is to say, to those realms of knowledge and praxis which had traditionally been differentiated from the realm of the aesthetic, with its disinterested judgments and its constitution as sheer appearance."[60] At the same time, "realism" is an art category and it is impossible to ignore the fictive character of artistic discourse. In addition, after Aristotle we have come to know that the possibilities of artistic forms are not unlimited. Many of those who write on the Holocaust struggle with what they see as binding and limiting literary forms. Stories of the Holocaust which adhere to the conventions of a specific narrative genre often betray the authentic reality. Narratives, in their different genres, are based on a stock of archetypes and prototypes, so there is always the danger, even in authenticated stories, of reading real characters in terms of archetypal literary figures.

To overcome these inherent constrictions of any art, especially narrative art, Holocaust film needs to retain a special relationship, aided by the unmatched recording power and transmitting effect of the photographic image, to historical reality. The facts and the incredible events are so disorienting that they repeatedly force us to take a fresh look at the meaning of what happened; the enormity of the evil was and is so terrifying that there should be no ambiguities about moral indignation. Finally, any treatment of the Holocaust is obligated to commemorate the sufferings of the victims with dignity and compassion, and to understand its monumental injustice to the Jewish people.

Notes

INTRODUCTION

1. George Steiner, *Language and Silence* (New York: Atheneum, 1967), p. 163.
2. Elie Wiesel, "For Some Measure of Humility," *Sh'ma* 5:100 (October 31, 1975), p. 314.
3. T. W. Adorno, "Engagement," in *Noten zur Literatur* vol. 3 (1965), pp. 109–135.
4. Michael Wyschogrod, "Some Theological Reflections on the Holocaust," *Response* vol. 25 (Spring 1975), p. 68.
5. Quoted in Seymour Chatman, *Story and Discourse* (Ithaca: Cornell University Press, 1978), p. 16.

CHAPTER I

1. Lawrence Langer, *The Holocaust and the Literary Imagination* (New Haven: Yale University Press, 1975), p. 54.
2. Ibid., p. 149.
3. Ibid., p. 43.
4. Ibid., p. 75.
5. Ibid., p. 3.
6. Ibid.
7. Ibid., p. 53.
8. Ibid., p. 57.
9. Alvin Rosenfeld, *A Double Dying* (Bloomington: Indiana University Press, 1980), p. 27.
10. Elie Wiesel, *Legends of Our Time*, trans. S. Donadio (New York: Holt, Rinehart and Winston, 1968), p. 8.
11. Sidra Ezrahi, *By Words Alone* (Chicago: Chicago University Press, 1980), p. 50.
12. Ibid., p. 51.
13. Pierre Julitte, *Block 26: Sabotage at Buchenwald*, trans. Francis Price (New York: Doubleday, 1971), p. viii.
14. Anatoli Kuznetsov, *Babi Yar*, trans. David Floyd (New York: Pocket Books, 1971), p. 1.
15. Rosenfeld, *A Double Dying*, p. 66.
16. Ibid., p. 65.
17. Michael Hamburger, *The Truth of Poetry* (London: Weidenfeld and Nicholson, 1969), chap. 9, pp. 220–66.
18. Rosenfeld, *A Double Dying*, p. 26.
19. Primo Levi, *Survival in Auschwitz*, trans. Stuart Woolf (New York: Collier Books, 1961), p. 112.
20. Roland Barthes, *Camera Lucida*, trans. Richard Howard (New York: Hill and Wang, 1981), p. 82.
21. David Roskies, *Against the Apocalypse* (Cambridge: Harvard University Press, 1984), p. 7. See also Sybil Milton, "The Camera as Weapon: Documentary Photography and the Holocaust," The Simon Wiesenthal Center Annual vol. 1 (1985), pp. 45–68.
22. Eli Mandel, "Auschwitz—Poetry of Alienation," *Canadian Literature* no. 100 (1984), p. 213.
23. Ibid., p. 216.
24. Roskies, *Against the Apocalypse*, pp. 294–96.
25. Susan Sontag, "Persona: The Film in Depth," in S. Kaminsky, ed., *Ingmar Bergman: Essays in Criticism* (New York: Oxford University Press, 1975), p. 226.

26. Roy Armes, *The Cinema of Alain Resnais* (New York: A. S. Barnes, 1968), p. 48.

27. Ibid., p. 48.

28. All the quotations are taken from the published script of *Night and Fog,* trans. Robert Hughes and Merle Worth, in Robert Hughes, ed., *Film: Book 2—Films of Peace and War* (New York: Grove, 1962), pp. 234–55.

29. Rosenfeld, *A Double Dying,* p. 156.

30. George Steiner, *The Death of Tragedy* (New York: Alfred A. Knopf, 1961), p. 352.

31. Armes, *Resnais,* p. 50.

32. Cited in Armes, pp. 50–51.

33. William Shirer, *The Rise and Fall of the Third Reich* (Greenwich, Connecticut: Fawcett, 1960), pp. 1247–48.

34. Robert Michael, "The Terrible Flaw of *Night and Fog,*" *Martyrdom and Resistance,* September-October 1981, p. 13.

35. Ibid.

36. See Roskies, *Against the Apocalypse,* pp. 294–96.

37. James Monaco, *Alain Resnais* (New York: Oxford University Press, 1978), p. 22.

38. M. Kinder and B. Houston, *Close-Up* (New York: Harcourt Brace Jovanovich, 1972), pp. 125–26.

39. Andrew Sarris, *Cinema and Politics* (New York: Columbia University Press, 1978), p. 86.

40. Monaco, *Alain Resnais,* p. 20.

41. François Truffaut, *The Films in My Life,* trans. Leonard Mayhew (New York: Simon and Schuster, 1978), p. 303.

42. Pauline Kael, *Deeper into Movies* (Boston: Little Brown, 1973), p. 428.

43. James R. MacBean, *Film and Revolution* (Bloomington: Indiana University Press, 1975), p. 255.

44. Ibid., p. 254.

45. Ibid., p. 255.

46. Stanley Hoffman, "Introduction" to the script of *The Sorrow and the Pity,* trans. M. Johnston (New York: E. P. Dutton, 1972), p. vii.

47. L. Furhammar and F. Isaksson, *Politics and Film,* trans. K. French (New York: Praeger, 1971), p. 104.

48. R. M. Barsam, *Filmguide to Triumph of the Will* (Bloomington: Indiana University Press, 1975), p. 26.

49. Siegfried Kracauer, *From Caligari to Hitler* (New Jersey: Princeton University Press, 1947), p. 301.

50. Susan Sontag, *Under the Sign of Saturn* (New York: Farrar, Straus, Giroux, 1980), p. 83.

51. Kracauer, *From Caligari to Hitler,* p. 301.

52. Sontag, *Saturn,* p. 83

53. Barsam, *Filmguide,* p. 17. Barsam, however, ignores Streicher's remark on racial purity. In general, Barsam's book is an unabashed sympathetic reading of Riefenstahl's work.

54. Ibid.

55. Brian Winston, "Was Hitler There?" *Sight and Sound* 50:2 (Spring 1981), p. 105.

56. Furhammar, *Politics and Film,* p. 104.

57. Ibid., p. 110.

58. The statement was made by the Czech author Ladislav Mnacko and was quoted by Jan Kadar in his article on *The Shop on Main Street,* "Not the Six Million, But the One," *New York Herald Tribune,* January 23, 1966, p. 21.

59. Lucy Dawidowicz, *The War Against the Jews* (New York: Bantam Books, 1976), p. 84.

60. For a good discussion of Nazi antisemitic films, see David S. Hull, *Film in the Third Reich* (Berkeley: University of California Press, 1969), pp. 157–77.

61. Furhammar, *Politics and Film,* p. 108.

62. See Joel Carmichael, "The Record Skewed," *Midstream*, 32:4 (April 1986), pp. 47–50.

63. The existing footage of the Warsaw ghetto was taken by Nazi crews. These films were designed—at times literally, for some of the scenes were staged—to denigrate the victims and show that they were subhuman. Ironically, they are among the most forceful pieces of visual evidence of the Nazis' inhumanity, as they show the subhuman conditions imposed by the Germans on the Jews.

64. Barthes, *Camera Lucida*, p. 82.

65. All quotations from the film are taken from the published script, *Shoah: An Oral History of the Holocaust* (New York: Pantheon Books, 1985).

66. Raul Hilberg is the only historian appearing in the film, and he serves as the voice of historical authority. In his influential massive study *The Destruction of the European Jews* (Chicago, 1967; rpts, 1967, 1985), Hilberg made some controversial observations on the Jews' complicity in the mass killing; Hilberg's compassionate analysis of Adam Czerniakow gives no hint of his objectionable assessment of the Jewish councils under the Nazis. However, Lanzmann only adopted Hilberg's cautious approach to the historical material (mostly apparent in the concentration on concrete details), and the attitude toward the Christian roots of antisemitism as a key causal origin to the incidence of the genocide.

67. Eugene Fisher, "The Holocaust and the State of Israel: A Critical Perspective," *Judaism* 35:1 (1986) pp. 18–19.

68. Quoted in Byron Sherwin, "Jewish and Christian Theology Encounters the Holocaust," in Byron Sherwin and Susan Ament, eds., *Encountering the Holocaust*, (Chicago: Impact Press, 1979), p. 426.

69. Claude Lanzmann spent eleven years working on his film. The work involved many adventures and ordeals, which will probably be the subject for a future book.

70. For this idea I am indebted to Professor Dan Diner and his lecture, "The Holocaust and Beyond," in the "After *Shoah*" symposium, the Tel Aviv Museum, December 18, 1986.

CHAPTER II

1. Christopher Williams, "Introduction," to *Realism and the Cinema* (London: Routledge and Kegan Paul, 1980), p. 7.

2. Ibid.

3. Stephen Heath, *Questions of Cinema* (Bloomington: Indiana University Press, 1981), p. 157. See also Seymour Chatman, *Story and Discourse*.

4. Quoted in Marianna Torgovnick, *Closure in the Novel* (New Jersey: Princeton University Press, 1981), p. 4.

5. Jonathan Culler, *Structuralist Poetics* (Ithaca: Cornell University Press, 1975), p. 207.

6. Henry James, "The Art of Fiction," in G. W. Allen and H. H. Clark, eds., *Literary Criticism: Pope to Croce* (Detroit: Wayne State University Press, 1962), p. 552.

7. Siegfried Kracauer, in his *Theory of Film* (London: Oxford University Press, 1960), argues that happy endings are an essential component of cinema, catering to its special nature and resources; see pp. 168–70. For a good summary of Hollywood's narrative style, see Peter Roffman and Jim Purdy, *The Hollywood Social Problem Film* (Bloomington: Indiana University Press, 1981), pp. 3–9.

8. Williams, "Introduction," p. 8.

9. Ibid., p. 9.

10. William Freidberg, "Nazi Concentration Camp Reactivated for Film," *New York Times*, February 20, 1949.

11. See Gene Moskowitz, "The Uneasy East," *Sight and Sound* 27:3 (Winter 1957), p. 137.

12. Susan Strasberg, *Bittersweet* (New York: G. P. Putnam's Sons, 1980), p. 130.

13. Quoted in Joan Mellen, *Filmguide to the Battle of Algiers* (Bloomington: Indiana University Press, 1973), p. 11.

14. *New York Herald Tribune*, June 2, 1964.

15. Quoted in Mellen, *Filmguide*, p. 11.
16. Robert Scholes and Robert Kellogg, *The Nature of Narrative* (London: Oxford University Press, 1966, rpt. 1978), p. 13.
17. See L. Langer, *Versions of Survival* (Albany: State University of New York, 1982), chapter 2, "Auschwitz: The Death of Choice," p. 74.
18. Steven T. Katz, *Post-Holocaust Dialogues* (New York: New York University Press, 1983), pp. 224–25.
19. Emil L. Fackenheim, "Reflections on Aliyah," *Midstream* 31:7 (August/September 1985), pp. 25–26.

CHAPTER III
1. See Saul Friedländer, *When Memory Comes*, trans. Helen R. Lane (New York: Avon, 1980), p. 4.
2. John Simon, *Movies into Film* (New York: Dial, 1971), pp. 278–79.
3. Antonin Novak, *Films and Filmmakers in Czechoslovakia*, trans. George Theiner (Prague: Orbis, 1968), p. 8.
4. In A. Liehm, *Closely Watched Films* (White Planes, New York: International Arts and Sciences, 1974), p. 38.
5. Jacob Talmon, *The Myth of the Nation and the Vision of Revolution* (London: Secker and Warburg, 1981), pp. 533–34.
6. Andre Bazin, "Le Ghetto Concentrationnaire," *Cahiers du Cinema* 2:9 (February 1952), p. 60.
7. Liehm, *Closely Watched Films*, p. 45.
8. In 1943 the Germans transported two hundred children from Bialystok in White Russia to Terezin, an unusual move of transferring from east to west which was part of an attempted bargain to sell Jews to Jewish aid organizations. When they were taken to the showers in Terezin, they cried "Gas!" This incident was evidently the source of the scene in Radok's film. The children remained in Terezin for nearly two months, secluded from the rest of the camp; when the negotiations with the Germans failed, they were all killed. See Friedländer, *When Memory Comes*, p. 117.
9. Bazin, "Le Ghetto," p. 60.
10. See Liehm, *Closely Watched Films*, p. 43.
11. See J. Blatter and S. Milton, *Art of the Holocaust* (New York: Rutledge, 1981). This book contains pictures of over 350 artworks created in ghettos, concentration camps, and in hiding places by victims of the Nazis.
12. Primo Levi, *Survival*, p. 29.
13. See discussion of Nemec's film, pp. 75–79.
14. R. Hughes, *The Shock of the New* (New York: Alfred A. Knopf, 1981), p. 299.
15. See *Art of the Holocaust*, pictures 71, 37, and 32.
16. Hughes, *Shock*, p. 298.
17. Bazin, "Le Ghetto," p. 59.
18. J. Skvorecky, *All the Bright Young Men and Women*, trans. M. Schonberg (Toronto: Peter Martin, 1971), p. 41.
19. *New York Times*, August 28, 1950.
20. *New Republic*, September 25, 1950, p. 30.
21. *New York Times*, August 28, 1950.
22. Bazin, "Le Ghetto," p. 61. Translation mine.
23. Skvorecky, *All the Bright*, pp. 40–41.
24. Novak, *Films . . . in Czechoslovakia*, pp. 29–30.
25. Herbert Luft, "Der Feuhrer Presents a Town to the Jews," *Films and Filming* 7:2 (November 1960), pp. 10–11.
26. Novak, *Films . . . in Czechoslovakia*, p. 31.
27. B. Crowther's review in the *New York Times*, February 8, 1967.
28. See Liehm, *Closely Watched Films*, p. 73.

29. Novak, *Films . . . in Czechoslovakia*, p. 32.

30. A. and M. Liehm, *The Most Important Art* (Berkeley: University of California Press, 1977), p. 230.

31. Ibid.

32. Novak, *Films . . . in Czechoslovakia*, p. 31.

33. Skvorecky, *All the Bright*, pp. 220–21.

34. R. Adler, *A Year in the Dark* (New York: Berkeley Medallion Books, 1971), p. 162.

35. Novak, *Films . . . in Czechoslovakia*, p. 32.

36. Simon, *Movies into Film*, p. 283.

37. T. Borowski, *This Way for the Gas, Ladies and Gentlemen*, trans. B. Vedder (New York: Penguin Books, 1976), p. 84.

38. Simon, *Movies into Film*, p. 283.

39. Novak, *Films . . . in Czechoslovakia*, p. 33.

40. In Adler, *A Year*, pp. 161–62.

41. Arnost Lustig, *Darkness Casts No Shadows*, trans. J. Nemcova (Washington, D.C.: Inscape, 1976).

42. Simon, *Movies into Film*, p. 286.

43. Ibid.

44. In the early sixties Robert Hughes asked several distinguished makers and writers of film to express their opinion on the social effectiveness of films dealing with peace and war. Jean Renoir's response was: "In 1936 I made a picture named *La Grande Illusion* in which I tried to express all my deep feelings for the cause of peace. This film was very successful. Three years later the war broke out. That is the only answer I can give to your interesting enquiry." In Hughes, ed., *Film: Book 2*, p. 183.

45. Rosenfeld, *A Double Dying*, p. 27.

46. Judith Crist's review of *The Shop on Main Street*, in the *New York Herald Tribune*, January 25, 1966.

47. The theme of Christianity is particularly important in *The Shop on Main Street* since the head of the collaborating Slovak state during the war was Monsignor Josef Tiso, a Catholic priest, and the ruling Fascist party was a right-wing Catholic nationalist group.

48. Kadar, "Not the Six Million," p. 21.

49. Ibid.

50. B. Crowther's film review, *New York Times*, January 25, 1966.

51. Ibid.

52. Crist's review in the *New York Herald Tribune*, January 25, 1966.

53. David W. Paul, ed., *Politics, Art and Commitment in the East European Cinema* (London: MacMillan, 1983), p. 58.

54. Rosenfeld, *A Double Dying*, p. 71.

55. Arnost and Joseph Lustig, "The Holocaust and the Film Arts," in Sherwin and Ament, eds., *Encountering the Holocaust*, p. 368.

56. Liehm, *The Most Important Art*, p. 284.

57. Skvorecky, *All the Bright*, pp. 219–20.

58. Novak, *Films . . . in Czechoslovakia*, p. 59.

59. Roy Armes used these Camus quotations as the motto for his book *Patterns of Realism* (New York: A. S. Barnes, 1971).

60. Rosenfeld, *A Double Dying*, p. 71.

CHAPTER IV

1. Oliver Claussen, "Weiss/Propagandist and Weiss/Playwright," *New York Times Magazine*, October 2, 1966, p. 132.

2. Rosenfeld, *A Double Dying*, p. 160.

3. *The Production Code*, Motion Picture Association of America (December 1956), Article X. The Production Code was adopted by the organization of Motion Picture Producers and Distributors of America (MPPDA) in 1930, to improve the image of the film industry

and in response to increasing pressures to create some form of film censorship. The document was a strict self-regulatory charter, providing specific guidelines to avoid moral and political scandals in the content of Hollywood movies. The Production Code became also known as the Hays Code, named after Will Hays, a former chairman of the Republican National Committee and U.S. Postmaster General in President Harding's cabinet. Hays was the head of the MPPDA from 1922 until 1945 and wielded much power over the motion picture industry. His Code, which was changed only in 1965, molded the content and image of Hollywood's movies for many years.

4. K. R. M. Short, "Documents," *Historical Journal of Film, Radio and Television*, October 1983, pp. 171–80.

5. Dawidowicz, *The War against the Jews*, p. 106.

6. In J. Morella, E. Z. Epstein, and J. Griggs, *The Films of World War II* (New Jersey: Citadel, 1973), p. 21.

7. Roffman and Purdy, *Hollywood Social Problem Film*, pp. 210–11.

8. Jack L. Warner, with Dean Jennings, *My First Hundred Years in Hollywood* (New York: Random House, 1965), p. 262.

9. John Belto, *The Hollywood Professionals, Vol. 3* (London: Tantivi, 1974), p. 108.

10. Ibid., pp. 103–4.

11. In *Professor Mamlock*, the Nazi oppression is presented as anti-Jewish and anti-Communist. On the whole, though, this Russian movie was used to convey Communist propaganda. At the end, after the death of the old Jew, his son is shown joining the Communists, completing a central dramatic process of ideological conversion. The son is embraced by an old comrade, the leader of the Communist resistance who becomes his new surrogate father.

12. Belto, *Professionals*, p. 108.

13. Lewis Jacobs, "World War II and the American Film," *Cinema Journal* 1 (Winter 1967–68), p. 21.

14. R. E. Shain, *An Analysis of Motion Pictures about War Released by the American Film Industry, 1930–1970* (New York: Arno, 1976), p. 213.

15. Elliot Paul and Luis Quintanilla, *With a Hays Nonny Nonny* (New York: Random, 1942), p. 155.

16. Lester Friedman, *Hollywood's Image of the Jew* (New York: Ungar, 1982), p. 107.

17. Jacobs, "WWII and American Film," p. 16.

18. Ibid., pp. 3–4.

19. Hull, *Film in the Third Reich*, p. 173.

20. Helen Fine, "Socio-political Responses during the Holocaust," in Sherwin and Ament, *Encountering the Holocaust*, p. 87.

21. Ibid., p. 88.

22. Ibid., p. 89.

23. Ibid., p. 93.

24. David Wyman, *The Abandonment of the Jews* (New York: Random House, 1984), p. 91.

25. Ibid.

26. Ibid., p. 92.

27. Ibid. See also Robert Skloot, "We Will Never Die: The Success and Failure of a Holocaust Pageant," *Theater Journal* 37 (May 1985), pp. 167–80.

28. *Time* magazine, February 10, 1941, p. 69.

29. Ibid., pp. 69–70.

30. Charles Chaplin, *My Autobiography* (New York: Simon and Schuster, 1964), p. 405.

31. Roger Manvell, *Films and the Second World War* (New York: Delta/Dell, 1976), p. 64.

32. Ibid.

33. Henry Popkin, "The Vanishing Jew of Our Popular Culture," *Commentary* 14 (July 1952), p. 52.

34. Fine, "Socio-political Responses," p. 102.

35. B. Wasserstein, Britain and the Jews of Europe, 1939–1945 (New York: Oxford University Press, 1979), p. 357.

36. Judith Crist, "The Aftermath," in Morella, p. 248.

37. E. E. Cohen, "The Film as a Social Force," Commentary 4:2 (October 1947), p. 113.

38. New York Times, November 12, 1947.

39. Irwin Rosen, "The Effects of Gentleman's Agreement on Attitudes toward Jews," Journal of Psychology 26 (October 1948), pp. 525–36.

40. Shelley V. Kraemer, 334 U. S. 1 (1948).

41. H. H. Wollenberg, "The Jewish Theme in Contemporary Cinema," Penguin Film Review 8 (1949), pp. 46–47.

42. John Mariani, "Let's Not Be Beastly to the Nazis," Film Comment 15:1 (January-February 1979), p. 51.

43. Henry Hart's review in Films in Review 2:8 (October 1951), pp. 50–51.

44. See David Irving, The Trail of the Fox (New York: Dutton, 1977).

45. Rommel was injured in the beginning of July 1944 and was not directly involved in the July 20 assassination attempt against Hitler, nor was he aware of any of the details of this operation.

46. New York Times, October 18, 1951.

47. New York Times, October 28, 1951.

48. Ibid.

49. Robert LaGuardia, Monty: A Biography of Montgomery Clift (New York: Arbor House, 1977), p. 168.

50. Alan Spiegel, "The Vanishing Act: A Typology of the Jew in Contemporary American Film," in S. B. Cohen, ed., From Hester Street to Hollywood: The Jewish-American Stage and Screen (Bloomington: Indiana University Press, 1983), pp. 262–63.

51. New York Times, April 3, 1958.

52. Ezrahi, By Words Alone, p. 186.

53. Irwin Shaw, The Young Lions (New York: Dell, 1976), p. 577.

54. The information on the filming of the concentration camp scenes is based on a private conversation with Edward Dmytryk. The details of the Commandant's speech are based on the facts of the camp. See Gordon Mork, "Confronting the Past: A Visit to the Struthof-Natzwiller Concentration Camp," Shofar 2:2 (Winter 1984), pp. 31–32; and K. G. Feig, Hitler's Death Camps (New York: Holmes and Meier, 1979), "Natzweiler/Struthof: A Skier's Paradise," pp. 215–26.

55. Look magazine, April 15, 1958, p. 55.

56. Shaw, Young Lions, p. 392.

57. Crist, The Private Eye, p. 159.

58. As noted by Crist, ibid., pp. 160–61.

59. Gordon Gow, Hollywood in the Fifties (New York: A. S. Barnes, 1971), p. 10.

60. Langer, The Holocaust, p. 77.

61. Rosenfeld, A Double Dying, p. 51.

62. Ibid., p. 52.

63. Ibid., p. 17. See also Ernst Schnabel, Anne Frank: A Portrait in Courage, trans. R. and C. Winston (New York: Harcourt, 1958).

64. Film Facts 2:10 (1959), p. 45.

65. Time magazine, March 30, 1959.

66. For a full explanation of the narrative structure of a tragic action, see Ruth Nevo, Tragic Form in Shakespeare (New Jersey: Princeton University Press, 1972), pp. 5–7.

67. Jacob Robinson wrote the following in his article "The Behavior of the Victims." "The behavior of the Jewish masses in the various stages of the Holocaust is in a general way what could have been expected from any group having to face all-pervading terror by the overwhelming power of a ruthless enemy such as the Nazi machine. In two respects it was, perhaps, above expectations. First, the instinctive will to live (in the ghettos where

families were not separated) developed resourcefulness and inventiveness in combating famine and oppression hardly found elsewhere in comparable situations. Second, in spite of
the continuous terror and bestiality of the persecutors, depersonalization only rarely reached
the lowest level of animalization." In Israel Pocket Library, *Holocaust* (Jerusalem: Keter,
1974), pp. 78–79.

68. Lawrence Langer, "The Americanization of the Holocaust on Stage and Screen," in
Cohen, *From Hester Street to Hollywood*, p. 213.

69. The makers of the movie *The Diary of Anne Frank* tried a different ending in a sneak
preview in San Francisco, showing Anne after her capture, in a concentration camp. The
viewers' reaction reinforced the producers' intention to create a film which would be "hopeful
after all." See *Variety*, April 1, 1959, "How 'Cheerful' is Anne Frank?"

70. Anne Frank, *The Diary of a Young Girl*, trans. B. M. Mooyaart-Doubleday (New
York: Doubleday, 1964), p. 245.

71. Ibid., p. 228.

72. Meyer Levin, *The Obsession* (New York: Simon and Schuster, 1973), p. 28.

73. Ibid., p. 35.

74. See Stephen Fife, "Meyer Levin's Obsession," *The New Republic*, August 2, 1982,
pp. 26–30.

75. In *The Obsession* Levin describes in detail the struggle over the *Dairy*'s dramatic
presentation.

76. Anne Frank, *The Diary*, p. 228.

77. Andrew Sarris, *Confessions of a Cultist* (New York: Simon and Schuster, 1970),
p. 200.

78. Sidney Lumet, "Keep Them on the Hook," *Film Quarterly* 2 (1966), p. 17.

79. Edward L. Wallant, *The Pawnbroker* (New York: Macfadden-Bartel, 1965).

80. Dorothy S. Bilik, *Immigrant-Survivor: Post Holocaust Consciousness in Recent Jewish-
American Fiction* (Middletown, Connecticut: Wesleyan University Press, 1981), p. 92.

81. Ibid., p. 94.

82. See Neil Hurley, *Theology through Film* (New York: Harper and Row, 1976), p. 129.

83. William Styron, *Sophie's Choice* (New York: Bantam, 1980).

84. Andrew Sarris, "Why 'Tootsie' Works and 'Sophie' Doesn't," *Village Voice*, December
21, 1982, p. 71.

85. *New York Times*, December 10, 1982.

86. Steiner, *Language and Silence*, p. 163.

87. Rosenfeld, *A Double Dying*, p. 14.

88. L. Epstein, "The Reality of Evil," *Partisan Review* 4 (1976), p. 639.

89. Sarris entitled his film review "To Cry or Not To Cry," *Village Voice*, December 28,
1982.

90. See Langer, *Versions*, p. 86.

91. *Time* magazine, May 1, 1978, p. 53.

92. Jean-Paul Bier, "The Holocaust and West Germany: Strategies of Oblivion 1947–
1979," *New German Critique* 19 (Winter 1980), p. 29.

93. Robin Wood, "Democracy and Shpontanuity," *Film Comment* 21:1 (January-February
1976), p. 9.

94. Langer, "The Americanization," p. 217.

95. LaGuardia, *Monty*, p. 174.

96. Steiner, *Language and Silence*, p. 150.

AN INTERLUDE

1. Chaplin, *My Autobiography*, pp. 424–25.

2. Manvell, *Films and the Second World War*, p. 38.

3. Theodore Huff, *Charlie Chaplin* (New York: Henry Schuman, 1951), p. 167.

4. Ibid., p. 264.

5. Gerald Mast, *The Comic Mind* (New York: Bobbs-Merrill, 1973), p. 72.

6. Ibid., p. 115.

7. Richard Grunberger, *The 12-Year Reich* (New York: Ballantine Books, 1972), pp. 455–56.

8. See Dawidowicz, *The War against the Jews*, p. 8.

9. Mast, *The Comic Mind*, p. 117. Mast is usually a very acute commentator, but his interpretation of Chaplin's words as "Marxism" is an erroneous reading of either Marxism or Chaplin's words.

10. Mast, *The Comic Mind*, p. 117.

11. Manvell, *Films and the Second World War*, p. 37.

12. Quoted in Jacobs, "World War II and the American Film," p. 8.

13. In Shirer, *The Rise and Fall*, p. 467.

14. Mast, *The Comic Mind*, p. 115.

15. Sarris, *Confessions*, p. 125.

16. See Edith Kern, *The Absolute Comic* (New York: Columbia University Press, 1980), especially chapter 2, "Carnivalesque Justice," pp. 39–84.

17. Chaplin, *My Autobiography*, p. 426.

CHAPTER V

1. See Peter Weiss, *The Investigation*, trans. J. Swan and U. Grosbard (New York: Simon and Schuster Pocket Books, 1967), pp. 201–02.

2. See Rolf Hochhuth, *The Deputy*, trans. Richard and Clara Winston (New York: Grove Press, 1964).

3. Quoted in John Russel Taylor, *Cinema Eye, Cinema Ear* (New York: Hill and Wang, 1964), p. 14.

4. Monica Stirling, *A Screen of Time* (New York: Harcourt Brace Jovanovich, 1979), pp. 192–93.

5. Ibid., p. 195.

6. Ibid., p. 198.

7. Luchino Visconti, *La Caduta degli Dei* (n.p.: Capelli, n.d.), p. 39.

8. Stirling, *A Screen*, p. 197.

9. Visconti, *La Caduta*, p. 31.

10. Simon, *Movies into Film*, p. 193.

11. Stirling, *A Screen*, p. 192.

12. Ezrahi, *By Words Alone*, p. 151.

13. Kinder and Houston, *Close-Up*, p. 173.

14. Ibid.

15. Richard Schickel, *Second Sight* (New York: Simon and Schuster, 1972), p. 292.

16. See Richard King, *The Party of Eros* (New York: Delta Books, 1972), pp. 52–62.

17. Clifford Kirkpatrick, *Nazi Germany: Its Women and Family Life* (Indianapolis: Bobbs-Merrill, 1938), p. 104.

18. Kinder and Houston discuss *The Damned* in their chapter "Views of Realism." See *Close-Up*, pp. 172–81.

19. Simon, *Movies into Film*, p. 192.

20. Monaco, *Alain Resnais*, p. 16.

21. George Steiner, *In Bluebeard's Castle* (New Haven: Yale University Press, 1971), pp. 30–31.

22. Chaplin's accounts of the special effects used in the big-crowd scenes is a wonderful example for the correlation between cinematic technique and ideological meaning. In *My Life in Pictures* Chaplin described the visual rendering of the faceless multitudes of Hitler's followers: "Some of the vast crowd effects were achieved by putting grape-nuts on a tray above a vibrator." (New York: Grosset and Dunlap, 1975), p. 270.

23. Mast, *The Comic Mind*, p. 116.

24. Cited in Stirling, *A Screen*, p. 191.

25. Sontag, *Saturn*, pp. 93–94.

26. For stimulating discussions of the exploitation of the Holocaust for aesthetic and erotic gratifications see: Susan Sontag, "Fascinating Fascism," in *Saturn*, pp. 73–105; Saul Friedländer, *Reflections of Nazism: An Essay on Kitsch and Death*, trans. Thomas Weyr (New York: Harper and Row, 1984); and Alvin Rosenfeld, *Imagining Hitler* (Bloomington: Indiana University Press, 1985).

27. George Steiner, *Language and Silence*, pp. 156–57.

28. Franco Solinas's allegorical story includes striking similarities to the real case of Pieter Menten, a Dutch war criminal who was sentenced to ten years in prison in the seventies after he was discovered by an Israeli journalist, Haviv Kanaan. In the thirties Menten lived in the Polish village Podhorodse and befriended many local Jews. A bon vivant art collector with a yellow sport car and mysterious business connections, he was to the Jews "an embodiment of much that was enlightened in Western culture." During the war he served the Nazis and organized the mass killing of the Jews in Podhorodse. Before coming to Palestine in 1935, Kanaan had a warm friendship with the Dutchman. When he found out that Menten was responsible for the death of his family members, Kanaan conducted a relentless manhunt to track down the war criminal and bring him to justice. For a full account of the story see Malcolm C. MacPherson. *The Blood of His Servant* (New York: Times Books, 1982).

29. *Time* magazine, 110:88 (November 14, 1977), p. 88.

30. *Mr. Klein*, published script in *L'Avant Scène du Cinema* no. 175 (November 1976), p. 46.

31. *Mr. Klein*, p. 52.

32. Foster Hirsh, *Joseph Losey*, (Boston: Twayne, 1980), pp. 188–89.

33. *Mr. Klein*, p. 31.

34. Langer points out a connection between *Moby Dick* and Holocaust literature in his comment that "Ilse Aichinger [in her *Herod's Children*] has put to excellent use Ishmael's ominous conjecture in *Moby Dick* that though 'in many of its aspects this visible world seems formed in love, the invisible spheres were formed in fright.' " (See Langer, *The Holocaust and the Literary Imagination*, p. 164). Melville's sentence can also serve as a motto for *Mr. Klein*.

35. *Mr. Klein*, p. 58.

36. Hirsh, *Losey*, p. 188.

37. Ezrahi, *By Words Alone*, p. 5.

38. Gershon Shaked, *Gal Hadash Ba-Siporet Ha-Ivrit* [A New Wave In Hebrew Narrative] (Tel Aviv: Sifriat Ha-Poalim, 1971), p. 73. Translation mine.

39. Rosenfeld, *A Double Dying*, pp. 23–24.

40. Hirsh, *Losey*, p. 187.

41. Steiner, *Language and Silence*, pp. 156–57.

42. *New Yorker* 53:87 (February 6, 1978), p. 78.

43. Rosenfeld, *A Double Dying*, p. 57.

44. Ibid., p. 59.

45. Giorgio Bassani, *The Garden of the Finzi-Continis*, trans. I. Quigly (New York: Atheneum, 1965). See especially Foreword, pp. 7–13.

46. David Denby, Film Review *New York Times*, January 2, 1972.

47. Ibid.

48. Ibid.

49. Bassani, *The Garden*, p. 254.

50. Pauline Kael, *Deeper into Movies* (Boston: Little Brown, 1973), p. 364.

51. Denby, Review, January 2, 1972.

52. Ibid.

53. *Time* magazine, May 1, 1978, p. 53.

54. See Lionel Trilling, "On the Modern Element in Modern Literature," in Irving Howe, ed., *The Idea of the Modern* (New York: Horizon, 1967), pp. 59–82.

55. Irving Howe, Introduction to *The Idea of the Modern*, p. 16.

56. Steiner, *In Bluebeard's Castle*, p. 29.

57. See Kracauer, *From Caligari to Hitler*.

58. Jacob Talmon, *Idan Ha-Alimut* [The Era of Violence] (Tel Aviv: Am Oved, 1974), pp. 289–90.

59. Aristotle, *Poetics*, trans. S. H. Butcher, in B. F. Dukore, ed., *Dramatic Theory and Criticism* (New York: Holt, Rinehart, Winston, 1974), p. 39.

60. Frederic Jameson, "Reflections in Conclusion," in R. Taylor, ed., *Aesthetics and Politics* (London: Verso, 1980), p. 198.

Bibliography

Adler, Renata. *A Year in the Dark*. New York: Berkeley Medallion Books, 1971.

Andrew, J. D. *The Major Film Theories: An Introduction*. New York: Oxford University Press, 1976.

Aristotle. *Poetics*. trans. S. H. Butcher, in B. F. Dukore, ed., *Dramatic Theory and Criticism: Greeks to Grotowski*. New York: Holt, Rinehart, and Winston, 1974.

Armes, Roy. *The Cinema of Alain Resnais*. New York: A. S. Barnes, 1968.

————. *Film and Reality: An Historical Survey*. Middlesex, England: Penguin Books, 1975.

————. *French Cinema Since 1946*. 2 vols. New York: A. S. Barnes, 1966.

————. *Patterns of Realism*. New York: A. S. Barnes, 1971.

Avisar, Ilan. "The Holocaust Film: 1933–1950." M.A. Thesis, Indiana University, 1980.

Barsam, Richard Meram. *Filmguide to Truimph of the Will*. Bloomington: Indiana University Press, 1975.

Barthes, Roland. *Camera Lucida: Reflections on Photography*. Trans. Richard Howard. New York: Hill and Wang, 1981.

Bassani, Giorgio. *The Garden of the Finzi-Continis*. Trans. Isabel Quigly. New York: Atheneum, 1965.

Battaille, Georges. *Death and Sensuality: A Study of Eroticism and the Taboo*. New York: Walker, 1962.

Bauer, Yehuda. *A History of the Holocaust*. New York: Franklin Watts, 1982.

Baxter, John. *Hollywood in the Thirties*. New York: Paperback Library, 1970.

Bazin, Andre. *What Is Cinema*. 2 vols. Trans. Hugh Gray. Berkeley: University of California Press, 1967 and 1971.

Belto, John. *The Hollywood Professionals, Vol. 3: H. Hawks, F. Borzage, E. Ulmer*. London: Tantivy Press, 1974.

Berger, Alan. *Crisis and Covenant: The Holocaust in American Jewish Fiction*. New York: State University of New York Press, 1985.

Bergman, Ingmar. *The Serpent's Egg*. Trans. Alan Blair. New York: Bantam House, 1977.

Bilik, Dorothy Seidman. *Immigrant-Survivor: Post-Holocaust Consciousness in Recent Jewish-American Fiction*. Middletown, Connecticut: Wesleyan University Press, 1981.

Birkos, A. S., comp. *Soviet Cinema*. Connecticut: Archon Books, 1976.

Blatter, Janet, and Sybil Milton. *Art of the Holocaust*. New York: Rutledge, 1981.

Bohn, T. W., and R. L. Stromgren. *Light and Shadows: A History of Motion Pictures*. Sherman Oaks, California: Alfred Publishing, 1978.

Borowski, Tadeusz. *This Way for the Gas, Ladies and Gentlemen*. Trans. Barbara Vedder, intr. Jan Kott. New York: Penguin Books, 1976.

Bottome, Phyllis. *The Mortal Storm*. Boston: Little Brown, 1938.

Brownmiller, Susan. *Against Our Will: Men, Women and Rape*. New York: Bantam Books, 1975.

Cayrol, Jean. *Night and Fog*. Trans. R. Hughes and Merle Worth, in Robert Hughes, ed., *Film: Book 2—Films of Peace and War*. New York: Grove Press, 1962.

Centerpoint: A Journal of Interdisciplinary Studies V. 4:1 (Fall 1980) "The Holocaust."

Chaplin, Charles. *My Autobiography*. New York: Simon and Schuster, 1964.

————. *My Life in Pictures*. New York: Grosset and Dunlap. 1975.

Chatman, Seymour. *Story and Discourse: Narrative Structure in Fiction and Film*. Ithaca: Cornell University Press, 1978.

Cohen, Sarah Blacher, ed. *From Hester Street to Hollywood: The Jewish-American Stage and Screen.* Bloomington: Indiana University Press, 1983.

Culler, Jonathan. *Structuralist Poetics.* Ithaca: Cornell University Press, 1975.

Dawidowicz, Lucy. *The Holocaust and the Historians.* Cambridge: Harvard University Press, 1981.

———. *The Jewish Presence.* New York: Holt, Rinehart & Winston, 1978.

———. *The War Against the Jews 1933–1945.* New York: Bantam Books, 1976.

Des Pres, Terrence. *The Survivor: An Anatomy of Life in the Death Camps.* 1970, rpt. New York: Pocket Books, 1977.

Dmytryk, Edward. *It's a Hell of a Life but Not a Bad Living.* New York: New York Times Books, 1978.

Doneson, Judith E. "The Jew as a Female Figure in Holocaust Film," *Shoah* 1:1, pp. 11–13, 18.

Erens, Patricia. *The Jew in American Cinema.* Bloomington: Indiana University Press, 1984.

Ezrahi, Sidra Dekoven. *By Words Alone: The Holocaust in Literature.* Chicago: University of Chicago Press, 1980.

Fackenheim, Emil. *To Mend the World.* New York: Schocken, 1982.

Feig, Konnilyn. *Hitler's Death Camps.* New York: Holmes and Meier, 1981.

Ferro, Marc. *Cinéma et histoire.* Paris: Denoel/Gonthier, 1977.

Ford, Charles. *Histoire du Cinéma Français Contemporain 1945–1977.* Paris: France-Empire, 1977.

Fox, Stuart, comp. *Jewish Films in the United States: A Comprehensive Survey and Descriptive Filmography.* Boston: G. K. Hall, 1976.

Frank, Anne. *The Diary of a Young Girl.* Trans. B. M. Mooyaart-Doubleday. New York: Doubleday, 1967.

Freud, Sigmund. *Civilization and Its Discontents.* Trans. and ed. James Strachey. New York: W. W. Norton, 1961.

Friedländer, Saul. *Reflections of Nazism.* Trans. Thomas Weir. New York: Harper & Row, 1984.

———. *When Memory Comes.* Trans. Helen Lane. New York: Avon, 1980.

Friedman, Georges. *The End of the Jewish People?* Trans. Eric Mosbacher, London: Hutchinson, 1967.

Friedman, Lester. *Hollywood's Image of the Jew.* New York: Frederick Ungar, 1982.

Friedman, M. R. "Exorcising the Past: Jewish Figures in Contemporary Films." *Journal of Contemporary History* 19:3 (1984), pp. 511–27.

Frye, Northrop. *Anatomy of Criticism: Four Essays.* 1957 rpt. New York: Princeton University Press, 1973.

Fuksievicz, Jacek. *Polish Cinema.* Trans. E. Gromck-Guzinska. Warsaw: Interpress Publishers, 1973.

Furhammar, Leif, and Folke Isaksson. *Politics and Film.* Trans. K. French. New York: Praeger Publishers, 1971.

Gennette, Gerard. *Narrative Discourse: An Essay in Method.* Trans. Jane E. Lewin. Ithaca, New York: Cornell University Press, 1981.

Goodman, Jack. *While You Were Gone: A Report on Wartime Life in the United States.* New York: Simon and Schuster, 1946.

Gow, Gordon. *Hollywood in the Fifties.* New York: A. S. Barnes, 1971.

Grant, B. K., ed. *Film Genre: Theory and Criticism.* Metuchen, New Jersey: Scarecrow Press, 1977.

Green, Gerald. *Holocaust.* New York: Bantam, 1978.

Grosman, Ladislav. *The Shop on Main Street*. Trans. Iris Urwin. New York: Doubleday, 1970.

Grunberger, Richard. *The 12-Year Reich: A Social History of Nazi Germany 1933–1945*. New York: Ballantine Books, 1972.

Guthke, Karl. *Modern Tragicomedy: An Investigation into the Nature of Genre*. New York: Random House, 1966.

Haft, Cynthia. *The Theme of Nazi Concentration Camps in French Literature*. The Hague, Netherlands: Mouton, 1973.

Hamburger, Michael. *The Truth of Poetry: Tensions in Modern Poetry from Baudelaire to the 1960's*. London: Weidenfeld and Nicolson, 1969.

Hanser, Reihe, ed. *Film in Der DDR*. Munchen: Carl Hanser Verlag, 1977.

Harel, Yehuda. *Ha-Kolnoah Me-Reshito Ve-Ad Ha-Yom (Cinema from its Beginning until the Present)*. Tel Aviv: Yavneh, 1956.

Heath, Stephen. *Questions of Cinema*. Bloomington: Indiana University Press, 1981.

Higham, Charles, and G. Greenberg. *Hollywood in the Forties*. New York: A. S. Barnes, 1968.

Hilberg, Raul. *The Destruction of the European Jews*. Chicago: Quadrangle Books, 1961.

Hirsh, Foster. *Joseph Losey*. Boston: Twayne, 1980.

Hochhuth, Rolf. *The Deputy*. Trans. R. and C. Winston. New York: Grove Press, 1964.

Howe, Irving. ed. *The Idea of the Modern in Literature and the Arts*. New York: Horizon, 1967.

Huff, Theodore. *Charlie Chaplin*. New York: Henry Schuman, 1951.

Hughes, Robert. *The Shock of the New*. New York: Alfred A.. Knopf, 1981.

Hughes, Robert, ed. *Film: Book 2—Films of Peace and War*. New York: Grove Press, 1962.

Hull, D. S. *Film in the Third Reich*. Berkeley and Los Angeles: University of California Press, 1969.

Hurley, Neil P. *Theology through Film*. New York: Harper and Row, 1976.

Insdorf, Annette. *Indelible Shadows: Film and the Holocaust*. New York: Random House, Vintage Books, 1983.

Irving, David, J.C. *The Trail of the Fox*. New York: Dutton, 1977.

Isaac, Dan. "Film and the Holocaust," in *Centerpoint* 4:1 (Fall, 1980).

Israel Pocket Library. *Holocaust*. Jerusalem: Keter, 1978.

Jacobs, Lewis. "World War II and the American Film," *Cinema Journal* Vol. I (Winter 1967–68), 1–21.

Jarvie, I. C. *Movies as Social Criticism*. Metuchen, New Jersey: Scarecrow Press, 1978.

———. *Towards a Sociology of the Cinema*. London: Routledge and Kegan Paul, 1970.

Jeavons, Clyde. *A Pictorial History of War Films*. New Jersey: Citadel Press, 1976.

Jones, Dorothy B. "Hollywood Goes to War," *Nation*, Jan, 27, 1945, pp. 93–96.

———. "Tomorrow the Movies: Is Hollywood Growing Up?" *Nation*, Feb. 3, 1945, pp. 123–125.

Kael, Pauline. *Deeper into Movies*. Boston: Little Brown, 1973. An Atlantic Monthly Press Book.

———. *Going Steady*. New York: Bantam, 1971.

Kahler, Erich. *The Tower and the Abyss: Inquiry into the Transformation of Man*. New York: Viking, 1957.

Kaminsky, Stuart, ed. *Ingmar Bergman: Essays in Criticism*. New York: Oxford University Press, 1975.

Katz, Steven T. *Post-Holocaust Dialogues*. New York: New York University Press, 1983.

Kaufmann, Stanley. *A World on Film: Criticism and Comment*. New York: Dell, a Delta Book, 1966.

Kaufmann, Walter, ed. *Existentialism from Dostoevsky to Sartre*. New York: New American Library, 1975.

Kern, Edith. *The Absolute Comic*. New York: Columbia University Press, 1980.

Keyser, Lester J. "Three Faces of Evil: Fascism in Recent Movies," *Journal of Popular Film* v. 4 (Nov. 1975), pp. 4–31.

Kinder, Marsha, and Beverle Houston. *Close-Up: A Critical Perspective On Film*. New York: Harcourt Brace Jovanovich, 1972.

King, Richard. *The Party of Eros: Radical Social Thought and the Realm of Freedom*. New York: Dell, a Delta Book, 1972.

Kirkpatrich, Clifford. *Nazi Germany: Its Women and Family Life*. Indianapolis: Bobbs-Merrill, 1938.

Kosinski, Jerzy. *The Painted Bird*. Boston: Houghton Mifflin, 1976.

Kracauer, Siegfried. *From Caligari to Hitler: A Psychological History of the German Film*. New Jersey: Princeton University Press, 1947.

———. *Theory of Film: The Redemption of Physical Reality*. 1960; rpt. New York: Oxford University Press, 1978.

Kren, M. George, and Leon Rappoport. *The Holocaust and the Crisis of Human Behavior*. New York: Holmes and Meier, 1980.

Kuznetsov, Anatoli. *Babi Yar*. Trans. David Floyd. New York: Pocket Books, 1971.

LaGuardia, Robert. *Monty: A Biography of Montgomery Clift*. New York: Arbor House, 1977.

Langer, Lawrence. *The Holocaust and the Literary Imagination*. New Haven: Yale University Press, 1975.

———. *Versions of Survival: The Holocaust and the Human Spirit*. Albany: State University of New York, 1982.

———. "The Americanization of the Holocaust on Stage and Screen," in S. B. Cohen, ed., *From Hester Street to Hollywood: The Jewish-American Stage and Screen*. Bloomington: Indiana University Press, 1983. pp. 213–30.

Leiser, Erwin. *Nazi Cinema*. Trans. G. Mander and David Wilson. New York: Collier Books, 1974.

Levi, Primo. *Survival in Auschwitz: The Nazi Assault on Humanity*. Trans. Stuart Woolf. New York: Collier Books, 1961.

Levin, Meyer. *The Obsession*. New York: Simon and Schuster, 1973.

Leyda, Jay. *Kino: A History of the Russian and Soviet Film*. New York: Collier Books, 1973.

Liehm, Antonin. *Closely Watched Films: The Czechoslovak Experience*. White Plains, New York: International Arts and Sciences Press, 1974.

Liehm, Mira, and A. J. Liehm. *The Most Important Art: Eastern European Film after 1945*. Berkeley: University of California Press, 1977.

Lusting, Arnost. *Darkness Casts No Shadows*. Trans. Jeanne Nemcova. Washington, D.C.: Inscape, 1976.

———. *Night and Hope*. Trans. George Theiner. Washington, D.C.: Inscape, 1976.

MacBean, James Roy. *Film and Revolution*. Bloomington: Indiana University Press, 1975.

MacCann, R. D., ed. *Film: A Montage of Theories*. New York: E. P. Dutton, 1966.

McConnell, Frank. *Storytelling and Mythmaking; Images from Film and Literature*. New York: Oxford University Press, 1979.

Malle, Louis, and Patrick Modiano. *Lacombe, Lucien*. Trans. Sabine Destree. New York: Viking Press, 1975.

Mann, Abby. *Judgment at Nuremberg*. London: Cassell, 1961.

Manvell, Roger. *Films and the Second World War*. New York: Delta, 1975.

Manvell, R., and H. Fraenkel. *The German Cinema*. New York: Praeger Publishers, 1971.

Mast, Gerald. *The Comic Mind: Comedy and the Movies*. New York: Bobbs-Merrill, 1973.

Matis, David. "Films of the Holocaust," *Yiddish* V.1 (Summer 1973), pp. 12–23.

Mellen, Joan. *Filmguide to The Battle of Algiers*. Bloomington: Indiana University Press, 1973.

Michatek, Boleslaw. *The Cinema of Andrezj Wajda*. Trans. Edward Rothert. New York: A. S. Barnes, 1973.

Monaco, James. *Alain Resnais*. New York: Oxford University Press, 1978.

Morella, J., E. Z. Epstein, and J. Griggs. *The Films of World War II*. New Jersey: Citadel Press, 1973.

Nevo, Ruth. *Tragic Form in Shakespeare*. Princeton, N. J.: Princeton University Press, 1972.

Nichols, Bill. *Ideology and the Image: Social Representation and the Cinema and Other Media*. Bloomington: Indiana University Press, 1981.

Novak, Antonin [Jan Zalman (pseud.)].*Films and Filmmakers in Czechoslovakia*. Trans. George Theiner. Prague: Orbis, 1968.

Ophuls, Marcel. *The Sorrow and the Pity*. Trans. Mirielle Johnston. New York: Outerbridge and Lazard, 1972.

Paul, David W., ed. *Politics, Art and Commitment in the East European Cinema*. London: MacMillan, 1983.

Paul, Elliot, and Luis Quintanilla. *With a Hays Nonny Nonny*. New York: Random, 1942.

Penkower, Monty Noam. *The Jews Were Expendable: Free World Diplomacy and the Holocaust*. Urbana and Chicago: University of Illinois Press, 1983.

Popkin, Henry. "The Vanishing Jew of Our Popular Culture." *Commentary* V. 14 (July 1952), 46–55.

Richardson, Robert. *Literature and Film*. Bloomington: Indiana University Press, 1969.

Roffman, Peter, and Jim Purdy. *The Hollywood Social Problem Film: Madness, Despair, and Politics from the Depression to the Fifties*. Bloomington: Indiana University Press, 1981.

Rosenfeld, Alvin. *A Double Dying: Reflections on Holocaust Literature*. Bloomington: Indiana University Press, 1980.

———. *Imagining Hitler*. Bloomington: Indiana University Press, 1985.

Roskies, David G. *Against the Apocalypse: Responses to Catastrophe in Modern Jewish Culture*. Cambridge: Harvard University Press, 1984.

Rubin, Steven Jay. *Combat Films: American Realism: 1945–1970*. Jefferson, North Carolina: McFarland, 1981.

Sarris, Andrew. *Cinema and Politics*. New York: Columbia University Press, 1978.

———. *Confessions of a Cultist: On the Cinema, 1955–1969*. New York: Simon and Schuster, a Touchstone Book, 1970.

Schickel, Richard. *Second Sight: Notes on Some Movies 1965–1970*. New York: Simon and Schuster, 1972.

Schnabel, Ernst. *Anne Frank: A Portrait in Courage*. Trans. R. and C. Winston. New York: Harcourt, 1958.

Scholes, Robert, and Robert Kellogg. *The Nature of Narrative*. 1966; rpt. London: Oxford University Press, 1978.

Shain, R. E. *An Analysis of Motion Pictures about War Released by the American Film Industry, 1930–1970*. New York: Arno Press, 1976.

Shaked, Gershon. *Gal Hadash Ba-Siporet Ha-Ivrit (A New Wave in the Hebrew Narrative)*. Tel Aviv: Sifriat Ha-Poalim, 1971.

Shaw, Irwin. *The Young Lions*. 1948; rpt. New York: Dell, 1976.

Shaw, Robert. *The Man in the Glass Booth*. New York: Grove Press, 1968.

Sherwin, Byron, and S. G. Ament, eds. *Encountering the Holocaust: An Interdisciplinary Survey*. Chicago: Impact Press, 1979.

Shirer, William. *The Rise and Fall of the Third Reich.* Greenwich, Connecticut: Fawcett, 1960.

Short, K. R. M., ed. *Feature Films as History.* Knoxville: University of Tennessee Press, 1981.

Simon, John. *Movies into Film: Film Criticism 1967–1970.* New York: Dial Press, 1971.

———. *Private Screenings.* New York: Berkeley Medallion Books, 1967.

Skloot, Robert, ed. with intro. *The Theatre of the Holocaust: Four Plays.* Madison: University of Wisconsin Press, 1982.

Skvorecky, Joseph. *All the Bright Young Men and Women: A Personal History of the Czech Cinema.* Trans. Michael Schonberg. Toronto: Peter Martin Associates, in association with *Take One* magazine, 1971.

tSolinas, Franco. *Mr. Klein,* in *L'Avant Scene du Cinema* No. 175 (November 1976).

Sontag, Susan. *On Photography.* New York: Farrar, Straus, Giroux, 1977.

———. *Styles of Radical Will.* New York: Farrar, Straus, Giroux, 1969.

———. *Under the Sign of Saturn.* New York: Farrar, Straus, Giroux, 1980.

Steiner, George. *The Death of Tragedy.* New York: Alfred A. Knopf, 1961.

———. *In Bluebeard's Castle: Some Notes towards the Redefinition of Culture.* New Haven: Yale University Press, 1971.

———. *Language and Silence: Essays in Language, Literature, and the Inhuman.* New York: Atheneum, 1967.

Stirling, Monica. *A Screen of Time: A Study of Luchino Visconti.* New York: Harcourt Brace Jovanovich, 1979.

Stoil, Michael Jon. *Cinema Beyond the Danube: The Camera and Politics.* Metuchen, New Jersey: Scarecrow Press, 1974.

Styron, William. *Sophie's Choice.* New York: Bantam Books, 1980.

Talmon, Jacob. *Idan Ha-Alimut (The Age of Violence).* Tel Aviv: Am Oved, 1974.

———. *The Myth of the Nation and the Vision of Revolution: The Origins of Ideological Polarization in the Twentieth Century.* London: Secker and Warburg, 1981.

Taylor, John Russel. *Cinema Eye, Cinema Ear: Some Key Filmmakers of the Sixties.* New York: Hill and Wang, 1964.

Taylor, Ronald, ed. *Aesthetics and Politics.* London: Verso, 1980.

Todorov, Tzvetan. *Introduction to Poetics.* Trans. Richard Howard. Minneapolis: University of Minnesota Press, 1981.

Torgovnick, Marianna. *Closure in the Novel.* Princeton, N.J.: Princeton University Press, 1981.

Tyler, Parker. *Chaplin: Last of the Clowns.* 1947; rpt. U.S. Horizon Press, 1972.

Visconti, Luchino. *La Caduta degli Dei (Gotterdammerung).* n.p.: Capelli, n.d.

Vogel, Amos. *Film as a Subversive Art.* London: Weidenfeld and Nicolson, 1974.

Wajda, Andrzej. *The Wajda Trilogy: Generation, Kanal, Ashes and Diamonds.* New York: Simon and Schuster, 1973.

Walker, Alexander. *Sex in the Movies: The Celluloid Sacrifice.* Baltimore: Penguin Books, 1968.

Wallant, Edward L. *The Pawnbroker.* New York: Macfadden-Bartel Books, 1965.

Wasserstein, Bernard. *Britain and the Jews of Europe, 1939–1945.* New York: Oxford University Press, 1979.

Weiss, Peter. *The Investigation.* Trans. Jan Swan and Ulu Grosbard. New York: Pocket Books, 1967.

Wertmuller, Lina. *Seven Beauties,* in *The Screenplays of Lina Wertmuller.* Trans. Steven Wagner. New York: Quadrangle, 1977, pp. 268–334.

Wiesel, Elie. *Night.* Trans. S. Rodway. New York: Avon, 1960.

————. *Legends of Our Time*. Trans. S. Donadio. New York: Holt, Rinehart and Winston, 1968.

Williams, Christopher, ed. *Realism and the Cinema: A Reader*. London: Routledge and Kegan Paul, 1980.

Wyman, David G. *The Abandonment of the Jews: America and the Holocaust 1941–1945*. New York: Random House, 1984.

Filmography

Address Unknown, U.S.A., 1943. Directed by William Cameron Menzies.

The Alien's Place, Holland, 1979. Directed by Rudolph van den Berg.

Ambulance, Poland, 1962. Directed by Janusz Morgenstern (short film).

And Now, My Love, France, 1974. Directed by Claude Lelouch.

Angry Harvest, West Germany, 1985. Directed by A. Holland.

As If It Were Yesterday, Belgium, 1980. Directed by Myriam Abramowitz and Esther Hoffenberg (documentary; hereafter only notable documentaries will be mentioned in this filmography).

Between Yesterday and Tomorrow, Germany, 1947. Directed by Harold Braun.

Birth Certificate, Poland, 1961. Directed by Stanislaw Rozewicz.

Black Thursday (*The Gates of the Louvre*), France, 1974. Directed by Michel Mitrani. Script by Mitrani an Albert Cossery, based on a book by Roger Boussinot.

The Blum Affair, Germany, 1947. Directed by Erich Engel. Script by Robert A. Stemmle.

The Boat Is Full, Switzerland, 1981. Directed and scripted by Markus Imhoof.

Border Street, Poland, 1948. Directed by Alexander Ford.

The Boys from Brazil, U.S.A., 1978. Directed by Franklin J. Schaffner. Script by Heywood Gould, based on Ira Levin's novel.

The Bride, Israel, 1985. Directed by N. Levitan. Based on Ladislav Grosman's story.

Brussels-Transit, Belgium, 1980. Directed and scripted by Samy Szlingerbaum.

Cabaret, U.S.A., 1975. Directed by Bob Fosse. Script by Jay Presson. An adaptation of Joe Masteroff, John Kander, and Fred Ebb's Broadway musical based on Christopher Isherwood's Berlin stories.

The Cellar, Israel, 1963. Directed by Natan Gross. Script by Shimon Israeli.

Charlotte, Holland/West Germany, 1981. Directed by Frans Weisz.

The Children of #67, West Germany, 1979. Directed and scripted by Usch Barthelmess-Weller and Werner Meyer.

The Condemned of Altona, Italy, 1962. Directed by Vittorio de Sica. Script by Abby Mann and Cesare Zavattini, from Jean-Paul Sartre's play.

Confessions of a Nazi Spy, U.S.A., 1939. Directed by Anatole Litvak.

Confrontation at Davos, Switzerland, 1975. Directed by Rolf Lyssy. Script by Lyssy and Georg Janett.

Conspiracy of Hearts, Great Britain, 1960. Directed by Ralph Thomas. Script by Robert Presnell.

The Cremator, Czechoslovakia, 1968. Directed by Juraj Jerz.

Crossfire, U.S.A., 1944. Directed by Edward Dmytryk.

The Damned, Italy, 1969. Directed by Luchino Visconti. Script by Visconti with Nicola Badalucco and Enrico Medioli.

Darkness at Daytime, Hungary, 1963. Directed by Zoltan Fabri.

David, West Germany, 1979. Directed by Peter Lilienthal. Script by Lilienthal, Jurek Becker, and Ulla Zieman, from an autobiographical novel by Joel Konig.

Diamonds of the Night, Czechoslovakia, 1964. Directed by Jan Nemec. Script by Arnost Lustig and Nemec, from Lustig's novel *Darkness Casts No Shadows*.

The Diary of Anne Frank, U.S.A., 1959. Directed by George Stevens. Script by Frances Goodrich and Albert Hackett, based on their dramatic version of the original diary.

Distant Journey (Ghetto Terezin), Czechoslovakia, 1948. Directed and scripted by Alfred Radok.

Dita Saxova, Czechoslovakia, 1968. Directed by Antonin Moshalyk. Script by Arnost Lustig, from his novel.

The Eighty-First Blow, Israel, 1975. Directed by Haim Gouri, Jacquet Ehrlich, and David Bergman (documentary).

The Enclosure, France, 1962. Directed by Armand Gatti. Script by Gatti and Pierre Joffrey.

Exodus, U.S.A., 1960. Directed by Otto Preminger. Script by Dalton Trumbo, from the novel by Leon Uris.

Fear Not, Jacob! West Germany, 1981. Directed by Radu Gabrea.

The Fifth Horseman Is Fear, Czechoslovakia, 1965. Directed by Zbynek Brynych. Script by Brynych and Hana Belohradska, from Belohradska's novella *Without Beauty, Without a Collar.*

The Garden of the Finzi-Continis, Italy, 1970. Directed by Vittorio de Sica. Script by Cesare Zavattini, Vittorio Bonicelli, and Ugo Pirro, based on the novel by Giorgio Bassani.

A Generation, Poland, 1955. Directed by Andrzej Wajda. Script by Bohdan Czeszko.

Genocide, U.S.A., 1982. Directed by Arnold Schwartzman. Written by Martin Gilbert and Rabbi Marvin Hier (documentary).

Germany, Pale Mother, West Germany, 1980. Directed by Helma Sanders-Brahms.

The Glass Cage, Israel/France, 1964. Directed by Phillippe Arthuys.

The Gold of Rome, Italy, 1961. Directed by Carlo Lizzani. Script by Lizzani with L. Battistrada, G. de Negri, and A. Lecco.

Grand Illusion, France, 1937. Directed by Jean Renoir. Script by Renoir and Charles Spaak.

The Great Dictator, U.S.A., 1940. Directed and scripted by Charles Chaplin.

High Street, Belgium, 1976. Directed by Andre Ernotte. Script by Ernotte and Elliot Tiber, from their book.

The Illegals, U.S.A., 1947. Directed by Meyer Levin (documentary).

Image before My Eyes, U.S.A., 1980. Directed by Josh Waletzky (documentary).

Jacob the Liar, East Germany, 1976. Directed by Frank Beyer. Script by Jurek Becker, from his novel.

The Jewish Wife, U.S.A., 1972 Directed by Jeff Young. Based on Bertolt Brecht's play (short film).

Judgment at Nuremberg, U.S.A., 1961. Directed by Stanley Kramer. Script by Abby Mann.

Judith, U.S.A., 1965. Directed by Daniel Mann. Script by John Michael Hayes, from a story by Lawrence Durrell.

The Juggler U.S.A., 1953. Directed by Edward Dmytryk.

Kapo, Italy, 1959. Directed by Gillo Pontecorvo. Script by Pontecorvo and Franco Solinas.

Lacombe, Lucien, France, 1974. Directed by Louis Malle. Script by Malle and Patrick Modiano.

Landscape after the Battle, Poland, 1970. Directed by Andrzej Wajda. Script by Wajda and Andrzej Brzozowski, based on stories by Tadeusz Borowski.

The Last Chance, Switzerland, 1945. Directed by Leopold Lindtberg.

The Last Chapter, U.S.A., 1978. Directed by Benjamin and Lawrence Rothman (documentary).

The Last Illusion, West Germany, 1949. Directed by Josef von Baky.

The Last Metro, France, 1980. Directed by François Truffaut. Script by Truffaut, Suzanne Schiffman, and Jean-Claude Grumberg.

The Last Sea, Israel, 1979. Directed by Haim Gouri, Jacquet Ehrlich, and David Bergman (documentary).

The Last Stop (*The Last Stage*), Poland, 1947. Directed by Wanda Jakubowska. Script by Jakubowska and Gerda Schneider.

Lili Marleen, West Germany, 1981. Directed by Rainer Werner Fassbinder.

Lisa, U.S.A., 1962. Directed by Philip Dunne. Script by Nelson Gidding, from the novel by Jan de Hartog.

Long Is the Road, Germany, 1947. Directed by H. B. Fredersdorf and M. Goldstein.

Love Camp Seven, U.S.A., 1968. Directed by R. L. Frost.

Lucky Star, Canada, 1980. Directed by Max Fisher.

The Man in the Glass Booth, U.S.A., 1975. Directed by Arthur Hiller. Script by Edward Anhalt, from the play by Robert Shaw.

Manon, France, 1947. Directed by Henri-Georges Clouzot. Script by Clouzot and Jean Ferry, an adaptation of the novel by Abbe Prevost.

Marriage in the Shadows, Germany, 1947. Directed by Kurt Maetzig.

The Martyr, Israel, 1976. Directed by Alexander Ford. Script by Josef Gross and Alexander Ramati.

Massacre in Rome, Italy, 1973. Directed by George Pan Cosmatos.

Me and the Colonel, U.S.A., 1958. Directed by Peter Granville. Script by S. N. Behrman and George Froeschel, based on the play by Franz Werfel.

Mephisto, Hungary, 1981. Directed by Istvan Szabo. Script by Szabo and Peter Dobai, based on the novel by Klaus Mann.

Morituri, Germany, 1947. Directed by Arthur Brauner.

Mr. Emmanuel, Great Britain, 1944. Directed by Harold French. Script by Louis Golding and Gordon Wellsley, from the novel by Golding.

Mr. Klein, France, 1976. Directed by Joseph Losey. Script by Franco Solinas.

The Mortal Storm, U.S.A., 1940. Directed by Frank Borzage. Script by E. West, G. Froeschel, and A. Ellis, based on the novel by Phyllis Bottome.

My Father's House, Israel, 1946. Directed by Herbert Kline. Script by Meyer Levin.

Naked Among the Wolves, East Germany, 1963. Directed by Frank Beyer. Script by Alfred Hirschmele, from the novel by Bruno Apitz.

Night and Fog, France, 1955. Directed by Alain Resnais. Script by Jean Cayrol (documentary).

The Night Porter, Italy, 1974. Directed by Liliana Cavani. Script by Cavani and Italo Moscati.

The Ninth Circle, Yugoslavia, 1960. Directed by France Stiglic. Script by Zora Dirnbach.

None Shall Escape, U.S.A., 1944. Directed by Andre De Toth.

The Odessa File, Great Britain, 1974. Directed by Ronald Neame. From the novel by Frederick Forsyth.

The Only Way, Denmark, 1967. Directed by Bent Christiansen.

Operation Eichmann, U.S.A., 1962. Directed by R. G. Springsteen. Script by Lewis Copley.

The Oppenheim Family, U.S.S.R., 1939. Directed by Gregori Roshal. Script by Serafina Roshal, from the novel by Lion Feuchtwanger.

Our Children, Poland and Israel, 1950. Directed by S. Goskind and N. Gross.

Our Hitler, a Film from Germany, West Germany, 1978. Directed by Hans-Jorgen Syberberg.

Paisan, Italy, 1946. Directed by Roberto Rossellini. Script by Federico Fellini (fifth episode).

Partisans of Vilna, 1986. Directed by Josh Waletzky (documentary).

La Passante, France, 1983. Directed by Jacques Rouffio.

The Passenger, Poland, 1962. Directed by Andrzej Munk. (Film completed by Witold Lesie-wicz.) Script by Zofia Posmysz and Munk, based on the novel by Posmysz.

The Pawnbroker, U.S.A., 1965. Directed by Sidney Lumet. Script by Morton Fine and David Friedkin, based on the novel by Edward L. Wallant.

Pebbels, Austria, 1982. Directed by Lukas Stepnik.

The Pedestrian, West Germany, 1973. Directed and scripted by Maximilian Schell.

Prayer for Katerina Horovitzova, Czechoslovakia, 1967. Directed by Antonin Moskalyk. Script by Arnost Lustig, from his story.

Professor Mamlock, U.S.S.R., 1938. Directed by Adolph Minkin and Herbert Rappaport. Script by Friedrich Wolf, from his play.

Professor Mamlock, East Germany, 1961. Directed by Konrad Wolf. A remake of the Russian film.

Raindrops, West Germany, 1981. Directed and written by Michael Haffman and Harry Raymon.

Reach for Glory, Great Britain, 1962. Directed by Philip Leacock. Script by Jud Kindberg, John Kohn, and John Rae, from John Rae's novel *The Custard Boys*.

Return from the Ashes, Great Britain, 1965. Directed by J. Lee Thompson. Script by Julius J. Epstein, from the novel by Hubert Munteilhet.

The Revolt of Job, Hungary, 1983. Directed by Imre Gyongyossy and Barna Kabay.

Samson, Poland, 1961. Directed by Andrzej Wajda. Script by Wajda and Kazimierz Brandys, from the play by Brandys.

Sanatorium, Poland, 1973. Directed by Wojciech Has. Based on the stories by Bruno Schulz.

Sandra, Italy, 1965. Directed by Luchino Visconti. Script by Visconti, S. Cecchi, di Amico, and E. Medioli.

The Search, U.S.A., 1948. Directed by Fred Zinnemann.

The Serpent's Egg, U.S./West Germany, 1977. Directed and scripted by Ingmar Bergman.

Seven Beauties, Italy, 1975. Directed and scripted by Lina Wertmuller.

Ship of Fools, U.S.A., 1965. Directed by Stanley Kramer. Script by Abby Mann, from the novel by Katherine Anne Porter.

Shoah, France, 1985. Directed by Claude Lanzmann (documentary).

The Shop on Main Street, Czechoslovakia, 1965. Directed by Jan Kadar and Elmar Klos. Script by Ladislav Grosman, from the novel by Grosman.

So Ends Our Night, U.S.A., 1940. Directed by D. L. Loew and A. Lewin. From the novel *Flotsam* by E. M. Remarque.

The Song and the Silence, U.S.A., 1969. Directed and scripted by Nathan Cohen.

Sophie's Choice, U.S.A., 1982. Directed and scripted by Alan Pakula. From the novel by William Styron.

The Sorrow and the Pity, France, 1969. Directed by Marcel Ophuls (documentary).

Stars, East Germany/Bulgaria, 1958. Directed by Konrad Wolf. Script by A. Vagenstein and C. Wernicke.

The Story of Chaim Rumkowski and the Jews of Lodz, Sweden, 1981. Directed by Peter Cohen. Written and co-directed by Bo Kuritzman (documentary).

Sweet Light in a Dark Room, Czechoslovakia, 1959. Directed by Jiri Weiss. Script by Jan Otcenasek.

A Tear in the Ocean, France, 1971. Directed and scripted by Henry Glaeser. Based on the novel by Manes Sperber.

The Tin Drum, West Germany, 1979. Directed by Volker Schlondorff. Script by Schlondorff, J. C. Carriere, and F. Seitz, from the novel by Gunter Grass.

To Be or Not to Be, U.S.A., 1942. Directed by Ernst Lubitsch. Script by Edwin Justus Mayer.

To Be or Not to Be, U.S.A., 1984. Directed by Mel Brooks.

Tobruk, U.S.A., 1967. Directed by Arthur Hiller.

Tomorrow the World, U.S.A., 1944. Directed by L. Fenton.

Transport from Paradise, Czechoslovakia, 1963. Directed by Zbynek Brynych. Script by Arnost Lustig, based on Lustig's book *Night and Hope*.

The Trial, Austria, 1948. Directed by G. W. Pabst.

Triumph of the Will, Germany, 1935. Directed by Leni Riefenstahl (documentary).

The 25th Hour, France/Italy/Yugoslavia, 1967. Directed by Henri Verneuil. Script by Verneuil, F. Bouer, and W. Mankowitz.

The Two of Us, France, 1966. Directed and scripted by Claude Barri.

Les Violins du Bals, France, 1973. Directed and scripted by Michel Drach.

Voyage of the Damned, Great Britain, 1976. Directed by Stuart Rosenberg. Script by Steve Shagan and David Butler, from the book by Gordon Thomas and M. M. Witts.

The Wandering Jew, Italy, 1948. Directed by G. Alessandrini.

War and Love, U.S.A., 1985. Directed by Moshe Mizrahi.

We Lived through Buchenwald, Belgium, 1947. Directed by E. G. DeMyest.

The Witnesses, France, 1962. Directed by Frederic Rossif (documentary).

The Young Lions, U.S.A., 1958. Directed by Edward Dmytryk. Script by Edward Enhalt, from the novel by Irwin Shaw.

Index